# WHITECHAPEL'S SHERLOCK HOLMES

# DICK KIRBY

## has also written

### Rough Justice – Memoirs of a Flying Squad Detective

'... the continuing increase in violent crime will make many readers yearn for yesteryear and officers of Dick Kirby's calibre'. POLICE MAGAZINE

### The Real Sweeney

'Its no-nonsense portrayal of life in the police will give readers a memorable literary experience'. SUFFOLK JOURNAL

### You're Nicked!

'In *You're Nicked!* he describes his hair-raising adventures ... with an equal measure of black humour and humanity'. NEWHAM RECORDER

### Villains

'This is magic. The artfulness of these anti-heroes has you pining for the bad old days'. DAILY SPORT

### The Guv'nors – Ten of Scotland Yard's Greatest Detectives

'They were heroes at times when heroes were desperately needed'. AMERICAN POLICE BEAT

### The Sweeney – The First Sixty Years of Scotland Yard's Crimebusting Flying Squad 1919–1978

'It's a rollercoaster ride; detectives took crime by the scruff of its neck and wouldn't let go'. EAST ANGLIAN DAILY TIMES

### Scotland Yard's Ghost Squad – The Secret Weapon against Post-War Crime

'... the fascinating true story of a talented squad of gang-busting detectives who were there when special deeds were essential. Dick Kirby ... knows how to bring his coppers to life on the page'. JOSEPH WAMBAUGH, AUTHOR OF THE CHOIRBOYS

### The Brave Blue Line – 100 Years of Metropolitan Police Gallantry

'Through a series of gripping, individual stories ... the author highlights the incredible courage often shown by officers on the front line'. DAILY EXPRESS

### Death on the Beat – Police Officers Killed in the Line of Duty

'... another book by the redoubtable Dick Kirby ... Nobody reading this book can fail to be sobered and impressed by the courage and humanity of the men and women working to keep our streets safe for us'. HISTORY BY THE YARD WEBSITE.

### The Scourge of Soho

'A gripping story, superbly told by a former Met policeman, turned crime writer.' BERTRAM BOOKS

# WHITECHAPEL'S
# SHERLOCK HOLMES

## THE CASEBOOK OF FRED WENSLEY OBE, KPM – VICTORIAN CRIMEBUSTER

### DICK KIRBY

PEN & SWORD
TRUE CRIME

First published in Great Britain in 2014 by
Pen & Sword True Crime
an imprint of
Pen & Sword Books Ltd
47 Church Street
Barnsley
South Yorkshire
S70 2AS

ISBN 978 1 78383 179 1

Typeset in Plantin by
Mac Style Ltd, Bridlington, East Yorkshire
Printed and bound in the UK by CPI Group (UK) Ltd,
Croydon, CR0 4YY

Pen & Sword Books Ltd incorporates the imprints of
Pen & Sword Archaeology, Atlas, Aviation, Battleground,
Discovery, Family History, History, Maritime, Military,
Naval, Politics, Railways, Select, Transport, True Crime,
and Fiction, Frontline Books, Leo Cooper, Praetorian
Press, Seaforth Publishing and Wharncliffe.

For a complete list of Pen & Sword titles please contact
PEN & SWORD BOOKS LIMITED
47 Church Street, Barnsley, South Yorkshire, S70 2AS,
England
E-mail: enquiries@pen-and-sword.co.uk
Website: www.pen-and-sword.co.uk

# Contents

*Acknowledgements* viii
*Author's Note* ix

**Chapter 1**    Beginnings    1

**Chapter 2**    Whitechapel    8

**Chapter 3**    Detective    14

**Chapter 4**    Learning Curve    24

**Chapter 5**    Detective Sergeant (Third-Class)    33

**Chapter 6**    Shootings and Mayhem    40

**Chapter 7**    The Embryo Flying Squad    48

**Chapter 8**    Murder and Gang Warfare in the East-End    64

**Chapter 9**    Gangsters from Eastern Europe    72

**Chapter 10**    Overlook Nothing!    79

**Chapter 11**    Conmen & Screwsmen    89

**Chapter 12**    Murders – Pointless & Squalid    98

**Chapter 13**    The Guv'nor    110

**Chapter 14**    Sailors and Prostitutes    123

**Chapter 15**    Anarchy    132

**Chapter 16**    The Man on Clapham Common    147

**Chapter 17**    Harding v Wensley: Round Two    166

**Chapter 18**    Chief Detective Inspector    174

**Chapter 19**    'Blodie Belgiam'    184

**Chapter 20**    The Flying Squad    189

**Chapter 21**    The Star-Crossed Lovers                    199

**Chapter 22**    Chief Constable of the CID                 208

**Chapter 23**    The Body in the Trunk                      216

**Chapter 24**    Scandals                                   221

**Chapter 25**    Time to Book off Duty                      233

*Epilogue*                                                   239
*Bibliography*                                               241
*Index*                                                      244

The book is dedicated to my late father,
Charles Albert Kirby, who
in common with the other East End street urchins
irreverently referred to Wensley as
'Old Boot-Nose'.

He also got too close to proceedings at the Siege of Sidney Street
and was clipped round the ear by a Scots Guardsman for his
impetuosity.

God bless his memory.

# Acknowledgements

First and foremost, I would like to thank Brigadier Henry Wilson of Pen & Sword Books for his unfailing enthusiasm and assistance. Next, my sincere thanks to my friend and fellow author, Stewart Evans, for his hospitality and enormous kindness in providing me with the vast majority of the photographs which feature in this book. The same applies to my friend of many years standing, Alan Moss, not only for providing photographs but also for his untiring and meticulous research, to which I am hugely indebted. I am most grateful to Donald Rumbelow for permitting the use of the photographs of the Houndsditch anarchists, and also to Delia Lorenson and Robert Clack for the use of the photograph of Stephen White. Every effort has been made to trace the copyright holders of the few remaining photographs, and the publishers and I apologise for any inadvertent omissions.

I would also like to thank Stefan Dickers of the Bishopsgate Institute, Paul Dew of the Metropolitan Police Historic Collection, Dr David Robinson, Bob Morris, David Whillock, Keith Skinner and George Chamier, my lynx-eyed editor, for their assistance.

I am indebted to my daughter, Sue Cowper, and her husband Steve for coming to the rescue when I was in danger of drowning in cyber-land, and also for the love and support of their children, Emma, Jessica and Harry, as well as my other daughter, Barbara Jerreat, her husband Rich and their children, Samuel and Annie Grace, and my two sons, Mark and Robert.

Most of all, my thanks go to my wife Ann for her unquestioning love and support, which has endured for over fifty years.

Dick Kirby
Suffolk, 2014

# Author's Note

The *Sunday Express* described Wensley as 'Sherlock Holmes in real life', and at first glance this could be dismissed as pure press hyperbole. Holmes was a fictional private detective who lived in Baker Street; Wensley, a public servant who lived in Whitechapel. In addition, Holmes was a bachelor who played the violin, infrequently injected himself with a 7 per cent solution of cocaine and in solving the most improbable crimes did his best to make Inspector Lestrade of Scotland Yard look like a halfwit.

But although Wensley would ironically say in later years that, unlike his fictional counterpart, he was unable to deduce the identity of a murderer by looking at a burnt matchstick, the two did have some traits in common. Both men utilised informants, disguises and logical reasoning. Both were pipe smokers and had a flair for showmanship. Neither man wasted time on rhetoric. 'He speaks with blunt vigour and stops when he has finished,' was how Wensley was described.

Holmes and Wensley could both be relied upon to acquit themselves nobly in a rough-house, with the private detective relying on *Bartitsu* – a combination of ju-jitsu, boxing and cane fencing – whereas Wensley used his fists. He was described as being 'a rare physical fighter when criminals showed fight'.

The similarities, such as they were, ended there. Holmes sometimes used firearms; Wensley abhorred them. And Holmes was prone to using a riding crop, whereas Wensley found himself on the receiving end of one.

★ ★ ★

Wensley knew the streets and the villains of the Whitechapel area inside out, as few other police officers did. The Jewish community experienced great difficulty pronouncing his surname so they referred to him as 'Mr Venzel'. Wensley's nickname was 'Weasel', and nowadays this epithet, together with its derivative, 'weasel words', is used to describe someone who is not to be relied upon. But a weasel is an animal noted for its ferocity in attacking inoffensive rabbits and poultry; and tempering that description to human proportions, it aptly described Wensley – someone who was single-minded and relentless in his pursuit of rather more offensive prey.

Wensley was a legendary detective in London's East End and during his forty-one years' service he would be involved in some of the biggest headline-grabbing cases – and some of the most controversial – in the history of the Metropolitan Police. Stinie Morrison was convicted of the murder of Leon Beron in 1911; but was he guilty of the crime or, as Morrison claimed, had Wensley framed him for the killing? Wensley took a notable part in the investigation of the triple police murder in Houndsditch, and during the siege of Sidney Street which followed he faced a fusillade of bullets from Russian anarchists as he rescued a wounded colleague across the rooftops; yet every person arrested in connection with that case was acquitted. Edith Thompson, together with her lover, was hanged for the murder of her husband; was it premeditated murder, as Wensley stated, or was Mrs Thompson, as her barrister suggested, 'a fanciful dreamer'? And right at the end of his career, Wensley oversaw the investigation into a case of police corruption which was so serious, so blatant, and with so many ramifications that reached into the heart of England's establishment, that after 100 years of that organization policing the capital, it threatened to topple the Metropolitan Police.

Wensley would also be responsible for introducing many innovations into London's Criminal Investigation Department – including the formation of the Flying Squad – so that he created a template which not only gave the CID a firm footing in the Metropolitan Police but provided Scotland Yard with the reputation of being the greatest crime-fighting police force in the world.

It was his expertise and sheer tenacity which would result in Wensley being dubbed 'The greatest detective of all time'. This is his story.

# CHAPTER 1

# Beginnings

Iff you had been born in the Pigmarket, would you have advertised the fact? No, and neither would I, nor did Fred Wensley. So he always settled for the fact that he was born in Taunton, Somerset.

A street market which received a mention in the Domesday Book was founded in 1086, south of the River Tone in Taunton; as well as dealing in market produce, silver coins had also been minted there. It was situated in an area known as Cornhill, where everything was sold – household goods and vegetables, as well as animals from the livestock stalls. By 1614 the Cornhill had become so crowded that a new market was set up, between the High Street and Paul Street, and this was renamed the Pigmarket. It was a busy, industrious area and it flourished; houses were built, tolls were charged and the streets were cleaned.

The Wensley family had lived in the area for generations; George Wensley was twenty-three when he married Jane Porter, who was aged twenty-one, at the Taunton Registry Office on 17 October 1858. George was a journeyman shoemaker and they lived in the High Street; within seventeen months their first child, George William, was born. By the time of their second son's birth, 28 March 1865, the family's business had prospered and they had been able to move to the rather more salubrious area of the Pigmarket. They named the new arrival Frederick Porter Wensley, and two years later a daughter, Matilda, was born.

Young Fred received a rudimentary education and left the village school, as was common then, at the age of twelve. Fred was said to be 'a loner' and during the 1880s he came to London, where he worked as a telegraph messenger. However, following a freezing experience delivering a telegram to Hendon, he decided to venture out of the capital and went to work at a large estate in Hampshire. But even though no member of his family was a police officer, nor did he know any, he had harboured a desire from boyhood to become a detective and he applied to join the Metropolitan Police at the end of 1887, giving his former occupation as 'gardener'. He was not alone; many of the applicants of that time came from the land, manual jobs or the military. However, Wensley fitted the criteria for police recruits: he was one and a quarter inches over the minimum height requirement of five feet eight, between twenty-one and thirty-five years old, physically fit and able to read and write.

At the time of Wensley's application conditions in London could only be described as grim. The commissioner of police was a former soldier, Sir Charles Warren GCMG, KCB, who, due to his dismissive views of his men's welfare and pensions, was not loved by the rank and file – he held office for barely eighteen months. Sir Charles was the first of seven commissioners under whom Wensley would serve.

The population of London was then 5,476,447 and the annual cost of policing the city was £1,542,812. The Metropolitan Police had been formed 59 years earlier and comprised twenty divisions with a force of 14,081 officers. However, 2,000 police officers were used on government and 'special duties', and when further deducting those officers who were on protection and station duties, on leave or sick, just 8,773 men were left to patrol the capital, 60 per cent on night duty, 40 per cent on days.

Wensley was one of the fifty-one recruits who lived at the section house at Kennington Lane police station – it was also known as the Renfrew Road section house, since it was situated at the junction with that thoroughfare, and had only just opened in October 1887 – and the training he received was two hours per day of drill for three weeks at Wellington Barracks, some very rudimentary lessons in criminal law and instruction in the perils of transgressing the disciplinary code. The recruits shared one large dormitory, no uniforms were yet issued and the pay was 15 shillings per week.[1] Lunch was bread and butter, there were no individual cooking facilities and the applicants were left to supply whatever food they could.

On 16 January 1888 Wensley was one of forty-eight applicants who were marched to Great Scotland Yard to be sworn in to become constables. He was allocated Warrant No. 73224 and two uniforms (both of very poor quality), plus an increased wage of 24 shillings a week. He was also furnished with one of the whistles which had been issued by J. Hudson & Co, Birmingham, four

---

1   Monetary values are notoriously difficult to compare across time, but £1 in the early 1900s had the purchasing power of about £100 in 2014. The pound then was divided into twenty shillings (thus worth 5p each, and abbreviated as 's') and each shilling was made up of twelve pence (thus 2.4 to each 1p, and abbreviated as 'd'). So the sum of money expressed as, for example, £5 10s 6d, was five pounds, ten shillings and six pence. A guinea was worth 21 shillings.

years earlier at a cost of 11 pence each to replace the constable's rattle, plus a truncheon made of Crocus wood. The latter had been introduced two years earlier to replace those made of Lignum Vitae (which tended to break when brought into smart contact with an adversary's head). Wensley was one of four officers sent to report for duty at the Divisional station of 'L' Division. His divisional number, to be shown on his collar, was originally recorded as 60 'L', but this number had already been allocated and it was therefore changed to 153 'L'.

There were just two police stations in 'L' Division, Kennington Lane and Kennington Road, and it was to the former that Wensley was posted, at 42 Lower Kennington Lane, where Superintendent James Brannan was in charge of 22 inspectors, 35 sergeants and 346 police constables.

Lambeth, in which Wensley now found himself, was an area of grinding poverty, drunkenness and violence. As he commenced walking the beat, so the Revd George W. Herbert, the first vicar of St. Peter's Church, Vauxhall, wrote of Lambeth: 'Our poverty is always great, whether trade is good or not; the sickness, the trials of old age and the helplessness are weighing us down.'

Patrolling police officers were considered suitable targets by the local criminals, as long as these tearaways were in sufficient numbers. They usually ensured that they were; and therefore it made good sense for these lone patrolling police officers to be very tough indeed. Many of them had seen service with the British Army in the Anglo-Zulu War of 1879 and/or the First South African War; they mostly stood over six feet tall, wore impressive medal ribbons, often sported aggressive-looking moustaches and were able to take care of themselves. This was just as well; if they displayed any sign of weakness in dealing with the local riff-raff, they might just as well have resigned – the hooligans would run their beat for them. You had to be tough simply to survive on those mean streets; grabbing hold of a constable and stuffing him head-first down a manhole was considered rare sport. During the first year of Wensley's service the reported number of assaults on the police was 2,094; however, many officers retaliated with their own brand of justice, and for obvious reasons these incidents were not recorded at all.

From his first outing on the beat Wensley was insistent that the uniform should be respected. In his case, however, it was not. He attempted to act as peacemaker in a drunken brawl and was picked up bodily and thrown through the window of a public house. Next, when a man suddenly unsheathed a swordstick and lunged at Wensley, he just as swiftly drew his truncheon and 'sticked' his adversary, which covered both of them in blood. 'You'll be on the report for this,' lugubriously muttered a colleague, but the swordsman turned out to be a lunatic who had previously assaulted police officers arresting him when he was making a raving speech in Trafalgar Square. On this occasion he attempted to attack the magistrate at the police court and was bundled off to an asylum.

Wensley's next confrontation was when he encountered a bunch of drunks who had emerged from a boxing match and insisted on obstructing him by linking arms across the pavement. In the ensuing fight the men knocked Wensley to the ground and jumped on him; he was only saved from even further serious injury after an off-duty officer who had just returned from holiday saw a colleague in trouble and waded in. This officer, too, was badly attacked, but other police officers arrived and the gang were sentenced to periods of imprisonment of up to six months each. Wensley had been so badly injured that he was placed on the sick list for 94 days. To add insult to injury, that was a time when to mark an officer's impertinence for going sick, one shilling per day was deducted from his pay.

However, the police were also determined to display their compassionate side. In *Police Orders* dated 28 April 1888 the following entry appeared:

### JUVENILE OFFENDERS

A new pattern birch-rod has been approved by the Assistant Commissioner. Great care is to be taken in whipping juvenile offenders that the birch-rod is not used too severely, especially in the case of small or delicate children.

This piece of advice undoubtedly brought home to the rough-and-ready rank and file that the Police Force was beginning to slide down a long and slippery slope towards rampant, tree-hugging liberalism.

\* \* \*

On 22 May 1888 Police Constable 153 'L' Wensley was patrolling Lower Marsh, which ran between Westminster Bridge Road and Waterloo Road. To the north of it was Waterloo station, erected forty years previously, and dingy, ill-lit alleyways, courts and yards branched off from Lower Marsh. A narrow thoroughfare, it was made to look even more restricted by the four-storey premises on either side of it. At 8.30 on that Tuesday evening Wensley saw a twenty-year-old printer named Thomas Adams with a group of men. They were merely talking and not causing any kind of a disturbance, so Wensley carried on with his two-and-a-half-mph patrol. However, Adams was a member of a gang which numbered between twenty and thirty and were the terror of the neighbourhood; they carried out street robberies in packs of four and five. In fact, the previous month, Adams had been sentenced to one month's imprisonment for larceny and had only just been released.

Barely fifteen minutes after initially seeing Adams and his cronies, Wensley was stopped by an agitated gentleman who told him that he had been jostled by three men, one of whom had pushed him against a wall and had attempted to steal his watch and chain. Having had Adams pointed out as the ringleader, Wensley approached the men, who turned and ran. Chasing after them, Wensley caught Adams – the other two escaped – and brought him back to the victim, who repeated his allegation. So all would have been well – except that Wensley and his prisoner were now surrounded by a large group of Adams' associates, and as they pulled Wensley and Adams apart, so Adams knocked Wensley to the pavement and subjected him to a violent kicking. Hemmed in by the mob, Wensley was unable to stop Adams escaping; by the time he pushed through the crowd, Adams had fled to his father's address in Victoria Court and then escaped via the back door.

Wensley, bruised, bloodied and furious, returned empty-handed to the scene of the incident, only to find that the victim of the attempted robbery had vanished – and Wensley had no idea of his name or address.

Adams was arrested four days later, when he denied ever being in Lower Marsh at the material time. But at Lambeth police court he was identified by Wensley, as he was by a waiter, Thomas Gray, who had witnessed the entire incident. The magistrate, Mr Slade, regretted that the victim could not be found, but on Saturday 3 June 1888, for the attack on Wensley, he sentenced Adams to two months' hard labour.[2]

★ ★ ★

On 1 October 1888 Wensley was one of 161 additional police constables and sergeants to be drafted into Whitechapel following

---

2 Hard labour was an additional form of punishment for sentences of up to two years' imprisonment. It included industrial work, oakum-picking and using a treadmill. It was abolished in 1948.

the murderous rampage of 'Jack the Ripper'. Some officers were in plain clothes, some dressed as prostitutes in the hope they would attract some (not all) of the Ripper's attentions, but Wensley, using some of the cunning which would soon become his trademark, nailed strips of old bicycle tyre to the soles of his boots to provide a silent approach for the day when he would leap upon the Ripper and become the most celebrated police constable of all time. Alas, it was not to be; neither Wensley nor any other police officer was able to bring the Victorian serial murderer to book.

But one thing was sure: Wensley thoroughly disliked the Whitechapel area of 'H' Division. It was filthy, it was squalid, it had the worst slums and some of the worst specimens of humanity in the capital; and when the tide of slaughter diminished, Wensley was relieved to be returned to Lambeth. And then something happened which set him on course as an aspiring detective.

\* \* \*

Two girls, Elizabeth Proud and Elizabeth Bartley, were inmates of the Salvation Army Home, Devonshire Road, Hackney, East London. During the early hours they stole a watch, a purse and some clothing belonging to Ellen Paul, a domestic servant at the home. They were heard to drop down from the dormitory on to the roof of the kitchen by the Matron, Annie Bambery, who saw them scale a garden wall and run off.

The following night, Wensley was on patrol in New Cut, Lambeth, when he saw the girls in company with two well-known local characters. Of course, he had no knowledge of the theft from the hostel, but when he saw the girls go into a coffee stall in Blackfriars Road, he followed them and heard them discussing their crime. He arrested them, and at the station pawn tickets were found in their possession which led to the recovery of the stolen property.

On 28 February 1890 at Dalston police court, the magistrate, Montague Phillips, told the girls they were guilty of 'base ingratitude' and sentenced each of them to three months' hard labour. He also commended Wensley, saying, 'I think the constable in this case displayed great intelligence and activity in arresting the prisoners'; a month later, the commissioner added his own commendation, together with an award of five shillings, a sum not to be sneezed at when Wensley's weekly wage was just nineteen shillings more than that. It was the first of many such commendations and rewards.

\* \* \*

By the end of 1889 police personnel had risen, very slightly, to 14,725, and there recruitment stopped. On 5 July 1890 there were demonstrations at Bow Street police station: 130 police officers refused to go on duty, demanding an increase in their pay, which had remained static for eighteen years, and it took two troops of Life Guards to disperse the crowd. The following day, the commissioner, Colonel Sir Edward Bradford Bt., GCB, GCVO, KCSI, had the 39 ringleaders paraded before him and promptly sacked the lot. ('I was out of the room, again,' one of them said, 'before I properly understood what had happened.') The remaining 91 protesters were packed off to different divisions, and Wensley was one of a number of other constables drafted in to fill the gap. As Police Constable 97 'E', he was posted to Bow Street police station.

In his autobiography, *Detective Days*, Wensley mentioned the posting and added that he was not there very long; he was quite right, but what he did not mention was the reason for his departure.

On 19 February 1891 Wensley and another officer, Police Constable 455 'E' Bishop, were both suspended from duty without pay. Four days later, both were reinstated, but Wensley was fined three days' pay (11s 9d) and transferred to another division, at an increased wage (thanks to the police strike) of 27 shillings per week; Bishop, being the younger and thus probably regarded as the less culpable of the two, was fined one day's pay (3s 6d) and permitted to remain on 'E' Division.

Whatever the disciplinary offence was, the details will now never be known. But it was possible that the senior officer sitting on the discipline board had heard of Wensley's loathing of the East End during his short spell there for the abortive attempt to catch 'Jack the Ripper'. If so, it seemed that sending Wensley to the Whitechapel area the following day was a suitable punishment for his transgressions.

# CHAPTER 2

# Whitechapel

Until now, Wensley had only seen Whitechapel under cover of darkness, two years previously. Now, on 24 February 1891, he saw it in all its glory. If Lambeth had been described as 'grim', Whitechapel was a hell-hole. Had Wensley consulted a fortune teller and discovered that 'H' Division would be his home for the next twenty-five years, it is likely he would have resigned on the spot. And if that soothsayer had added that not only would he come to love the area and, furthermore, resist all efforts to remove him from those reeking streets, he would undoubtedly have thought it his duty to have this obviously unbalanced creature committed to an asylum.

At that time, Whitechapel had an official population of 32,326, but that was only the number registered on the census forms; since the 1840s thousands of Irish had descended into the area, together with many more Jews and Eastern Europeans fleeing persecution, and the true population figure was probably in the region of 122,000. It turned what had been predominantly a market area into an industrial one, not that there were many factories. The residents were crowded into houses which were often used as their workplace – hermetically sealed sweatshops which were a breeding ground for disease. Houses which were originally meant for one family now accommodated three or four, often with seven or eight people to a room, and the landlords charged extortionate rents. Insanitary conditions had brought about the cholera epidemic of 1866, as well as typhoid fever. Infant mortality rates were very high and the average life expectancy for a man was forty; suicide became common, many seeing it as a release. Little wonder that the Revd James Adderley wrote of Whitechapel as having, 'a dullness and a sadness in East London, peculiarly its own'.

There were hundreds of disreputable public houses – they were open from 4 in the morning until 12.30 at night – and also lodging houses, the breeding ground for every kind of villainy, interlinked by cellars and a whole network of courts and alleyways; this made both committing crime and escaping from the authorities easy. The police had been given powers in 1851 to supervise these lodgings – they were known as 'doss houses' – but although they closed down over 700 of the worst of the establishments, it was not until 1894 that the London County Council took over control. It did little good.

Unemployment was high, as was alcohol consumption and domestic abuse. Begging, stealing, robbery with violence and pickpocketing were rife, and many of the children were born to be criminals. Since 1860, 20,000 prostitutes had been working in London; a large proportion gravitated to Whitechapel, to accommodate the sailors emerging from their ships after a long voyage. The environment also presented dangers to the prostitutes, from the attentions of drunken vagrants who inhabited the unlit, stinking alleyways to those of the more murderous variety, as 'Jack the Ripper's' victims found to their cost. However, it was a two-way street: many of the prostitutes' customers found themselves infected with a colourful variety of antisocial diseases, with the extra options of being robbed of their wages or murdered by the woman's pimp if they showed signs of offering resistance. Murders were common, and quite often, where a victim was discovered having been bashed over the head in the absence of witnesses, what had been a murder was not recorded as such.

With a dozen different languages being screamed at the top of their speakers' lungs, plus the filth, the disease and the lawlessness, Whitechapel must have appeared to be a madhouse to a newcomer like Wensley. One century later, the author L. Perry Curtis Jr wrote, with considerable conviction, of those times as, 'a breeding ground for criminals, prostitutes and layabouts; a centre for depravity, degradation and disease'.

Police officers were a target for the local tearaways, just as they had been in Lambeth. Fred Sharpe (later to become head of the Flying Squad) was posted to Whitechapel and was told, 'Fred, they used to hit you on the head with a chopper, *for a lark*!' And that wasn't all: Police Constable Henry Windebank was medically discharged on 30 January 1891 after being hit so hard with a coal-heaver's shovel that it caused insanity and led to his early death in a lunatic asylum. Since he had no further need of his Divisional number – 402 'H' – three weeks later it was passed on to Wensley, 'H' Division's newest addition.

\* \* \*

At that time, 'H' Division had a workforce of 587 officers, and within weeks of Wensley's arrival the newly built five-storey police station at 76 Leman Street was operational; it was there that Wensley set to work with a will.

Street robberies were common: when George Rumsby, a seaman, was drinking at the Blakeney Head, Cable Street on 13 December 1893, he had already lent fifteen shillings to Francis Victor Mygren, and now he lent him a further half-crown. In his purse, Rumsby had £7 in gold and a £5 note; he later admitted, 'Mygren might have seen that money.' As he left the pub at 11.15 pm, Mygren grabbed hold of Rumsby, and an associate, Thomas Richford, tore his trouser pocket out and grabbed the purse; the men then ran off.

Five days later, Wensley was on patrol in Ship Alley when he saw Mygren and arrested him from the description he had been given. Mygren replied, 'I was there but I didn't rob him; the others robbed him.' And five days after that, Wensley arrested Richford, who indignantly replied, 'What old lag is putting me away?' At the Old Bailey, each man blamed the other; Richford was sentenced to eighteen months' hard labour and Mygren to three.

As William Douglas was crossing Whitechapel High Street he consulted his watch and it was almost snatched from his hand by James Hammerman, aged thirty-five. Only part of the chain was taken, but William Schennick, aged thirty, knocked Mr Douglas to the ground. Wensley was patrolling Leman Street at the time and saw the two men, whom he well knew as local tearaways, hurrying along the road from the direction of the High Street. He knew nothing of the robbery at that time, but within minutes he had heard, and searched unsuccessfully for them. At 7.30 that evening he and his close friend, Police Constable 442 'H' Henry Richardson, changed into plain clothes, and at 10.20 they saw the men in the High Street and arrested them. Although Schennick told the officers, 'I know nothing about it', the jury at the Old Bailey thought differently. The stolen piece of watch chain was valued only at tuppence, but both men had a number of previous convictions recorded against them; Schennick was sentenced to five years' penal servitude[3] and twenty strokes of the cat, and Hammerman to seven years' penal servitude.

Twenty-eight-year-old Thomas Cantwell and Charles Thomas Quinn, a twenty-six-year-old printer, made a seditious speech at Tower Hill in which they incited an assembled crowd to murder members of the Royal Family. One witness told Cantwell, 'You dirty dog; you ought to be ashamed of yourself for speaking like

3   Penal Servitude replaced transportation; its purpose was to punish the prisoner. It covered terms of imprisonment from three years to life, and the prisoners worked for private contractors, often in quarries. It was abolished in 1948.

you have. Are you an anarchist?' When Cantwell replied that he was, the onlooker told him, 'A bright specimen, too; you ought to be shot!'

Cantwell shoved the witness, telling him, 'Get away.'

He was joined by Quinn and chased by a very hostile crowd, one of whom shouted, 'Get out of it, you dirty dog; I'll give you anarchist!'

Wensley stepped in, which resulted in a commendation at the Guildhall Justice Rooms, and at the Old Bailey Mr Justice Lawrence sentenced both men to six months' hard labour.

But all the time, Wensley was building up his store of knowledge of the villains of the area, their ways of working, their haunts and their associates. He discovered how to surreptitiously follow suspects, both in uniform and plain clothes, and learnt the ways of running informants, when to let them have a free rein with their activities and when to exert pressure. He studied the criminal law. He worked long hours; having finished a tour of duty, he thought nothing of changing into plain clothes and going out to hunt down the thieves and robbers who infested the area. None of this extra work was for payment; when the matter of paying gratuities to the police who worked beyond their eight-hour shift was brought up at a Commons sitting on 17 June 1890, Henry Matthews (later 1st Viscount Llandaff PC, QC), the Secretary of State for the Home Department, told his fellow MPs:

> These demands were made on several occasions. They involved the principle that the police had an equitable right to be paid for loss of leave or for overtime beyond their usual spell of eight hours' duty. This principle has not hitherto been admitted in the administration of the police. It appears to me contrary to the terms on which the police are employed. It carries with it the consequence of payment for all overtime beyond an eight hours' day. I did not feel justified in allowing this novel claim.

Wensley was desperate to become a detective and he was commended by magistrates, judges and the commissioner, time and time again. The usual way to get accepted into the Criminal Investigation Department (CID) was by first becoming a 'Winter Patrol' – this was the forerunner of the 'Aids to CID' system which would commence thirty years later. The Winter Patrols dressed in disreputable clothing, were paid 2s 6d per week extra and hunted down the thieves and tearaways of the area. But although Wensley had been doing just this in his spare time, to be sanctioned to

perform the duty full-time and officially required the consent of
the divisional detective inspector (DDI) – in those days known as
local inspectors – and this was not forthcoming.

Edmund John James Reid was Whitechapel's DDI and he
had joined the Force in 1872. In 1884 he had been promoted to
inspector, had set up the CID on the newly-formed 'J' Division, and
in 1887 had arrived on 'H' Division. He had taken a very active role
in the hunt for 'Jack the Ripper', but perhaps he perceived Wensley
to be a troublemaker, citing his three changes of division – from 'L'
to 'E' to 'H' – all within a space of seven months, plus a disciplinary
board and a fine. As far as he was concerned, Wensley's aspirations
to become a detective were going nowhere.

It was during this time that Wensley married the girl he had met
several years previously: Laura Elizabeth Martin, who was always
known as 'Lollie'. Wensley had written to her father in May 1891,
asking permission to court her, and the small, hazel-eyed girl,
four years his junior, who came from Eastbourne, Sussex, became
Wensley's wife on 3 August 1893 when they were married at the
parish church of Hadlow in Kent. It was a union of great happiness
which would last until Lollie's death, fifty years later. The couple
moved into rooms in Fair Street, Stepney, then shifted to Smith
Street until the spring of 1897, when they finally settled into 98
Dempsey Street, Stepney, where they would remain for the next
sixteen years.

Not that Lollie would see much of her husband (neither did
their son, Frederick Martin, born the following year); Wensley
relentlessly pursued the criminals of those unfriendly streets, and
his contribution to law and order did not go unnoticed. Whilst
on patrol he was stopped by Superintendent Charles Dodd, who
had joined the police twenty-five years previously. Discovering
that Wensley had almost eight years' service as a uniformed police
constable, and fully aware of his successes as a thief-taker, Dodd
demanded to know why he had not joined the CID. According to
his memoirs, Wensley replied, 'I don't think I'm wanted, sir.'

That reply probably touched a nerve, because Dodd snapped,
'*I'm* looking after this division', and told him to put his application
through DDI Reid, adding, 'I'll see to it.'

Quite obviously, he did. Within days of Wensley submitting his
application an old detective named Payne was pensioned off, and
on 4 October 1895 Wensley was appointed a permanent patrol, the
forerunner of the detective constable. It was a parting gift from
Dodd; within a month he would be gone, posted to 'S' Division.
His superintendent had to report on Wensley's qualifications within
three months, so the report would therefore not come from Dodd;

but nor would it be DDI Reid who would interfere with Wensley's career. Within two months, Reid was gone as well; he was posted to 'L' Division and two months after that he would resign with twenty-three years' service. Reid received a No. 3 Certificate as to his conduct – which can be described as 'not too bad' and a long way from being 'exemplary' – and it may have had something to do with having been admonished by the Assistant Commissioner, James Monro, the day before his transfer to 'H' Division.

If Wensley congratulated himself upon his good fortune at being parted from Reid, he was being rather premature; Reid's successor, who commenced duty on 9 December 1895, was DDI Stephen White – and he was a *really* nasty piece of work.

# CHAPTER 3

# Detective

If White (whose background will be dealt with later) disliked Wensley, the feeling was mutual. However, there was a multiplicity of talent in the CID for Detective Wensley (as he was now known) to work with and learn from. Detective Sergeant John W. Gill had three years' seniority over Wensley and was a year younger; they became firm friends and invariably worked together. There was Detective Sergeant William Brogden, who had joined just prior to Wensley. The son of Yarmouth's chief constable, Brogden had been commended on 135 occasions; unfortunately, he put a bet on with a bookmaker, on behalf of another, and was busted to constable. Other detective sergeants were Jack 'Jew-Boy' Stevens, who drew his pension until the ripe old age of ninety-one, and Henry Dessent, whose poor health prevented further advancement. Eli Caunter was the detective sergeant (first-class); known as 'Tommy Roundhead', he would soon retire after twenty-six years' distinguished service, taking with him eighty commendations. Detective Sergeant William Thick had joined the Metropolitan Police twenty years before Wensley; he dressed flamboyantly in loud checks, and although he had a reputation as a 'holy terror' to the local tearaways, he was also held in great affection, possessing an unusual nickname. On one auspicious occasion, he was greeted by a lady of his acquaintance with the words, 'Why, fuck me if it ain't Johnny Upright!' Wensley referred to him as 'one of the finest policemen I've ever known'.

It was men like these from whom Wensley learnt his trade and honed his skills. It was just as well, because there were few other aids to detective work. That was not all. Whatever the preconceptions about detective work harboured by the young Wensley growing up in Taunton, it is certain that it bore little resemblance to the grim reality of what was then Scotland Yard's detectives' department.

The plain-clothes Detective Branch had been formed in 1842; it consisted of just eight officers who worked from Scotland Yard. There were no other detectives, either in the Metropolitan Police or any of the country's constabularies; it was just these officers who were called upon to investigate serious crimes, at home or abroad. It took twenty-six years for the Detective Branch to be increased, to a total of twenty-eight. The following year, 1869, the new commissioner, Colonel Sir Edmund Henderson KCB, RE, introduced detectives to the divisions. It was a disaster. The divisional superintendents took the opportunity to rid themselves of their dross, officers who were bone-idle, incompetent and barely-literate. These 197 'detectives' were supervised by twenty sergeants, whose educational capabilities were on a par with their subordinates, and were left to their own devices; in 1871 when it was suggested that the officers might be made more accountable by keeping a daily diary, the head of the detectives, Superintendent Frederick Adolphus Williamson, was obliged to inform the commissioner:

> I am afraid the keeping of a daily journal by officers employed in investigating criminal matters is with the present stamp of men impracticable, as a number of them who are employed as divisional detectives would, from their want of education, find it impossible to make a daily comprehensible report of their proceedings.

Williamson was experienced and popular, but in 1877, following 'The Trial of the Detectives', when three of his colleagues were sent to prison for two years each, his reputation was severely damaged. In March 1878 Sir Charles Edward Howard Vincent KCMG, CB was appointed Director of Criminal Intelligence and created the new Criminal Investigation Department. A former soldier and Home Office official, Vincent went to Paris, studied the way the French police worked and sent a report with recommendations to the Home Office in which he outlined a semi-independent department, which he had modelled on the *Sûreté*.

Within months, the new department consisted of 280 officers, of whom 254 were to be based in division, under the control of 'local inspectors'. Sensibly retaining Williamson to provide the hands-on experience which he lacked, Vincent held the reins of the CID for six years and made many much-needed changes.

But the CID still had a long way to go; there were divisional boundaries which were jealously guarded, together with pettifogging rules and regulations. Many of the detectives were very good at their work, developing a 'nose' for criminals, but when it came to obtaining advice in other than routine cases, help was not always forthcoming.

In the 1890s Tom Divall, then a detective, wanted advice on how to tackle an enquiry into a case of a long-firm fraud, and he turned to his local inspector. He was told:

I am not here to tell you what to do in making your enquires; if I advise you what to do, and it turns out wrongly, I shall get into trouble. You are a detective and are expected to know your work and if you cannot carry out your duties, tell me and I'll soon deal with you.

Of course, this reply was a conglomeration of ignorance, stupidity and spinelessness, and although Divall went on and used his common sense to solve the investigation – and, incidentally, thought his local inspector had given him the correct advice – it is interesting to note that had he wanted further information on how to crack the case, the next rung up the ladder would have been to pose the question to Superintendent Williamson.

This was the CID of which Wensley had become a member.

★ ★ ★

One year before Wensley's appointment, the Anthropometry Department (using principles set out by a Frenchman, Alphonse Bertillon) was formed at the Yard; it included measuring the length of a suspect's bones, noting the colour of his eyes, and so on. It had a few successes in identifying criminals who claimed they had no previous convictions and led to a notable miscarriage of justice in the case of Adolf Beck, but at the time it was the best system available.

When criminals were imprisoned, their photograph was taken by the penal authorities and one copy would be sent to what became known as the 'Rogues Gallery' at Scotland Yard. This unit proved immensely helpful to Wensley after he arrested a man for stealing a purse who immediately claimed that it was Wensley who was the thief. Since Wensley had pocketed the purse to safeguard the evidence, and this was witnessed by both the victim and the crowd which had rapidly gathered, it appeared that the man's allegation might have some basis in fact. The prisoner repeated his allegation at the police station and at the police court, where he called witnesses to say that he was a man of good character. He was nevertheless committed for trial to the North London Sessions, and Wensley, who was convinced the man had previous convictions, spent days poring over photographs contained in the Rogues Gallery. Eventually, he identified the man and discovered that in the past he had used the same trick, which had resulted in several acquittals and censure for the officers who had arrested him. Wensley took grim delight in informing the court how the thief had endeavoured to frame him and had, indeed, framed officers in the past, and saw him sentenced to eighteen months' hard labour. It almost beggars belief that the routine photographing of criminals, following charging at Metropolitan Police stations, would take another *eighty years* before it was finally implemented.

The Fingerprint Bureau was set up in 1901 but it was not until 1905 that its worth was shown in a murder trial; fortunately, the jury was sufficiently impressed with the weight of the evidence to convict, unlike the judge, Mr Justice Channell, who was extremely wary of placing any reliance on the prisoners' incriminating fingerprints. Until then, a prisoner either admitted his previous convictions or, if they happened to be known to the officer in the case, a warder had to be produced from the prison in which the defendant had last served his sentence, in order to prove the conviction.

Blood grouping was non-existent; the best the doctors and pathologists could say when examining bloodstains were that they were probably human or, at the very least, belonged to one of the family of 'great apes' – which must have been amazingly helpful to a murder investigator. There was little if any preservation of a crime scene; detectives, uniformed police officers, pressmen and general members of the public wandered into the scene of a crime and crunched their way through what was probably a whole mass of evidence. In 1924 Chief Inspector Percy Savage was treated to a furious verbal broadside from the eminent pathologist Sir Bernard Spilsbury, who discovered him handling portions of a murder victim's putrefying flesh with his bare hands instead of wearing rubber gloves, thus running a very high risk of contracting septicaemia; Savage rather gormlessly replied that he had not been issued with any. Thus, the 'Murder Bag' (at Spilsbury's instigation) came into being; it was not until 1934 that a forensic science laboratory was opened.

It can therefore be seen that Wensley and his contemporaries were in a tight corner regarding the war against crime; but what they did possess were speed, experience and intuition, which seldom let them down.

Wensley demonstrated these skills when he was on patrol in Whitechapel Road during the late evening of 4 May 1896. Bernard Weber, an enameller, was walking past the East London Music Hall when he was set upon by what he described as 'three roughs'; Thomas Marshall grabbed him by the neck and another man snapped and made off with Mr Weber's watch-chain. Managing to retain a hold on his watch, Mr Weber tried to chase after the thug, but the third man blocked his way and Marshall grabbed his hands. The three men ran off down Mary Street, which was a very dark thoroughfare, but Wensley had witnessed the attack and, as Mr Weber later told an Old Bailey jury, 'in about half a second the detective came and caught him'.

In his defence, Marshall stated that he had heard the cry, 'Stop thief!' and was erroneously arrested by Wensley, even though Mr Weber had told him that he was not responsible. In turn, this was repudiated by Mr Weber, and Wensley denied that he had 'taken Weber to one side and had a talk with him at the police station'; this was accepted by the jury, who found Marshall guilty. It was then revealed that he was the possessor of seven previous convictions, the last in the name of William Needham, and was still on licence, which would not expire until January 1897. Marshall was sentenced to three years' penal servitude and Wensley was once more commended.

It was another good result for Wensley; however, exactly two weeks later he would carry out an arrest which was so sensational it would propel him into the public domain. What was more, Wensley was not even on duty.

* * *

If young William Seaman had been a literary type of child, he might have read a certain Charles Dickens novel, published a dozen years before he was born, entitled *Oliver Twist* – and if he had, he might have come to the conclusion that the brutal, manipulative and murderous arch-villain of the piece, Bill Sikes, was a suitable role model. Whether he did or not is of course a matter of conjecture, but if Seaman did see Sikes as an iconic figure and set out to model himself on one of Dickens' more repellent characters, he had certainly succeeded.

Seaman – he was also known as William King and William Saunders – moved into the first division of crime when, aged twenty, he appeared at the Old Bailey and was sentenced to seven years' penal servitude for burglary. Hardly had he been released when in December 1876 he once again appeared at the Old Bailey, this time for robbery with violence; on this occasion he was sentenced to fourteen years' penal servitude, to be followed by seven years' police supervision. Seaman was released slightly early, and this was a mistake on the part of the penal commissioners, because in 1888 he walked into a chemist's shop in Berners Street, asked for the loan of a hammer and promptly smashed the proprietor over the head with it. He was caught at the scene and this time he received seven years' penal servitude. Seaman had only been released for a few months prior to his next offence.

* * *

Martha Lawton lived at 35 Turner Street and on Saturday, 4 April 1896 at 1.00 pm she went to no. 31 to see her cousin, John Goodman Levy, aged seventy-five. She had had supper with Mr Levy and his housekeeper, Mrs Sarah Ann Gale, aged thirty-seven, the previous evening and had intended to join them for lunch on the Saturday. There was no answer, so she knocked next door, at no. 29, and spoke to the occupier, William Shafer, who went into his back yard; over the wall he saw the bearded William Seaman and shouted, 'What are you doing there?' Seaman promptly hid. Police were called, Police Constable 231 'H' Walter Atkinson arrived, followed by another constable, and they entered Mr Levy's premises. A shocking sight confronted them there: Mr Levy's body was half in and half out of the ground-floor lavatory, and an eight-inch wound in his throat had severed his windpipe and gullet and also one of his arteries; his head had been smashed in by a blunt instrument and six ribs had been broken. In the front bedroom on the top floor was the body of Mrs Gale; her throat, too, had been cut and her head had also been battered. Blood was splattered everywhere and the premises had been ransacked. The two officers went immediately to Arbour Square police station to report the double murder.

Wensley and his friend Henry Richardson were off duty and strolling along Commercial Road, when some youngsters shouted, 'There's been a murder at Turner Street!' Breaking into a run, the officers arrived at the junction of Turner Street and Varden Street, where a crowd had already gathered. Entering no. 31, they searched the premises and found the corpse of Mr Levy; in the top-floor bedroom, as well as the body of Mrs Gale, they discovered a large hole in the ceiling. Richardson climbed through the hole and then along the roof space until he found another hole in the tiles. Looking out, he saw Seaman on the roof and to Wensley he shouted, 'Look out – he's about to jump!'

Wensley rushed downstairs and was in time to see Seaman leap from the parapet and land on some of the crowd who had gathered in Varden Street. Wensley seized hold of Seaman, who was unconscious, having suffered head injuries, as well as a broken arm and leg, in the forty-foot fall; Dr Lewis Smith, the house surgeon at the London Hospital, would later tell a coroner that, 'Nine out of ten men would assuredly have been killed by such a jump.'

There was a rumour at the time that the murderer had an accomplice, and Wensley in his dishevelled state, covered in soot and plaster, appeared to the crowd to fit the bill. As he struggled to pull Seaman indoors, the crowd ripped the coat right off Wensley's back, and it was only the presence of uniformed officers that prevented Seaman – and possibly Wensley too – from being lynched.

A constable helped carry Seaman indoors; as he did so, Mr Levy's gold spectacles, a seal and some money fell from his pocket. Seaman was also seen by Dr Charles Le Sage, who noticed that his clothing was very dirty; his overcoat was covered in lime and plaster but there were no bloodstains on it. The rest of Seaman's clothing was a very different matter. All the front of his jacket, its sleeves and his waistcoat, both inside and out, were covered in blood, as were both trouser legs, front and back; blood was also clotted on both boots. An Inspector searched Seaman and found gold chains, a gold ring and a diamond and opal pin – and these and many other items found in Seaman's possession and around him were later positively identified as belonging to Mr Levy and Mrs Gale.

Meanwhile, Richardson had searched the roof and discovered a hammer broken in two with plaster on it, some money and a sovereign purse; whilst Wensley went upstairs, made a thorough search and in between the ceiling and the tiles found a brown cloth cap with a woman's hat pin attached to it – later identified as belonging to Mrs Gale – and in the top back bedroom, a bloodstained knife, a chisel and an overcoat.

When Seaman was asked his name, he replied, 'I shan't tell you'; and when his address was requested, he said, 'I refuse to tell you; you will find that out.'

The knife, hammer (used in committing the murders) and chisel were the property of the Bowater family, who lived at Millwall, and it was there that Seaman had lodged since his release from prison. When his erstwhile landlady, Rebecca Bowater, saw him in the London Hospital, she asked him if it was possible that he had done such a terrible crime. 'I did do it,' Seaman replied, and when asked his motive, said, 'Revenge'.

'What revenge could you have against that poor old gentleman?' asked Mrs Bowater, and received the reply, 'He did me the greatest injustice that one man can do another.'

'Why?' said Mrs Bowater. 'Was that woman your wife?'

'No, she was no man's wife,' replied Seaman, before the police stepped in and put an end to this melodramatic gibberish.

Mrs Bowater also told the Press regarding her former lodger that, 'If a mouse was caught in a trap, he would plead with me to let it go' – although it is not entirely clear whether this tribute to his character was made before or after hearing his surly confession.

Police Constable 359 'H' Ernest Bacchus appeared to be a rather humane officer, because at the hospital the following day he gave Seaman some milk, telling him, 'That will do you good.'

'Oh, don't bother much about that,' replied Seaman. 'I could go to the scaffold and swing for what I've done, without fear. I know what's in front of me and I can face it; if a man takes a life, he must suffer for it. I don't value my life a bit; I've made my bed, I must lie on it.'

Seaman appeared at the Old Bailey in May 1896 before Mr Justice Hawkins and pleaded not guilty to Levy's murder. He rejected the offer of a defence counsel since that would have inhibited his last performance; he was clearly guilty, the evidence was overpowering, but now it was time for a little showboating.

Seaman sneered at the evidence and jeered at the witnesses. Police Constable 140 'H' William Elliott was one of the officers guarding Seaman at the hospital, and on 12 April he recorded the following statement:

I have been a frequent visitor in Turner Street where the job was done, and if the fucking old Jew had given me the £70 he owed me, the job would never have happened. You don't know the half what there has been between old Levy and me; nobody else knows now and I will keep it to myself. You don't know what I have to put up with from the two bastards but this finishes the lot. This morning I knocked at the door, old Levy himself answered it and I walked in. He said the girl was upstairs. I then went upstairs and found her in her own bedroom; she had just got her dress on and was leaning over her own bed, which appeared to me not to have been slept in. She always slept with old Levy. When she saw me she shouted and began struggling, but I soon stopped her kicking. I then came downstairs and soon put the old Jew's lights out. After the job was finished I heard someone keep knocking at the door. I stood behind the door, considering whether to let them in or not. If I had opened the door I would soon have floored them so they would not have walked out of that house again, alive – they would have been carried out stiff with the others. I then got on the roof from the inside and saw my only chance was to dive down off the roof, head-first. If it had not been for someone breaking my fall, I should not be lying in here. But there it is. Everyone has to die sometime. I know I am going to get hung and would not care if it was now, for I am tired of my life.

This was just one of several incriminating statements made by Seaman, attempting to justify but at the same time glorifying in the murders, and it was also a first-rate opportunity to attack the credibility of the police, because in cross-examination Seaman told PC Elliott, 'The whole of your evidence is a fabrication. Either I'm a madman to make such a statement or you're a rogue. You've been sworn on the Bible but they ought to have sworn you on a pack of cards.' Asked by the judge if he wished to ask PC Elliott any further questions, Seaman pompously replied, 'No. He's the greatest liar I have ever had in front of me. He's a disgrace to the police force.'

Seaman's defence consisted of challenging trivialities – inaccurate newspaper reporting regarding his past – and of lies; he was keen to put the blame for the crime on Levy because of non-payment of the fictitious £70 owed to him and on Mrs Gale for her alleged immorality. However, none of Seaman's assertions held water; inevitably, he was found guilty and sentenced to death.

There is a curious appendix to this story. All the time he was in custody, Seaman insisted on seeing newspaper reports regarding the arrest of two fellow thugs, Albert Milsom and Henry Fowler, who had brutally murdered seventy-nine-year-old Henry Smith. Whilst the jury was considering their verdict on both men at the Old Bailey, Fowler attacked Milsom in the dock and almost throttled him before they were separated; both were found guilty and sentenced to death, but it was feared that at their execution on 9 June – this date coincided with Seaman's hanging – a further attack would be launched. Therefore Seaman was placed between them, and he told the small audience, 'Well, this is the first time in my life I've ever been a bloody penitent.' As an added precaution, four warders surrounded the scaffold; unfortunately, the assistant hangman, Mr Warbrick, who was busy pinioning the feet of one of the prisoners, was obscured from the view of the hangman, James Billington, who pulled the lever to release the three trapdoors rather prematurely. Warbrick vanished, head-first, into the void with the three murderers, saving himself only by hanging on to the legs of one of them.

This marked the last triple execution at Newgate Prison; in fact, it could have been a quadruple execution, because fifty-eight-year-old Amelia Elizabeth Dyer, the notorious 'baby farmer', who had pleaded guilty to murdering one infant (but was thought to be responsible for the deaths of 400 others), was also due to be hanged on that day. Instead, she was hanged the following day, with Billington carrying out the execution alone – his traumatized assistant being indisposed.

\* \* \*

William Whittaker, a boy who had not yet reached his eighth birthday, did not give evidence at the Old Bailey but he had at the

Coroner's Court. He had been sent by his mother on an errand to the home of Mr Levy on that Saturday morning. There was no answer to his repeated knockings, but as he was about to leave he heard a noise inside the premises. He was met by Mrs Lawton, who also knocked on the door, and it was their knocking that Seaman had referred to in his disputed statement to PC Elliott. Had Seaman opened the door to Mrs Lawton and the little boy, would he have carried out his threat ('they would not have walked out of that house again, alive – they would have been carried out stiff, like the others')?

Without being disproportionally uncharitable to the late Mr Seaman, on the balance of probabilities I think he would have.

# CHAPTER 4

# Learning Curve

Despite being feted by the courts over his input to the Seaman case, Wensley had no intention of resting on his laurels. As a detective, he was just getting started.

It was Wensley's business to know who associated with whom and who went where, so on the morning of 8 January 1897, when he glanced through the window of the Bricklayers' Arms, Cable Street, he saw Charles Hutchings, a local villain, and also noticed William Stevens, a particularly slimy individual, serving behind the bar. He filed that piece of information away in his memory, just as he had noticed Michael Callaghan in company with Hutchings in the same pub, almost on a daily basis, for the previous three weeks.

At about three o'clock that afternoon, James Duggan, a ship's fireman who had just been paid off from his ship, entered the pub. Duggan barely had time to swallow his first sip of porter before he was followed in by Hutchings, who said to a group of men, 'Has he done it yet?' Whatever it was that was thought to have occurred, and whoever was supposed to have carried it out, was sufficient for one of the bar's clientele to reply, 'No', and Duggan was seized by the men. He shouted to the barman, Stevens, to blow his police whistle, but Stevens told the gang, 'Don't do anything like that, or take him outside and do it.'

Hutchings pulled £2 from Duggan's pocket and said, 'I've got to let the bastard go; if you let him outside, he'll make an alarm and get away.'

To this Callaghan replied, 'I'll see he don't bloody well get away', and punched Duggan in the head, who fell through the pub entrance and summoned a police officer; but by the time it took the latter to run the 100 yards to the Bricklayers' Arms, the miscreants had fled.

The slippery barman, Stevens, told Wensley he had never seen or indeed heard of Hutchings before, but from Duggan's description of his attackers Wensley knew better, and the following day at 9.00 pm, he saw Callaghan in Leman Street and arrested him; Hutchings, too, was arrested an hour later, saying, 'I wasn't there; I'm innocent.'

The Old Bailey jury thought otherwise. Hutchings had six previous convictions and Callaghan four, and both were sentenced to hard labour – Callaghan to twelve months and Hutchings to fifteen.

A deeply unpleasant robbery occurred when Ann Tofler was walking along Cable Street at 4.00 pm with her purse in her hand and found herself surrounded by five young desperadoes. One of them, William Downes, aged nineteen, who had been sentenced to six months' hard labour for burglary the previous year, punched her in the back; but although he then took her purse containing sixteen shillings, she grabbed Downes by the collar and snatched it back. To mark her insolence, Downes repeatedly punched her in the face, blacking her eye, twice cutting her lips and badly bruising her nose, whilst his twenty-year-old accomplice, James Cronin, punched her on her back and shoulder. The five men then fled.

Once again, Wensley knew exactly who he was looking for, and five hours after the robbery he arrested Cronin in Leman Street. Cronin told him he knew nothing about it, so Wensley blandly replied, 'Then you need not be frightened.' And as Downes was walking along Cable Street an hour later, as he quaintly put it, 'Detective Wensley came and took me.'

Despite a spurious alibi, the cowardly pair were convicted and each awarded twelve months' hard labour and 'a bashing' – twelve strokes with the cat-o'-nine-tails. The court awarded Miss Tofler £1 as a mark of 'her courageous conduct'.

So these were two cases where Wensley's personal knowledge brought about the arrest of the guilty parties. The next was one in which plodding police work resulted in the arrest of a thief and a receiver – and a jury let go five certainly guilty parties.

Charles Miles, aged eighteen, was employed by a clothing manufacturer, who instructed him to deliver forty dozen blouses on a barrow to Jacob Littmann, a job buyer of 56 Leman Street, on the evening of 16 March 1897. But when Miles handed over just a few boxes, Mr Littmann demanded to know where the rest of the consignment was, only to be told that someone had stolen Miles' barrow and the rest of the blouses with it. However, several witnesses had seen Miles with another boy, William Ford, aged seventeen, before the delivery; one heard Miles say, 'You go on with the truck; I'll take the boxes in.' Later that evening, a witness saw Ford take the barrow to 125 Shepherdess Walk, where the occupants, Edgar Cornwall Jnr (aged sixteen) and Edgar Cornwall Sr (aged thirty-nine) unloaded the boxes and took them inside. The following day, Frederick Vilben, aged forty-nine, hired a van and together with Cornwall Sr. loaded it with forty to fifty boxes and instructed a driver to take them to a job buyer, who later heard Cornwall say to Vilben, 'Get as much cash as you can.'

The buyer was suspicious and called the police. Vilben and Cornwall Sr were arrested. Ford, too, was arrested by Wensley and Gill, and on 18 March at 3.00 am, both officers paid a visit to 125 Shepherdess Walk. There they found sisters Ellen West, aged thirty-eight, and Rose Wilson, aged thirty, who denied any knowledge of any blouses; eight of them were found in a tin box belonging to West, another was behind a curtain. Cornwall Jnr was also in the premises; another sixty blouses were found, and he was also arrested.

All of the prisoners pleaded not guilty, with the exception of Cornwall Sr, who pleaded guilty to receiving. A letter had been found in his possession, which read as follows:

Dear Bill,

I have seen the boy again. He says about thirty-four dozen, so we may have two dozen each. That will leave thirty or more for 'H'. Bring me a dozen down as early as you like, in time for seven. I can sell your dozen at a good price.

Tom

It is quite possible that 'H' referred to Edward Hartley, a receiver of stolen goods who on 27 May had been sentenced to seven years' penal servitude for receiving stolen property on a widespread scale.

However, in his defence Vilben called Cornwall Sr to testify to his good character and the latter was subjected to cross-examination, which provoked this astonishing outburst:

I do not tell you my address; you won't get it. I ask the jury to believe me and refuse to tell it. I won't give my reason – I won't write it down, even if his Lordship and the jury only are to see it. I don't mind the police going when I'm there but they are not going when I'm out. I left the goods at Wilson's because my boys live there … I never went under the name of Wilson. I am a clerk – I'm employed nowhere … I do not tell you when I was last employed because enquiries might be made; eighteen months ago I was in employment – I decline to tell you where – I will not write it down … A letter was found on me – I won't tell you who wrote it; I don't know anything about it – I mean to incriminate nobody. I do not know who 'H' means – I do not know Hartley – I decline to answer – I do not know 'Tom' … I never lived at 4 Clarence Street with Mrs Wilson as my wife, or Clarence Square or Clarence anything else – I have never lived with her as my wife … I cannot tell you how long I've known her but I knew her brother intimately, better than I should like to know you.

And after all this, Frederick Vilben, Ellen West, Rose Wilson, Edgar Cornwall Jnr and William Ford (who was positively identified by several witnesses as Charles Miles' co-thief) were all acquitted. Charles Miles was convicted but the jury made a recommendation for mercy, since they considered that he had been the tool of Cornwall Sr, and he was sentenced to four months' hard labour. And Cornwall Sr – who must have come across as a near-hysterical, thoroughly shifty, not to mention arrogant piece of work – received his just deserts when he was sentenced to five years' penal servitude.

Receivers were ten a penny, but convicting them was something else. On 20 December 1897 a driver took a van containing six chests of tea to Lower East Smithfield and went upstairs. When he returned, the van and contents had vanished. Quite obviously, Wensley's informants had been burrowing deep, because the following day he and Detective Charley Smith went to Princes Street to interview Samuel Solomons.

Wensley was also accompanied by his senior officer, Divisional Detective Inspector Stephen White. It must have seemed inexplicable to Wensley that White should have chosen to accompany him on such a mundane task – DDIs absolutely never left their desks for operational police work unless it was a case of murder. But learning the name of the person that Wensley was going to visit, White wanted to hear, first-hand, what it was that Samuel Solomons was going to say. If it was something to his detriment, he would not want someone like Wensley to be the recipient of it; and given what was to happen at the forthcoming trial, this was a prudent move.

Speaking to Solomons alone, White told him he had reason to believe he had a quantity of tea at his premises. Solomons replied that he had some stables but that they belonged to his son, Isaac. If any other conversation passed between them, it was not recorded, but it was only then that White brought Solomons out into Princes Street, where he met up with Wensley and Smith. Solomons' sons Henry and Isaac were spoken to and denied that they were in possession of tea or that they had a key to the stables; the door was forced, and it was revealed that the stables contained the six chests of stolen tea.

'They are our stables, I'm not here very often, if there is anything wrong, it is the fault of my son,' Samuel told White, and turning to Isaac, he said, 'You are the man they want, you brought the stuff here, you know you did, I have told you before you will get us all into trouble, I wish I was dead; why don't you speak the truth and save me in my old age?'

Not unsurprisingly, Henry retorted, 'Why don't you shut up?'

Isaac said, 'The tea was brought here by a man named Brown, I know where he lives.' But when White asked for his address, Isaac replied, 'I don't know.'

Henry then offered an alternative explanation. 'No,' he told White. 'It was brought here by a man named Morris. I don't know where he lives.'

It was all compelling evidence to support a charge of receiving, and at the Old Bailey Isaac pleaded guilty, his father and brother pleaded not guilty, and a sustained attack was carried out on the character of DDI White by the barrister appearing for Samuel Solomons.

It appeared that Solomons was someone White had known for twenty years, undoubtedly as a receiver of stolen goods and quite possibly as an informant as well; he had given evidence for Customs and Excise in a smuggling case and, as was revealed during the trial, he was not slow in pointing the finger of blame at his own son. White was asked about allegations of impropriety made against him by the Association of Carmen which resulted in the possibility of questions being raised in Parliament. He admitted that some of his subordinate officers had been degraded and added that Brogden was one of them; 18 December 1897 was the date of his downfall with the bookmaker.

White denied that an officer named Lapsley had arrested him for being drunk (it had probably been an Inspector Montgomery), but Lapsley had made a complaint against him. Detective Sergeant Harry Lapsley had been busted to constable and as Police Constable 124 'X' had resigned from the Force on 20 February 1896 – his conduct was given, simply, as 'Good'. It all added up to White being conspicuously unpopular with his subordinates and, furthermore, rather shifty, after he admitted that 'only one' complaint had been made in respect of his conduct in the Hartley case, the previous year – even though he never gave evidence in it. 'I'm a chief inspector [sic],' said White, 'and hope I shall be for a long time.'

It is probably just as well that a note found during the Hartley investigation was not produced during Solomons' trial. It read:

Dear Sam,

Have sent a quantity of cutlery, say £10 the lot. I am going to send you some parcels from Smith, and as I do not want him to know your address, as the goods will go away from his place in Cotton Street, I have send them in the name of Archer to Milnes; so anything that comes in that name, accept, and settle with me.

Yours faithfully, Ted

So seventy-five-year-old Samuel Solomons tottered from the dock, acquitted by the jury. His sons were not so fortunate: the oddly named Mr Justice Latrine flushed them away to terms of penal servitude – four years for Henry and three for Isaac.

★ ★ ★

If the judge in the Solomons trial was strangely named, the girl who featured in Wensley's next case possessed a name which many a modern-day porn star might crave. Sheena Suck, aged twenty-two, and her associate Rose Greenbaum, aged seventeen, were two young women who had captured the attention of Wensley, Richardson and Detective Sergeant Henry Whitbread, because on 11 November 1897 the officers followed them from 11.00 am to 3.00 pm. The girls visited shops in Commercial Road and High Street, Whitechapel, before taking an omnibus to Tottenham Court Road, where they visited premises which included a jeweller's and manufacturers of fans and corsets. They then returned to Liverpool Street and as they walked along High Street, Whitechapel, they threw away two cardboard boxes marked 'J. Rosenburg & Co', the name of a company selling corsets. As Whitbread and Wensley stepped in front of the girls, so Suck dropped two corsets, saying, 'Not mine!' She was also carrying a fan, valued at £5 10s 0d, as was Greenbaum, who dropped her fan as she was arrested.

Both girls were dressed very fashionably and expensively: Suck was wearing a green three-quarter-length cape, and in her possession were £7 and a valuable diamond brooch. Greenbaum was in possession of two pairs of corsets, a gold chain in a satchel and also a pawn ticket for a sealskin cape. Wensley found another sealskin cape, plus a lot of satin and silk and other valuable property, in a drawer at the rooms at 23 Watney Street rented by the girls; the capes, they said, were theirs.

Not so. Enquiries revealed that both capes, valued together at £24, were stolen by the girls the previous day from a furrier's at St Paul's. Herbert Barnard, the proprietor, told an Old Bailey jury that Suck had represented herself to be a Madame Schneider, a court dressmaker of 12 Upper Rathbone Place, had said she wished to buy a cape for Greenbaum but had stated that none of the capes he had shown them were of sufficiently high quality. He had then gone off to find capes of a better grade; the two stolen capes were not even missed until the detectives showed them to Mr Barnard, the following day.

The girls were both represented by barristers who ran the unwise defence of saying that all of the property was theirs and that the detectives had stolen their receipts. It merited sentences of hard labour: fifteen months for Suck and nine months for Greenbaum.

Although the girls had carried out a series of shopliftings, this type of offence was officially known as larceny – as was the crime, commonly referred to as 'the jump-up', committed by thirty-two-year-old Robert Crundle. George Chilvers was driving his van through Ayr Street, loaded with eleven chests of tea; one – containing a hundredweight (112 lbs) of tea – was on the tailboard, and when he looked again, it had vanished. He then saw Crundle putting the chest on to his hired van. Chilvers chased the van and stopped its horse. Crundle jumped from the van and disappeared.

Some brisk questioning of the van's owner by Wensley and Charley Smith resulted in Crundle being identified as its hirer. Four days later he was run to ground in a pub in New Road; he told Wensley, 'I hope you will act fair and not put me away.' To Smith, he said, 'I shall plead guilty and try to get it settled here.'

Unfortunately, he did not, and at the Old Bailey he ran the defence that he had lent the van to 'some other chap'. A previous conviction for felony, even though it had happened six years previously, failed to mitigate his actions, and he went away for three years' penal servitude.

And all this happened the same year that Wensley's second child was born: a girl who was named Edith Mercy – known as Edie – who was fated to see as little of her father as her mother and sibling did.

* * *

Wensley had now been a detective for almost three years and thought, quite rightly, that he had achieved considerable success. He felt his efforts merited promotion to sergeant; after all, he had passed all of the necessary examinations, having been encouraged by Lollie to supplement his education by taking lessons from a retired schoolmaster. In addition, he had learnt a smattering of Yiddish so as to be able to converse with many of the East Enders. Nevertheless, he was passed over for promotion. Wensley now had over ten years' total service and he was the most effective thief-taker on 'H' Division. He had been commended on twenty-five occasions and been granted thirteen monetary awards. It all depended on a recommendation from his divisional detective inspector; but since that person was Stephen White, it was not forthcoming.

White's basis for refusal was given in a particularly wily fashion. It was usual when an officer was promoted for him to be posted to another division. So, in refusing to recommend Wensley he told him, firstly, 'I'm not going to have you transferred after I've taught you all you know.' This, of course, was nonsense. It was highly debatable whether White had taught him anything; it was simply an excuse to refuse advancement to an officer whom he thoroughly disliked.

White then added, 'You must wait until a vacancy occurs in this division.' He may well have been aware that no such vacancy would arise in the foreseeable future; and as and when it did, he could find a fresh excuse to deny Wensley the promotion he so richly deserved.

If White congratulated himself for placing a seemingly insurmountable barrier in Wensley's way, he had underestimated his junior officer's cunning and tenacity. Wensley refused to give up; he simply went right over his senior officer's head.

Wensley had originally gained admittance to the CID through his old superintendent, so now it was the new superintendent, John Mulvany, whom he approached. However, Mulvany was not about to side with a junior officer against a senior one. Not that this deflected Wensley from his promotional crusade by one jot, because he told Mulvany, 'Very well, sir; I will appeal to Scotland Yard.'

This probably took the wind right out of Mulvany's sails; such an action was practically unheard of. Having leapfrogged right over the head of his divisional detective inspector, a man regarded in the CID as God, this young upstart was proposing to do exactly the same with his superintendent. Mulvany told Wensley to go ahead, 'If you want to take the risk,' adding, 'It's a daring thing to do'.

And Mulvany was right; it could have cost an impetuous detective his career. However, what he did not know was that Wensley possessed a wild card. He enjoyed the friendship and patronage of the Chief Constable of the CID himself, Sir Melville Macnaughten CB, KPM.

* * *

Born in 1853, Sir Melville had been a tea planter in India before returning to England; due to his friendship with James Monro CB (later to become commissioner of police from 1888 to 1890), Sir Melville was appointed assistant chief constable of the CID in

1888 and chief constable two years later. He took an active interest in the 'Jack the Ripper' case and was regarded a most humane man, one who took a great interest in the careers and welfare of his detectives. The Assistant Commissioner, Sir Basil Home Thomson KCB, said of him, 'He knew the official career of every one of his 700 men and his qualifications and abilities.'

Wensley and the chief constable had first met during the Seaman case; Sir Melville heard that Seaman had an accomplice in the double murder and when he strolled into Leman Street police station, Wensley – the only CID officer there – explained the position to him. Wensley was enormously impressed with the officer's tact and charm and accompanied him at his request to 31 Turner Street so that he could personally view the murder scene.

However … although Wensley had carried out the arrest, the officer in charge of the case was none other than DDI White, who had doubtless heard from his predecessor precisely how Wensley had gained admittance to the Department. If White's dislike of Wensley had not commenced there and then, it was certainly present four months later, because he had instructed Jacob Myers, the murdered man's stepson, to let nobody into the house, 'not even the commissioner himself'. Wensley managed to persuade Myers to let them enter, but when White discovered what had happened, he was furious with Wensley for flouting his orders. Following a court commendation – as Wensley had been commended by the jury at the inquest in the Seaman case – it was unheard of for the officer not to be automatically commended by the commissioner. Not in this case, though. Refusing to put Wensley's name forward for official recognition was the very least that White felt he could do.

But Wensley had gained a true friend; and now he approached Sir Melville with his dilemma. Of course, to that diplomatic man there was no problem. He would ensure his protégé's promotion and at the same time be careful not to offend the sensibilities of DDI White, who was so keen not to lose such a valuable member of his staff.

On the very same day that Wensley approached him, Sir Melville ensured that the following day, 4 July 1898, Wensley would be promoted to detective sergeant (third class) and would remain on 'H' Division – now one man over strength.

# CHAPTER 5

# Detective Sergeant (Third-Class)

In the ten years since Wensley had joined the police, their annual running costs had only risen to £1,812,735, an increase of less than £270,000; but the crime figures had rocketed to 18,838. A proper punishment for Wensley's sleight of hand in obtaining promotion would have been to relegate him to mundane office duties, but White took the wrong course of action entirely; with the increased crime statistics he felt justified in putting a massive workload on Wensley's shoulders. Wensley, of course, could have asked for nothing better.

A month after his promotion, Wensley and Gill were keeping observation on four disreputable members of a racetrack gang, all of whom had been convicted of violent assaults. In the Mile End Road the quarry turned on their pursuers, with one of them, James Jackson, saying, 'What the fuck are you watching us for? Do you think we don't know you?' His associate, John Chatfield, then said, 'What are you following us for? You'll have to go through it now, you bastard!', whereupon the gang attacked both officers using a stick and their fists.

The men appeared at Thames police court on 27 August 1898, where it was revealed that Chatfield had previously served six months' imprisonment for assaulting a detective sergeant; this had possibly been a more sustained attack than that carried out on Wensley and Gill, because on this occasion Jackson and Chatfield were fined just twenty shillings each.

Within weeks Wensley and Gill were in action again, arresting Sam Karmaryzn of Catherine's Buildings, Cartwright Street who was in possession of a large quantity of ladies' clothing, jewellery and German currency. The property had been stolen from a railway station whilst its owner was in transit, travelling from one part of Europe to another; therefore, at Bow Street police court, a request was made for the prisoner to be discharged, since he was going to be extradited to Germany. Nevertheless, the magistrate stated that both officers 'had acted with great skill and zeal and he wished to commend them.'

Wensley and Gill were unstoppable; they kept observation on a team of industrious 'dips'[4], two men and two women, outside

---

4 Pickpockets.

the Royal Oak public house, Whitechapel Road, watching them 'rub down' potential customers. One of the men struck Wensley when he found a stolen compass in his pocket, but the magistrate at Thames Court on 16 March 1899 decided that whilst there was insufficient evidence to justify a charge of larceny, there was enough to convict them of being 'suspected persons'. Ellen Crawley, Catherine Smith and John Beattie all received three months' hard labour, and Henry Rogers, two months.

A jeweller's shop in Old Street, Shoreditch – part of 'G' Division's area – was the subject of a robbery by five men, and a considerable amount of property was stolen. William Bailey, a twenty-three-year-old fishmonger from Hare Alley, Shoreditch, had been involved in the planning of the offence and was supposed to have been included in the raid. When he was not, he found his associates in a public house spending their ill-gotten gains quite freely and demanded 'a corner' – or cut – of the money. Not only did they refuse, two of them threatened him with revolvers, so Bailey borrowed ten shillings, purchased a revolver of his own and on 15 January 1899 confronted the men in Hanbury Street, Spitalfields. There was an argument and Bailey shot one of the gang, John Long, in the neck.

Bailey was arrested and taken off to be charged with attempted murder, and Long was taken to the London Hospital where the house surgeon, Mr Gregory, described his injuries as being of 'a serious character'. In his coat pocket there was found the substantial sum of £51, and this discovery was communicated to Wensley.

Long's wife, accompanied by his brother Samuel, arrived at the hospital and requested the coat containing the money, which was handed to her. As the couple left the hospital, Wensley caught up with them and engaged them in conversation. Samuel Long said that his brother had been shot, following 'a row in the street'. Wensley mentioned that he had heard the man in hospital had been in possession of a considerable sum of money. Long agreed, saying it was £51 and that he had given it to his brother in order that he could buy some cloth. At this point Wensley revealed his identity and arrested Samuel Long for unlawful possession of the money.

At Worship Street police court the following day, Wensley was asked, amidst laughter in court, if he had initially represented himself as a press reporter in order to obtain the information. To this Wensley (showing every sign of indignation) replied, 'Certainly not!'

During a remand hearing, the injured John Long was called; the shooting had left him paralyzed in his left arm. He stated that prior to the shooting he had been hit over the head and that when, the following day, he demanded to know who was responsible, Bailey refused to say. Long had hired a group of bullies to teach him a lesson, and it was then that Bailey shot him.

The gang were determined to get the money back; their legal representative told the court that, 'it was ridiculous for the police to say it was the proceeds of a jewel robbery.' Samuel Long was discharged from receiving the stolen property, a summons under the provisions of the Prisoners Property Act 1869 was served on the police to recover the money and the case was heard before Sir James Vaughan, Bow Street police court's chief magistrate. Long stated that on the day of the shooting he had given his brother the £51 in order to purchase a business in Essex Road, Islington, and this was corroborated by John Long. A statement made by William Bailey (who, with four previous convictions, had on 8 February at the Old Bailey been sentenced to nine months' hard labour for the shooting) gave the correct version of the events.

The summons was thrown out, and although a High Court action was threatened, it never came to fruition. Wensley was perfectly aware of the identities of the rest of the gang but there was insufficient evidence to convict them. On the plus side, the offences happened on another division's ground – that, and the police got to keep the £51.

Burglars, next: Marks Rosenberg, aged thirty-two and a cabinet maker, broke into the Whitechapel home of Isidor Nash with another man and stole £170 in banknotes, two watches and some jewellery. When Wensley arrested him, not only did Rosenberg refuse to name his accomplice, he refused any information at all. Things did not go well for him at the North London Sessions when he appeared on 19 April 1899: his sentence was one of eighteen months' hard labour.

During the early hours of 2 May 1899, Frederick Brown and Herman Baungart, both of St George's-in-the-East, removed the glass from a window of 21 Albany Mansions, Battersea, the home of Herbert Henry Spencer, and stole a bicycle valued at eight guineas. Four hours later, Wensley and Richardson were on patrol when they stopped the couple. Wensley, wondering how a scruff like Brown could have afforded such a conveyance, was not impressed when Brown pointed vaguely in the direction of Tower Bridge, saying, 'I found it over there.' By the time they reached the police station, both men had made a full confession to the burglary, and Mr Spencer was so delighted at being reunited with his bicycle, which had been recovered almost as soon as he had discovered its loss, that he told the magistrate he wanted to commend the officers. The magistrate agreed and told them, 'The arrest was a smart piece of work.'

John Buller was a twenty-one-year-old carman[5] employed by Pickfords who had a very nice sideline of business in selling his consignments to fifty-four-year-old Aaron Cavalho, described by the police as being 'a fair old crook'. On 21 June Buller was arrested at Pickfords depot at 7.30 pm by Wensley and Gill and in a rash error of judgement assaulted both officers. Three hours later, Carvalho, having been seen in Union Street in possession of a parcel containing curtains and petticoats, was arrested at his home at Tewkesbury Court, a second-floor flat above 100 High Street, Whitechapel. Asked the origins of the goods, he replied, 'I shan't tell you'.

The following morning, as the cab containing Carvalho and Buller was about to enter the yard of the police court, Carvalho's daughter called out, 'You'll be all right, father', but he replied, 'Your father's done, my girl; look, here's the carman who brought the things to me,' indicating Buller. These comments were overheard by Gill.

Buller pleaded guilty at the Old Bailey to stealing the property and was probably lucky to be sentenced to nine months' hard labour. Although Carvalho had no previous convictions, he was weighed off with four years' penal servitude.

★ ★ ★

Receivers were often the most difficult of criminals to convict, few more so than William George Hearn, aged forty-two, of 10 Alexander Buildings, St. Luke's. Known as 'Fatty' Hearn, this appallingly slimy character frequently disposed of property stolen by means of vicious street robberies. Wensley decided on an innovative plan to trap him by persuading thieves who had sold him stolen property to give evidence against him. This was not a case of 'turning King's Evidence', where a prisoner in the dock would give evidence against a co-accused in return for a lighter sentence; this was a case where the thief had already been convicted, much in the same way that Supergrasses would be used, seventy years later.

Dr Henry Archibald Stonham had visited a patient at 5 Twine Court on 15 June 1899 and left at 4 pm; as he was walking through a passageway he was surrounded by five men, an arm encircled his throat and his head was jerked backwards. His gold watch and

---

5   Driver of a horse and van.

chain – a family heirloom and valued at 100 guineas – was stolen, as was a matchbox and fifteen shillings. Within a week, Henry Marsh, aged twenty-three, was arrested as was Thomas Thompson, aged twenty-one, and at the Old Bailey they were found guilty of robbery with violence. Each had six previous convictions. Marsh – also known as William Andrews – was sentenced to eighteen months' hard labour. Thompson, who also called himself Henry Wright, was sentenced to three years' penal servitude. Both men were additionally sentenced to twenty strokes of the cat-o'-nine-tails.

Wensley now went to work. He spoke to Marsh at Chelmsford Prison, where he was serving his sentence, and perhaps suggested that his 'bashing' could be deferred (or possibly even forgotten about) if important information was forthcoming.

John Levy was also arrested for the robbery and was sentenced to six months' hard labour – but most importantly, so was Hearn, the receiver, who was not only charged with receiving Dr Stonham's property but also receiving a twenty-guinea gold chain belonging to the victim of another robbery. Upon his arrest, Hearn told Wensley, 'It's got to be proved. My word is as good as theirs.'

At the police court Wensley described the arrest as 'most important', and Marsh came from jail to inform the court that, following the robbery, they had gone to the Black Swan public house, where they received £6 15s 9d from Hearn for the watch which they divided amongst themselves. Hearn had asked if it had been 'a shoe-fly'[6], and Payne, another of the gang replied, 'Yes, we searched a mug in Shadwell.'

Unfortunately, the question of credibility came into the equation. During his own trial Marsh had pleaded not guilty, stated he knew nothing about the robbery and offered an alibi, provided by his stepmother, Catherine Marsh, who got thoroughly confused and told the court, 'I cannot account for his story not being the same as mine.' Furthermore, he accused Wensley's chum Richardson of assault and intimidation, whereas Thompson told the jury, 'I've never been in Twine Court in my life. I swear before God, I'm innocent.'

Hearn was committed for trial, but the case was thrown out, the jury being told that if Marsh had committed perjury before, he could certainly do so again – particularly if it meant saving himself from a 'bashing'. It was a let-down but the concept of the scheme

---

6  Robbery.

had been good, particularly when coming from a newly-promoted detective sergeant (third class).

However, there were plenty more thieves and receivers waiting for Wensley to come and claim them. Receivers like Michael Lipman, a fifty-year-old lodging house keeper, who was visited at his home address by Wensley and Detective Smart. There they discovered four cases of brandy, two jemmies and a hammer. Lipman told Wensley, 'A lodger who slept here for nine nights brought ten cases here last Wednesday night and asked me to let him leave them here until the morning, as he was too late to deliver them. He took six away on Thursday morning and I have not seen him since.'

Thomas Keating, an eighteen-year-old carman who was responsible for the theft of the ten cases of brandy, valued at £125, was later picked up in Aldershot, and his comments rather knocked a hole in Lipman's explanation. 'I was led to do it,' he told Wensley. 'I took the ten cases to Lipman and he promised me £3 when he sold them,' adding sorrowfully, 'I've not had the money yet.'

With Christmas on its way, the demand for Yuletide gifts increased, especially those which had, in modern parlance, 'fallen off the back of a lorry'. In the case of James Morris, aged twenty-nine and Daniel Hayes, aged twenty-eight, they had delivered a whole van-load of goods directly to stables used by the receivers.

They had stolen a horse and van, and the commodities to be disposed of were confectionery, port wine, tea, cigarettes and firewood, valued collectively at £180. Wensley found the wine in a stable belonging to a Mr Deppe, who pointed him in the direction of 12 Lower Chapman Street. The occupiers, Hugo and Berthold Friday and Morris Kuttner, denied any knowledge of the goods, but this was contradicted by Mr Deppe, who reminded them that Kuttner had asked him to store the goods and Berthold Friday had rolled the casks into the stables.

Mr Mead, the magistrate at Thames police court, discharged Hugo Friday on 29 November but committed the others for trial. It was not a very Merry Christmas for any of the parties involved.

It was even less of a festive time for Kate Shannon and Frances Neville, who, on 23 December stopped a mariner named William Owen in the Commercial Road, asking him to 'treat them'. The virtuous Mr Owen refused but gave them twopence 'to get rid of them'. However, this beneficence was considered insufficient by the ladies; Neville put her arm around his neck, Shannon snatched his watch, and both women ran off. Their escape did not take them very far, however, because the whole incident had been witnessed by Wensley and Gill.

At the police station Neville told Shannon, 'You've got me into a nice mess.' But Shannon rightly replied, 'You were as much in the mire as I was.' And on Christmas Eve both women were sentenced to hard labour: three months for Shannon and six weeks for Neville. Since the matter was disposed of at the police court, it is possible that a deal was struck; prostitutes often made very good informants.

The year was coming to a close and 1899 had been a good one for Wensley. His promotion had been more than justified, he had brought in some impressive results and, furthermore, his third child, Harold William, had been born.

By the end of the year police numbers had risen to 15,763, to protect the capital which now contained a population of 7,000,000. But morale was poor, and there was a high rate of suicide amongst the officers, due to the harsh discipline and insensitivity of their senior officers.

Rigorous treatment extended beyond the police, of course; at the Old Bailey, Alfred Robert Soane and Samuel Robert Bone were convicted of committing an act of gross indecency. Judgement was respited and the judge granted them bail on the understanding that their fathers had them flogged.

So whilst the curtain was coming down on the 1800s, the early years of the new century would result in Wensley achieving spectacular successes, both in cleaning up the East End of London and in winning promotion, commendations and awards, all of which propelled him firmly into the public eye. But with success came controversy, over some of the most bitterly contested cases of the twentieth century.

# CHAPTER 6

# Shootings and Mayhem

While Wensley carried out his daily battle against Whitechapel's ne'er-do-wells he was unaware of the existence of Gustavo Franci, a violent eighteen-year-old Argentinian who arrived in England on 22 January 1900; it was not long before he was involved with two equally dangerous German citizens – Ernest Reuter, aged nineteen and Frederick Braun, aged twenty. All three were in possession of loaded revolvers, and on 3 February during the last of a string of burglaries in Dulwich, South London, the police were called and the men opened fire. Franci shot an officer in the leg, then ran off and fired again, hitting the metal plate on the helmet of a constable, who promptly 'sticked' him. Braun was disarmed, and when another officer approached Reuter and told him, 'Put it down or I'll knock you down', the gunman wisely did as he was told.

The trio were induced to describe how they had disposed of the stolen property; the receivers lived in Whitechapel, hence Wensley's involvement. Nathan Musheat, a tailor, agreed after some prevarication that he had originally received the goods, which were worth £150, and had sold them on to Lazarus Shapiloff, a jeweller, who allegedly told Musheat, 'I'll give you £15 for the lot, but don't say anything about it.'

Shapiloff later told the police, 'Well, the stuff is gone and you cannot get it back. You cannot do much to me; you cannot prove that I knew it was stolen.'

Famous last words, as the saying goes; in spite of the receivers being represented by barristers at their Old Bailey trial and Shapiloff calling three dodgy witnesses for his defence, both were found guilty and sentenced to hard labour – twelve months for Shapiloff and, with a recommendation for mercy from the jury, six months for Musheat.

There was no such plea for clemency in respect of the three armed burglars, however, who were each sentenced to eight years' penal servitude.

★ ★ ★

Thomas Rochford, at the age of sixty-two and in possession of ten previous convictions, really should have known better than to rob somebody he had known for years. He was one of a group of men who waited until William Wilson, a ship's boatswain, emerged from a urinal late in the evening of 25 June 1900 and then robbed him of £7 10s 0d. It was entirely likely that Rochford had been aware that Wilson was flush with money, since the latter had stood him a drink earlier that evening.

It took little time for Wensley to trace Rochford; at 2 am the following morning he arrested him in a lodging house at Shadwell and found he had £1 10s 0d in gold in his possession. 'I don't know anything about it,' he told Wensley. 'I wasn't there.' Pointing to another man who was also arrested, he added, illogically, 'He wasn't there.' But of one matter the jury was sure, and that was that Rochford *had* been there. He was sentenced to four years' penal servitude.

There must have been a large number of 'unfortunates'[7] who heaved a sigh of relief when a twenty-four-year-old German tailor named Edwin Hansen (also known as Arthur Esener) was locked up. In September 1899 Anna Grandahl had been living with Hansen but became alarmed at his unpredictable behaviour and left him; he showed three men a knife of Russian manufacture and told them, 'I've sharpened this knife today for three girls I want to kill; Anna, Lizzie and Lily.' Unfortunately for Anna, she was top of the list, and he stabbed her three times. She was so terrified of giving evidence against him that her friends set up a subscription list to raise money in order that she might leave the country.

Hansen originally pleaded not guilty at the Old Bailey to wounding Miss Grandahl with intent to murder her, but then changed his plea to guilty. Wensley told the court that he had seven previous convictions, including stabbing a police sergeant and breaking a man's arm, as well as having convictions in Germany. He added that Hansen lived on the immoral earnings of the women whom he terrorized, and that twenty such women had been threatened.

On 12 December 1900 Hansen learnt the hard way the advisability of keeping his mouth shut – not only that he should avoid bragging to his friends of his murderous intentions but also that it was not really prudent to tell an Old Bailey jury, 'When I stab people, I mean to kill them.' He was sentenced to ten years' penal servitude.

★ ★ ★

---

7   Prostitutes.

What follows is the strange and disturbing case of Police Constable 240 'H' William Ernest Thompson.

The story began on 13 February 1891. PC Thompson had joined the police two months previously and this was his first night out on the beat alone. He was patrolling Chamber Street at 2.15 am when suddenly a man dashed out of a side turning, Swallow Gardens; seeing the officer, he turned and ran off towards Mansell Street. Entering Swallow Gardens, PC Thompson turned his lantern on to the body of a woman; it was Frances Coles (aka 'Carroty Nell') an attractive twenty-one-year-old prostitute who had been working the area of Whitechapel for eight years, and she was dying. Her throat had been cut and blood was flowing freely from the wound, but she was still alive because she opened and shut one eye. Thompson was in a quandary: was this a victim of 'Jack the Ripper' and should he give chase? But the woman was still alive, and he felt it was his duty to stay and give aid if he could. His indecision – highly understandable, given his inexperience – would haunt him for the rest of his life.

The years passed, and PC Thompson was still a constable on the beat, now aged thirty-two and married with four children. He was popular with his colleagues, a willing and courageous officer and not inclined to be quarrelsome towards members of the public. At one o'clock in the morning of 1 December 1900 PC Thompson was patrolling his beat when there was a disturbance at a coffee stall at the junction of Union Street and Commercial Road. Seven men and two women were arguing loudly, and PC Thompson ordered them to disperse. So they did, with the exception of Barnet Abrahams, a forty-one-year-old cigar maker, who was both drunk and belligerent. 'What have I done?' he truculently demanded of PC Thompson, who in time-honoured tradition told him to 'move on'.

At that moment, Police Constable 400 'H' David Tittle was one of six constables in the Commercial Road conveying prisoners to Arbour Square police station, when he saw Abrahams advance towards PC Thompson, raise his arm and strike him on the left side of his neck. Thompson grabbed hold of Abrahams by his lapels and threw him to the ground, falling on top of him. As well as witnessing the assault, PC Tittle was quite definite about one matter: PC Thompson had not struck Abrahams.

PC Tittle and the other officers, including Police Constable 414 'H' Zieba Beckett, who saw blood spurting from PC Thompson's neck, rushed over to their mortally wounded comrade, who told them, 'I'm done. He's stabbed me – hold him', before he became unconscious, but his grasp was so tight on Abrahams' coat that it took several of the officers to release his grip.

Abrahams was pulled to his feet by PC Beckett and Police Constable 231 'H' Walter Atkinson; he struggled violently, and the incident was exacerbated by the arrival of about twenty aggressive tearaways. Police Constable 51 'H' Harry Harding caught hold of Abrahams by the back of his neck and PC Beckett hit the prisoner on his shoulder with his truncheon. Abrahams pulled himself partially free and struck PC Beckett in the chest. PC Atkinson then punched Abrahams straight between his eyes, twice – 'As hard as I could', he later told the coroner.

Abrahams had knifed PC Thompson – the weapon was recovered at the scene. The puncture wound in Thompson's neck was three-quarters of an inch long and the knife had penetrated his neck to a depth of two inches, severing the jugular vein and the carotid artery. He died shortly after reaching London Hospital.

At Leman Street police station Abrahams was seen by Inspector Frank Spencer, to whom he whimpered, 'They have knocked me about, cruel.' And so they had. He had two black eyes, his nose was broken and he had lacerations on both sides of his head and bruises on his shoulder and thigh.

Charged with PC Thompson's murder, Abrahams told Wensley, 'It is quite possible. I don't remember anything about it; I had no reason or cause to do any injury to anybody.' But later he said, 'I did do it; it was an unlucky moment for me.' After a pause, he added, 'May his soul rest in peace,' and, 'I regret it; it cannot be helped.'

At the Old Bailey, Abrahams' barrister, Charles Gill KC, argued that it had been PC Thompson who had been the aggressor, that he had pushed, punched and kicked Abrahams along the street before drawing his truncheon and hitting him across the head with it, and that Abrahams had drawn his knife simply to protect himself. Abrahams told the credulous jury that they had grappled and fallen to the ground with PC Thompson on top and that he had no idea how the officer had received his injury. It was difficult for him to remember, he added, since he was in such a daze after being hit by PC Thompson's truncheon.

Every injury inflicted upon Abrahams had falsely been attributed to PC Thompson, whose truncheon had never been drawn, since it was still in his pocket. Furthermore, no officer who struck Abrahams following his arrest attempted to deny or minimize their actions. But the jury accepted the defence: they convicted Abrahams of manslaughter, not murder, and Mr Justice Phillimore sentenced him to twenty years' penal servitude.

It was a most unhappy coincidence that Thompson's career had started with a young woman being knifed in the throat and that his own life had been terminated in the same way.

★ ★ ★

The case of Michael Cronin demonstrates the enormous difficulties and dangers of policing the streets of Whitechapel during the first year of the twentieth century.

Police Constable 279 'H' William Clarke was patrolling Commercial Road at 9.30 pm on 10 December when he saw Cronin, aged twenty-seven, and three other roughs interfering with pedestrians on the other side of the road. He kept observation on the gang and saw George Nixon, a seaman from Newcastle who had been paid off from his ship that day, walking towards them. He had been drinking, although as he later told an Old Bailey jury, 'I wasn't silly drunk'. But he appeared the perfect prey for Cronin & Co.

Cronin grabbed hold of Nixon, the others started rifling his pockets and Nixon shouted for help. He was thrown to the ground, Cronin knelt on him and snatched his pocket book containing a money order and some seaman's discharges from his inside pocket. His trousers were ripped right down and £2 18s 6d was taken from his pockets. When Cronin got to his feet, he kicked Nixon in the ribs. As PC Clarke dashed towards the four men, they took to their heels, and the officer chased them through several streets before he caught Cronin, who dropped Nixon's pocket book just as he was entering a lodging house.

The gallant Cronin screamed for help and about twenty men soon filled the lobby of the house. Cronin struggled furiously and PC Clarke wrenched 6s 6d in silver out of his hand. He was now behind Cronin, with an arm around his throat; someone knocked the top of his knuckle off with an iron bar, and Cronin received a blow which split his head open, although it was intended for PC Clarke. The officer was kicked on both sides; he drew his truncheon and, as he later said, 'used it freely on the crowd'. Cronin tried once more to escape and this time PC Clarke hit him on the head with his truncheon, so hard that Cronin's blood spurted into his face.

Assistance arrived, the heroic crowd melted away and at the police station Cronin stated that he was out of work and that he had pawned a ring that day, which accounted for the money in his possession. It was not really convincing, and after Cronin had swiftly been found guilty, Wensley told the court that he had twelve previous convictions and described Cronin as being 'a member of a dangerous gang of criminals who had been terrorising the neighbourhood'. This was sufficient to ensure that the Common Serjeant imposed a sentence of five years' penal servitude and fifteen strokes of the cat – and issued a very well-deserved commendation for the plucky PC Clarke.

\* \* \*

But it was not all violence on 'H' Division's streets; there were plenty of the common or garden types of offence being committed as well.

Henry Turner, aged forty, was delivering three hogsheads of whisky with his horse and van but made a detour to Devonshire Street, Mile End, where he was met by William Somerton, aged forty-five, who handed three bottles and two large jars to him. Whisky was siphoned into them and the two men continued to 13 Hedger's Grove, which was where Somerton lived, who went inside, taking the bottles with him. The whole episode had been witnessed by Wensley and Gill – it resulted in sentences of hard labour, four months for Turner and three for Somerton.

Next it was the turn of Thomas Pearman, a twenty-three-year-old carman, who on 26 September 1900 obtained employment by means of a forged character reference with agents of the Great Central Railway Co. Within days he had stolen a case containing cotton damask valued at £25 2s 1d which he passed to a receiver named Pinkus Green (described sinisterly as 'a foreign Jew'). The two men were seen by Wensley and Gill, who followed them to Green's address at Old Gravel Lane. There was the stolen property; the case showing the owner's address in Manchester had been broken open and was in the process of being burnt.

At the North London Sessions on 17 October the Chairman called the case 'a bad one', and he was right, especially when Wensley informed him that Pearman had used the same ruse to obtain employment in August 1899 and had then been sentenced to twelve months' hard labour. This time, Pearman received four years' penal servitude, and Green, who had served three prison sentences and who, Wensley told the Chairman, 'had long been suspected of receiving stolen goods', was sentenced to twelve months' hard labour.

\* \* \*

Lord Belper chaired a five-man Home Office committee in 1900 to consider whether or not the anthropometry system of identifying suspects could be improved by the addition of fingerprinting; once Edward Henry demonstrated the use of fingerprints from his collection of 7,000 prints, the committee was convinced. Their recommendation was that fingerprints should be routinely taken and added to anthropometric cards, and in the following year Scotland Yard's Fingerprint Bureau was up and running.

There was a further step forward in criminal investigation during 1900, although this only affected the CID personnel of 'H' Division. Stephen White, the detested DDI, retired with 123 commendations on 15 October after twenty-five years' service in the following circumstances. White had been arrested by Inspector John Boustred for being drunk and improperly arresting two men. He was taken before the commissioner and the matter was deferred for six weeks; however, after fourteen days White resigned and was fined one day's pay. And seven months after his resignation, White was arrested again, for being drunk and assaulting Inspector Boustred; this time he was fined forty shillings.

White's successor was a rather different kettle of fish.

Tom Divall had joined the Force in 1882. The first question asked by his inspector was, 'Can you fight?' – and this was put to the test shortly afterwards on the streets of Deptford when Divall encountered a group of drunken hooligans whom he told to disperse. They duly ambled away – save one, who stood his ground and received a right-hander from Divall. Seconds later, it was Divall who was clumped on the head; turning, he discovered that his assailant was none other than his inspector, who told him, 'I'll teach you better than to hit a man under a street lamp!'

Divall rose through the ranks and during a thirty-year career he would collect 216 commendations, reaching the rank of chief detective inspector; amazing really, since he had started work when he was eight years of age and had never been to school. He simply attended board school and taught himself to read and write at night whilst his wife and children were asleep. This appeared to have the desired effect; after a stiff examination and with eighteen years' service, Divall was promoted to inspector and replaced White as head of the CID on 'H' Division.

★ ★ ★

On 26 June 1901 both Divall and Wensley were involved in the investigation of the murder of Mary Ann Austin, a twenty-eight-year-old prostitute. She had been fatally stabbed at 35 Dorset Street, Spitalfields, a very common lodging house, and the manner of her killing – ten stab wounds below the waist, one in her womb, another in her rectum – prompted press reports that 'Jack the Ripper' was at work again. In fact, he almost certainly was not, and although the investigation was extremely thorough and Divall and Wensley were commended by the coroner's jury for their conduct of the case, the inquest was bedevilled by a string of witnesses who experienced the greatest difficulty in telling the truth. They 'only told another story when they were found out', sourly commented the coroner, Mr Wynne E. Baxter, and the verdict was one of 'wilful murder by some person or persons unknown'.

★ ★ ★

It was clear that Wensley was a superb all-round detective. However, in the coming months he would conduct two cases which were not only brilliantly investigated; they would also begin to completely reshape the whole concept of the Metropolitan Police's criminal investigation. The first would be the robbery of Frederick Cox. The offence did not take place on 'H' Division. Those responsible for the robbery did not live on 'H' Division. What was more, nobody believed that Mr Cox had been robbed in the first place.

The next chapter tells the story of what happened.

# CHAPTER 7

# The Embryo Flying Squad

Frederick Cox was a seventy-one-year-old jeweller whose shop was situated at 54 Clerkenwell Road. On 3 October 1901 the premises were undergoing refurbishment, and by 7.30 pm that evening the men carrying out the improvements had left. The watches repaired by Mr Cox's assistants were put into a box, prior to his taking them down to the safe. One of Mr Cox's employees had left, leaving two others, Edwin Craggs and Edwin Nicholls, who were about to leave, when a well-dressed man with an air of respectability entered the shop. This man was William Smith, aged thirty-nine, a criminal with two previous convictions, and he asked Mr Cox to show him the works of some watches. The two employees left, and Mr Cox served Smith, who to all intents and purposes was a genuine customer.

The door then suddenly burst open and two men, their faces masked with crepe material, joined Smith; the three then surrounded Mr Cox and told him they had come to rob, not kill him. Graciously permitting Mr Cox to remove his false teeth before thrusting a handkerchief into his mouth, they blindfolded him and tied his arms with ropes and straps which they had brought with them, before laying him on the floor. The two men were James Connor (alias James Shrimpton), aged sixty-six, a man with three previous convictions, and Frederick Lewis, aged forty-four, who had previously been convicted of a felony.

They robbed Mr Cox of his personal possessions, took the keys to the safe and emptied it, and removed anything else of value in the shop. Much of the property was gold, including watches, bracelets, seals, pins, rings and charms, valued together at £350. Before they left, the robbers said, 'We must hold him tightly', and bound Mr Cox to the banisters on the stairway.

Fortunately, Mr Cox managed to free himself quite quickly – had he not, it is more than likely that he would not have been found by his employees until the following morning, twelve hours later. If that had been the case, because of Mr Cox's age, the amount of force that had been used and the trauma it had caused, the robbery could well have turned into a murder investigation. As it was, the unfortunate Mr Cox had his work cut out to convince the police that a robbery had actually occurred; it was initially thought that he had dreamt up the scheme to swindle his insurance company.

Clerkenwell Road was part of 'G' Division's ground, so it was there that the matter was investigated and the description of the stolen property was circulated. It was nothing to do with Wensley, who already had his hands full; before, during and following the robbery at Mr Cox's premises, he was fully engaged in following and gathering information about the Weiner gang, of whom more later.

But this did not stem the flow of information coming into Wensley's office, because Detective William Brogden received a tip-off that one of Mr Cox's employees had been involved in the robbery and was also told the identities of the rest of the gang.

Therefore Wensley was now in possession of information about a gang of villains who lived on 'L' Division and who had carried out an offence on 'G' Division – which was nothing whatsoever to do with 'H' Division. Consequently, it was Wensley's duty to pass that information over to 'G' Division, so that the superintendent might contact his opposite number on 'L' Division, with all the attendant inter-divisional problems, bickering and jealousies which that would entail.

Typically, Wensley did nothing of the kind, and this was the reason why. As a junior detective, he had arrested a man who had shot a police officer on another division during the course of a robbery. Using his own ingenuity and contacts, Wensley had tracked the culprit down, arrested him, still in possession of the stolen property, and taken him to the local detective inspector of the division where the offence had occurred – who then claimed all the credit. Wensley was furious, and ensured it would never happen again.

Wensley discovered that the suspects were accustomed to meet in Clapham Park Road in South London, so that area was kept under observation by him, Detective Inspector Divall and his men, until 2 December, when he saw James Connor, together with his twenty-two-year-old son, Gaius Shrimpton, walking along Clapham Park Road. The two men were followed until they reached Carfax Square; the father entered no. 13 whilst the son waited outside.

When Connor emerged from the house father and son set off together, but once they were some distance away Divall and his men moved in. Shrimpton tried to escape, as well he might have, since he was in possession of a set of housebreaking implements. Both men were arrested and taken to the local police station, where Connor said, 'My boy knows nothing about it. I'm guilty and I don't care what becomes of me but I'm sorry for the boy.' In turn,

Shrimpton told Divall, 'I live with my father, but I don't know what he's been doing.' In Connor's possession Divall found keys, one of which fitted a box on the top floor of his lodgings which contained diamond seals and other items belonging to Mr Cox.

As soon as Connor and Shrimpton had passed out of sight along Clapham Park Road, Wensley and his officers rushed into the house at Carfax Square, where they confronted Frederick Lewis. 'My wife knows nothing about this,' Lewis told Wensley. 'Nicholls has shopped us. I was a fool to have anything to do with it. It looks bad for me, as I have a lot of the stuff at my place.' Feeling he might have left something out, he quickly added, 'It was not me who gagged Mr Cox.' Lewis certainly did have 'a lot of the stuff' – in his possession Brogden found three ladies' and one gentleman's watch and in a black bag in his room, seventy-two watch movements and eight watch cases, all the property of Mr Cox. He also found a jemmy and a centre bit.

With Messrs Connor and Lewis hotly denying that their son and wife respectively knew anything about the robbery, it seems highly likely that a little horse-trading was entered into; possibly as a result of this, Detective Sergeant Rose and Detective Brogden went to 43 Penton Place, Kennington, where they arrested Mr Cox's bogus customer, William Smith, who told the officers, 'That's all right.' Whilst the premises were being searched, Smith commented to his wife, 'This is a bad job, my dear. The old man has done this. I wish now I had never seen him.'

Another person who was implicated was William Henry Lawrence, aged sixty-one, a general dealer of 1 Gray's Place, Lambeth. When Detective Smart knocked on his front door, Lawrence looked out of the first-floor window and called out, 'Who's there?'

'The police,' shouted Smart, whereupon Lawrence vanished from the window and a great deal of noise appeared to come from the rear of the premises.

Ten minutes later, Lawrence opened the door. 'I expected this,' he told Smart. 'I had a good try to escape at the back of the house but I see you have some coppers there. I'm very timid and I thought you were going to shoot me as there are some queer things done now. I suppose the old man or "Long Fred" has shopped me. Give me a fair chance; you will not be able to charge me as I was not on the job with the others.'

In his room a life preserver was found, as was a gimlet and window wedges. It is likely that as well as carrying out the robbery in question, the men were a team of housebreakers, given the burglarious implements found in both Shrimpton and Lawrence's possession and the fact that other stolen property was found in Connor's possession. So after thirty-four hours' continuous duty, the majority of the robbers had been arrested.

However, Smith told the officers, 'Lawrence and Shrimpton know nothing about it'; and as Divall would later tell the Clerkenwell police court, 'The evidence against Shrimpton and Lawrence is weak.' Both men were later discharged, with Shrimpton becoming a witness for the prosecution.

And that left Mr Cox's assistant, Edwin Nicholls, aged forty-eight, who had set up the robbery. He had returned to the shop on the morning following the robbery and upon being questioned by the police provided a description of the 'customer', saying, after he was asked if he could recognize him again, 'I do not think I would'. Thereafter, he continued at his job, for which he was paid 28s 0d per week, until 16 November, when he terminated his employment.

Wensley now sent Nicholls a telegram, in the name of one of his accomplices, asking to meet him on 10 December at York Road; when he arrived he was met by the investigating officer, Detective Sergeant Henry McKenna of 'G' Division, who had previously seen and spoken to him. Told he would be arrested for being concerned with Connor, Lewis and Smith in robbing Mr Cox, Nicholls replied, 'I don't know Connor. I have known Lewis for the past ten years; he's a watchmaker.' At City Road police station, Nicholls said, 'What did you say you were going to charge me with? Does Mr Cox say I robbed him?'

'No,' replied McKenna. 'You will be charged with being concerned with Connor, otherwise Shrimpton.'

'I have known Lewis about six years,' said Nicholls. 'He introduced me to Shrimpton and a short dark man in the Criterion public house the night before the robbery. I have seen them all since the robbery but I am not going to say anything to convict myself.'

McKenna mentioned that he had seen Nicholls with Lewis in the Clerkenwell Road, eleven days after the robbery, to which Nicholls replied, 'Yes, I have often met him since.'

Nicholls had indeed met the others previously: at the Old Bailey in January 1902 before Mr Justice Jelf, where Connor, Smith and Lewis pleaded guilty, Edwin Craggs, Nicholls' erstwhile colleague, gave evidence that he had seen Nicholls and Lewis together, up to six months prior to the robbery. Alice Driver, the landlady at 57 South Island Place, Brixton, where Connor lodged, had seen Nicholls outside the house with Connor a day or two before the robbery, and Gaius Shrimpton gave evidence that at about the time of the robbery he and his father had visited four public houses with

Lewis, Smith and Nicholls and at the conclusion of these visits Nicholls walked off accompanied by Smith and Lewis.

And when another of Mr Cox's employees, Thomas Ellis, told the jury that he had seen Nicholls outside the jeweller's talking to Lewis two months before the robbery, and that furthermore, Nicholls had been obliged to borrow half-a-crown prior to the robbery but was wearing a different suit 'and a nice new hat' afterwards, it made Nicholls' assertion ('I had only seen the prisoners occasionally and they must have planned the robbery, but I had no hand in it') seem a little shallow. So did the fact that he was in possession of £2 in gold at the time of his arrest.

Nicholls was found guilty of conspiracy to rob, Mr Justice Jelf commenting that he regretted that Nicholls could not be sentenced to penal servitude, which he richly deserved, for morally he was as guilty as the others. Instead, Nicholls was sentenced to the maximum allowed by the law: two years' hard labour.

Not so the others, who additionally pleaded guilty to robbery with violence: Lewis and Smith were each sentenced to ten years' penal servitude and Connor to twelve.

The officers were highly commended, both by the judge and the commissioner, and quite rightly so; it had been a brilliant investigation. And what was more, the kudos had gone to the right officers.

★ ★ ★

The same year, Wensley set an operation in motion that in many ways mirrored the Cox enquiry and would also be echoed in the successes of the Flying Squad, when it was formed eighteen years later. It was an investigation of great complexity and it all began in July 1901, when Wensley was making an enquiry in the Shadwell area and happened to notice a group of Germans, mostly in their twenties. Some of them he had seen before but they were not known criminals; however, they did appear to have quite a lot of free time on their hands and a sufficiency of cash. It was enough for Wensley to keep an eye on them, and over the next few months, sometimes alone, sometimes working with Gill and Detective Ben Leeson, and inevitably utilising a variety of disguises, he started following them to see where they went and who they met up with …

Many of the group lived in a four-bedroom house at 5 Albert Street, Shadwell. Wensley discovered that the rent of the premises was paid by a woman named Bertha Weiner, a fifty-one-year-old German Jewess, who lived a mile away at 13 Ship Alley with a twenty-seven-year-old German seaman named Max Rebork, who would be finally discharged from his ship on 4 September. Bertha Weiner was a frequent visitor to Albert Street and from time to time she was accompanied by her brother Ludwig Weiner, aged fifty, and his two sons, Willie, aged twenty-two and Adolph, aged eighteen. Their profession was given as 'auctioneer' and they lived at 51 Tredegar Square, Bow.

It was impossible to constantly keep observation on the houses or to follow the occupants all the time, but occasionally some of the men would be missing from Albert Street for a couple of days. Clearly, they were up to no good, but what? Even if Wensley or his men could get close enough to overhear snippets of conversation, the men invariably spoke in German. Wensley therefore set his informants to work; one was especially close to the group, and the information which was forthcoming was that the men from Albert Street were a team of professional night-time burglars of dwelling houses – and not locally, either. They committed offences all around the London suburbs, usually working in groups of four or five, and they made some rich pickings. This was why Wensley had been unaware of their activities – crime in the commuter belt would have been of little concern to detectives working in London's East End. Bertha Weiner orchestrated the burglaries and disposed of much of the common or garden stolen property, but the more expensive commodities were dealt with by her brother and nephews.

So Wensley was not aware that during the night of 31 July the gang had broken into the home of Ernest Hatch at Beachwood House, Hampstead and stolen property valued at £400 – or that three weeks later, the gang had moved their attentions to 4 Endsleigh Gardens, Ilford. Early on 23 August, the householder, William James Brown, discovered he had been burgled and that property including a fish slice and fork were stolen.

Just over one week later, Warwick Dean at Ealing Common was broken into – the occupier, Lucy Millar, would later tell the jury at the Old Bailey, 'I missed a good many things', which included a music box.

And then, for a while at least, matters quietened; perhaps the gang were rejoicing at Max Rebork's return from sea. But at any event, the next recorded burglary was on 6 October, when Londerry, Chingford Hall was broken into and amongst the property belonging to George Phillips which was stolen were a pair of marine glasses. As if to make up for lost time, the gang then moved right across London to Middlesex, because the following night, 7 October, from 11 pm onwards, they ransacked the property of John Parsons and his son-in-law Montague Sharpe, at Brent Lodge, Hanwell.

Less than two weeks later, they struck again in the same area, at 19 Emmanuel Avenue, Acton. Colonel Carrie Fulton was furious to discover his house had been burgled; amongst the property stolen was a tea service, a seal with his coat of arms and most importantly, his medals.

Three nights later, the burglars were back across London again, this time in Barkingside; when Henry Durrell came downstairs he discovered that the door to his conservatory had been forced and possessions which had not been stolen were smashed and scattered about. Much of the tea service and silverware – and other items valued at £150 – were identifiable, as the gang would later discover to their cost. During the same night, the gang struck at nearby Wanstead, where they broke into the home of Sidney Maddocks at 8 Oak Hall Road. In the night he thought he had heard a match struck, and he was right; in the morning he found the gas alight in the kitchen, the previously secured back door wide open, the hall stand stripped of its coats and umbrellas and a great deal of other property stolen.

On 23 October, two days later, Emily Hartman, the wife of the licensee of the Royal Crown public house, St George's-in-the-East, performed a small service for her friend of two years' standing, Bertha Weiner. Mrs Hartman agreed to look after a parcel for her, since she confessed that she was afraid that her paramour, Max Rebork, would steal it. It was only after Mrs Hartman heard of the arrest of Bertha Weiner and her associates that she thought it prudent to hand the parcel to police. She did so, and it was opened in her presence; it contained a picture frame, a sofa cushion, a yellow silk piano cover, a tablecloth and a butter dish and cover. Some of the property belonged to Mr Durrell and some to Mr Maddocks.

The following day, William Rowe, an assistant at Dicker's Pawnbrokers at 300 Commercial Road, advanced 6s 0d on a jacket and vest (the property of Mr Durrell) and an overcoat (belonging to Mr Maddocks). The person bringing these items swore that the clothing was his to dispose of and he truthfully gave his name as Charles Yates and his address, which was 5 Albert Street.

Later the same day, Thomas Swift, an electro-plater and gilder from Oak Hall Gardens, Hornsey, received a visit from Willie and Adolph Weiner, who, it appears, were old customers of Mr Swift's business, where ready-money transactions were the norm. Swift had removed initials from silver items before for the Weiners, and this is what he did on this occasion; the property involved was part-proceeds from the burglary at Mr Durrell's.

The next night, 25 October, the burglars struck again; this time at 47 Kidbrook Road, Blackheath. The occupier, Arthur

Frederick Sturdee, discovered the following morning that several silver and plated articles had been stolen, as well as some wine and champagne. Some of the wine had been drunk on the premises, and a pipe from the Pan-American exhibition had been taken.

On 28 October, Willie and Adolph Weiner called upon Woolf Myers, the manager of Freeman's Jewellers, 26 Clerkenwell Road. Here too they were old customers, and they had a great deal of Mr Durrell's silver to sell. Mr Myers wanted to know if the items were 'all right' but he must have been assured that they were, because although Willie asked for 2s 10d per ounce, Mr Myers persuaded him to accept 2s 7d instead, and he eventually parted with £5 9s 0d. In fact, Mr Myers was a plausible sort of fellow; when the police pointed out that the receipt for Willie Weiner was made out in the name of 'Hymens' he was able to persuade them that this was an error by his clerk. It also secured his attendance at the Old Bailey as a witness for the prosecution, rather than an appearance in the dock to face a charge of receiving.

★ ★ ★

It had been Wensley's intention to carry out synchronized arrests on that day; however, a personal tragedy intervened. His father, who had been unwell for some time, died of phthisis, a wasting disease associated with tuberculosis, aged sixty-seven at his home at 16 Western Terrace, Kensington, and of necessity the raids had to be postponed.

In fact, this delay proved providential; the gang had begun to suspect something was amiss, and some of the stolen property was hidden away. But when nothing happened, they were lulled into a sense of false security. The following night, they carried out two more burglaries. The first was at Dorris Hill House, Willesden, where the occupant, Sir Hugh Gilzean Reid, disturbed the burglars at 4 am and they fled, taking with them a silver mug and a trowel which had been presented to Sir Hugh for laying a foundation stone. On the dining room table were many valuable items put there ready to take away.

But even though they had been disturbed, the thieves next struck at 234 Willesden Lane, the house belonging to Athelstan Dangerfield. A great deal of clothing was taken, as well as china and silverware. The scullery window had been forced as had the kitchen door, and as Mr Dangerfield told an Old Bailey jury, 'It must have taken them hours to do all this'. It probably had; one of the gang was discovered in the kitchen by the cook, Mary Lemmer, when she came downstairs at 6.45 am. The man ran off and the alarm was raised; the police were called, but of the intruders there was no sign.

Just before 6.00 am on 31 October, Wensley led his men to 5 Albert Street and went straight into the front room on the ground floor where he found three men in bed: twenty-two-year-old Conrad Blaschke, Matthias Hauten, aged eighteen and Franz Peters, aged nineteen. 'We're police officers,' said Wensley, 'and we're going to arrest you on suspicion of being concerned with others in committing burglaries in and around London during the past three months.' None made any reply, and Wensley entered a back room on the ground floor where he found William Wald, aged twenty-six, in bed with a woman; he then went up to the first floor front room, where he saw Charles Yates also in bed with a woman, and continued to the top floor, where he discovered Otto Braum and August Salveskie, both aged twenty-five and Saul Muller, aged twenty, in bed. All of them were similarly informed of their arrest, and since none of them had anything to say, Wensley left the premises, leaving the prisoners with other officers who made some interesting finds.

Detective Sergeant Alfred Gould found two spoons, eight odd socks and an umbrella in the room occupied by Blaschke, Hauten and Peters. In addition, in a cupboard in that room was a coat belonging to Mr Durrell and in the pocket a cold chisel, later found by Detective Inspector Divall to correspond exactly with the marks made at the burglary at Mr Dangerfield's house. In the room occupied by Wald he found Mr Dangerfield's coat, four small spoons, the property of Mr Durrell, the seal belonging to Colonel Fulton and a magistrate's badge. In addition, there was a photograph of Wald wearing the badge; he was a wrestler and liked to boast to his friends that he had been awarded the medal for winning a wrestling bout. In fact, it had been awarded to Montague Sharpe when he was Deputy Chairman at the Middlesex Sessions by his fellow magistrates and had been part of the haul from Brent Lodge, Hanwell.

Detective Sergeant Gill was present when Muller got dressed – later, at the police station, Gill realized that Muller was wearing a pair of bicycle stockings belonging to Mr Dangerfield. Detective Sergeant Roland Thornell was a little quicker off the mark than his contemporary; he noticed that the socks that Peters was putting on bore the initials 'AD' and deducing correctly that these belonged to Athelstan Dangerfield, he told Peters to remove them. It was not until they reached the police station that Detective Sergeant John Allam of 'S' Division realized that Salveskie was also wearing a pair of Mr Dangerfield's socks; in addition, he had Dangerfield's leather cigar case in his pocket.

Socks also featured in the search carried out by Detective Thomas Rose; in the back room where Muller, Salveskie and Braum were sleeping, he too noticed that Braum was starting to insert his feet into a pair of Mr Dangerfield's socks and made him take them off. He also found a hard black felt hat, a dagger in a case and a pair of scissors – all the property of Mr Dangerfield – as well as a tea cloth and a cream jug, a black felt hat and coins, the property of Mr Durrell. In Yates' room Rose found a basket, the property of Mr Dangerfield, as well as two silver spoons. In the front room on the top floor Rose found a bottle of champagne – identified by Mr Sturdee as being his property.

On the way to the police station Blaschke told Detective Frederick Stevens, 'Me no thief; they are all thieves. I have only been with them three months; I only went with them twice, once to Willesden and once to Wanstead. I did not go into the house – I only carried the stuff.' He had, quite literally 'carried the stuff' – the hat he was wearing en route to the station belonged to Mr Maddocks.

The other garrulous prisoner was William Wald; he told Detective Ben Leeson, 'I would not get into other people's houses, only they told me I would make lots of money like them.' He neglected to tell Leeson that the waistcoat he was wearing belonged to Mr Durrell.

*   *   *

In the meantime, Wensley and Detective Inspector Divall had gone straight to 13 Ship Alley. Wensley shouldered the door to the front room on the ground floor where he beheld Bertha Weiner and Max Rebork in bed. Divall told them, 'We are police officers' and asked Weiner, 'Do you rent No. 5 Albert Street, Shadwell?'

She replied, 'Yes.'

Divall said, 'I have caused eight men to be arrested there for committing burglaries in London.'

Weiner replied, 'They have brought a lot of things to me; I do not know where they did get them.' She added, 'I do not know nothing' – which, as Divall told an Old Bailey jury, he interpreted as meaning, 'You won't get anything out of me.'

Wensley told Rebork that he was under arrest for burglary and Weiner for receiving stolen goods. Weiner responded, 'You have got to prove that I knew it was stolen.'

Police Constable 175 'S' Thomas King, a fluent German speaker, was present when Rebork was dressing, and heard him say in German, 'I do not know anything about these affairs; these men from 5 Albert Street bring all sorts of things here which the old one buys but I do not know where they get them from or what she does with them. Now and again, she gives me a shilling out of the things; there are eight of them lodging there, and they all come here with stuff.'

Detective Sergeant Gill discovered that Weiner's and Rebork's English was quite intelligible when he searched their room. He found two of Mr Dangerfield's tablecloths as well as a purse containing sixteen pawn-tickets. Bertha Weiner said, 'Some of those tickets belong to me and some to my lodgers at 5 Albert Street.'

Upon Gill finding a sugar sifter (Mr Durrell's property), Rebork said, 'That is mine; I bought it with a lot of other things from Mrs Weiner's lodgers in Albert Street.' Gill also found a pipe (the property of Mr Sturdee), to which Rebork said, 'That is mine.'

When Gill found Lucy Millar's music box, Bertha Weiner claimed, 'That is mine, I have had it for years', and when he found George Phillips' marine glasses, Rebork told him, 'That is my property; I am a seaman.'

★ ★ ★

Whilst the arrests and the searches were being carried out, Detective Charlie Smith and other officers had gone to 51 Tredegar Square, arriving there at 9.30 am, just in time to see furniture and hampers being loaded into a large pantechnicon. In the passageway of the house were Ludwig, Adolph and Willie Weiner, and Smith told them, 'We're police officers and have reason to believe you have stolen property in your possession, the proceeds of burglaries.'

Ludwig replied, 'I have got nothing, only what is my own.'

Willie said, 'I do not know what you mean.'

Adolph said, 'You have made a mistake.'

Smith took a hamper out of the van, which Adolph stated was his. In it was a mug, serviette ring, teapot, sugar basin, milk jug and tobacco jar belonging to Mr Dangerfield. In another hamper and a large box at the front door – of which Willie claimed ownership – Smith found a trowel, a cup (the property of Sir Hugh Reid), a dozen knives, a cruet stand and two overcoats, belonging to Mr Dangerfield. In a leather bag in the passageway – 'That bag is mine,' said Ludwig – Smith discovered six fish knives and forks, a fish slice and fork (the property of Mr Brown), a salad spoon and fork, a sugar basin and tongs, a milk jug and snuff box, all the property of Mr Durrell.

Detective Smith invited the men to account for this property and they obliged him. Adolph quickly passed the buck, saying, 'I bought the things from my brother Willie.'

Willie responded, 'I bought them from some man who came to the door, I forget how much I paid for them', and added that he had forgotten to get a receipt.

Ludwig's reply rather sunk him, because he said, 'They are my wedding presents and were given to me on my wedding, about twelve months ago.'

★ ★ ★

Back, now, to Leman Street police station. When Wensley arrived there with his prisoners from 13 Ship Alley, he saw Yates, part of the haul from Albert Street, who told him:

> I never stole the things, it's not my game. If you had come yesterday, you would have found a lot of stuff; they were frightened of seeing you about there and took a lot of it away. They asked me to pawn a suit of clothes for them, which I did. One of the officers found the ticket on me; the worst of it is, I told the pawnbroker that they belonged to me. All the men you have got here went out together about nine o'clock in the night, last Monday week; they came home early on Tuesday morning and brought the clothes and some silver and nickel-plated stuff with them; they told me that they broke into a house somewhere off the Edgware Road.

All of which information, gratuitously given, was of great assistance to Wensley; later, in cross-examination, he denied that he had told Yates, 'If he would give me information about those other fellows, I would let him off.' That, said Wensley, 'was absurd, as I had no authority to do so.'

But what was extraordinary were the conversations recorded by PC King. He mingled with the other prisoners, they, of course, being quite oblivious of his ability to speak and comprehend German.

Hauten said, 'I am sorry I did not put my own jacket and vest on, I have left my own socks and boots behind and hope they won't find out whose they are.'

Braum asked him, 'Did you not take the name out of the socks?'

Hauten replied, 'No', but Peters said, 'I did.'

Wald said, 'What a lucky thing Max fetched all those things away the night before last; if they had found all that, what a job it would have been.'

Yates said, 'I think the old woman will hold her tongue for her own sake; anyhow, neither of us have sold her anything, you understand that, don't you? I hope they won't find the other stuff in the hole under the table and the lot under the stone; I say, Hauten, they will see the holes in the doors where you have practised with your drills.'

Hauten replied, 'Yes, we left them behind, and I suppose they have found them.'

Salveskie said, 'Look here, it is no good talking, we must deny everything and hold our tongues.'

Muller said, 'I expect they will find the music box at the old woman's and the marine glasses.'

Hauten said, 'Let me see, the yellow silk handkerchief, the two table cloths and the umbrellas all come from the same place, so as it stands they only have the one case against us.'

Muller said, 'I wonder whether they will find me out at Holloway? When I was there before I gave the name of Richard Dresser. I expect there will be someone there who will recognize us.'

Braum said, 'Oh well, my liberty has not lasted long, I have only been out three or four months.'

Peters said, 'I am curious to know whether they will arrest Salveskie.'[8]

When Yates said, 'What do they know about me?' Hauten replied, 'Quite enough, for they have no doubt kept observation on us and have seen us go there drinking.'

Yates said, 'I do not think the old woman has much about her place; I dare say Max has taken most of it round to Smith.'

To this, Salveskie said, 'Smith may call at Albert Street today, and he will find himself collared by one of the blue ones.'

Muller responded, 'Don't you worry, he knows about this affair long before now. There, you see, they will both get off, and we shall have to do time.'

Baume stated, 'If they ask me how long I have been here, I shall tell them I have only just returned from South America.'

It was, thought the investigating officers, quite an illuminating series of conversations.

★ ★ ★

At 12.30 pm Wensley went to 51 Tredegar Square, where in the front room of the house he saw the three Weiners who had been

---

8  Since Salveskie had already been arrested, it is possible that the word 'arrest' was used in the sense employed by East End criminals, to ask the arresting officer, 'Am I nicked?' meaning, 'Am I going to be charged?'

detained. He told them, 'You will be charged with being concerned with Bertha Weiner in receiving the proceeds of burglaries and housebreaking during the past three months', and none of them replied – except that, on the way to the police station, Willie Weiner told Wensley:

> About three months ago, Mrs Weiner who lives at 13 Ship Alley, and is my aunt, sent me down some plated stuff which she said she had got from her lodgers at no. 5 Albert Street; I bought the articles and she afterwards introduced me to the men, and I have had several deals with them. When they got anything, they used to send for me and I used to go to no. 5 Albert Street and buy it. My aunt was always there and I thought it was all right; a lot of the plated and silver stuff had initials on, and it was unsalable, so I had the initials taken out. You will find two forks, two jam spoons, two salt spoons and a large spoon at Mr Swift's, a jeweller in Percival Street, Clerkenwell Road. I have had the initials taken out and replated.

Willie Weiner had been as helpful to Wensley as Yates had been earlier, but there was more to come: at the police station, in the absence of his father and brother, Willie pointed to Muller, Yates and Blaschke and told Wensley, 'These are three of the men I bought the stuff from.'

All of the prisoners were then charged, and at the police court Hauten told the magistrate, 'I can prove I was in Germany till three months ago.' Wald stated, 'I am innocent'; Salveskie said, 'I bought the stuff I gave to Yates'; Bertha Weiner said, 'I had two gentlemen staying in my house. One of them had a box he left; I never knew the things were stolen'; and Rebork summed up matters for everybody by saying, 'The evidence is false.'

However, the magistrate thought otherwise and committed the thirteen prisoners for trial; on 16 December 1901 they appeared at the Old Bailey, before Mr Commissioner R.L. Smith KC. All of the prisoners, with the exception of Muller and Peters, pleaded not guilty.

The defence unwisely prompted Wensley and Gill to explain the association between the defendants; this they were able to do in great detail, giving evidence of their observations and describing who met whom, and when.

The case for the defence was that much of the property could not be accurately identified by the victims in the case. Mr Dangerfield positively identified most of his belongings but admitted he was unable to do so in respect of the tablecloth which had been found in 13 Ship Alley. His wife Susannah was able to identify the tablecloth and a serviette, and when Mr Morris, appearing for nine of the defendants, suggested otherwise, she turned on him, furiously. 'I say they are mine, because they *are* mine!' she snapped. 'They are not English, they are French; the pattern may be common in France but not in England.' She went on to point out that the 'D' on the serviette was not a laundry mark, but her own initial.

Mr Maddocks also identified much of his property and saw that his hat, which he had seen Blaschke wearing at Arbour Square, had had its lining, upon which were his initials and the maker's name, Towley of Fenchurch Street, torn out.

George Phillips identified the marine glasses found in Rebork's possession and told the court he had owned them for twenty years, noting they were slightly bent on one side, having fallen on deck. 'The sort of accident that could have happened to any such object?' slyly asked Mr Morris, to which Mr Phillips tartly replied, 'It did to mine.'

Having shot himself in the foot twice, Mr Morris compounded the matter by questioning PC King's ability to speak and understand the German language. Unfortunately, PC King cut an impressive figure in the witness box, stating firmly that there was no mistake in his statement and he had not confused one prisoner for another. After that crushing defeat, Mr Morris sat down and left the nine prisoners in his charge to their fate. He was not alone; the other barristers appearing for the rest of the defendants fared just as badly.

It was a miserable defence, with the prisoners blaming each other, denying having made incriminating statements, and giving nonsensical reasons for being in possession of the stolen property. It was inevitable that they would be found guilty.

Wensley told the court that the defendants were a most dangerous and clever gang of burglars and that they were able to connect the gang with thirty-six burglaries, although there may have been many more. They were connected with some of the worst characters in London, added Wensley, and for good measure he mentioned that the Weiners had received stolen property valued at £1,000, although only £150 of it had been recovered.

On 20 December the judge passed sentence. Adolph Weiner received twelve months' hard labour, but everybody else – with one exception – was sentenced to five years' penal servitude. The exception was Bertha Weiner – as ringleader, she was sentenced to seven years' penal servitude. At that, the prisoners erupted with fury and did their best to attack Wensley; it took the efforts of several very large City of London policemen to assist the dock officers and prison officials in getting them into the waiting prison vans.

Wensley and his men were highly commended by the trial judge 'for being instrumental in breaking up this dangerous gang of burglars', and it was a commendation that was echoed by the commissioner of police.

But it was more than a good job well done; it made its mark on Wensley – it showed what could be achieved by a group of men carrying out observations, using disguises and cunningly using informants to secure the arrest of a dangerous gang. The birth of the Flying Squad was getting nearer.

# CHAPTER 8

# Murder and Gang Warfare in the East-End

There had been a silly, pointless, drunken quarrel in a coffee house during the evening of 10 October 1901; Henry 'Scotty' Wilson, a commercial traveller, had got in a fight with a man whom he had knocked out; then he turned his attention to Edward Palmer, a thirty-one-year-old steward, blacked both his eyes and knocked him out too. The management ejected all of the combatants into the street.

The fighting continued, however. Wilson now took on Edward Palmer's brother George, and this time Wilson got the worst of it. Edward Palmer had meanwhile gone into a barber's shop to get his face bathed and emerged to help Wilson to his feet; but far from expressing gratitude, Wilson stated that he intended to 'cut the Palmer brothers' heads off'. In fact, Wilson stabbed George Palmer, and this was witnessed by his brother, who had acquired a knife of his own from a nearby chandler's shop. Edward Palmer shouted, 'You've stabbed my brother – take that!' and plunged a knife with a foot-long blade into Wilson's heart. As he ran off, Palmer, perhaps unnecessarily, told a passer-by, 'I've done it.'

Palmer was arrested by Wensley and Gill and charged with murder, but nobody was particularly surprised when he was convicted of manslaughter and sent to penal servitude for three years.

Wensley now had a whole string of successes behind him, especially the robbery of Mr Cox and the arrest of the Weiner gang – as well as a senior officer without the hostility of Reid or White – and after three and a half years he was promoted to detective sergeant (second class) on 1 January 1902; and retained on 'H' Division – naturally!

Two nights later, there was a rather curious incident. Wensley, Divall and Detective Thomas Rose were walking along New Road. Perhaps they had been celebrating Wensley's promotion, but in any event, five men, including Arthur Levine and Ezekiel Rose, obstructed the footway, Levine loudly stating, 'Here are three splits' [detectives].

Divall told them, 'I'm an inspector of police – behave yourself!' but Levine ignored this warning and punched Wensley in the face, knocking out a tooth; and as Wensley fell to the ground, he was kicked all over his body. Levine was arrested, as was Rose, for obstructing police and using bad language, and Rose gave the rather ambiguous statement, 'I'm sorry I attempted to interfere with Levine', the meaning of which depended on whether a full-stop or comma was inserted after 'sorry'.

At Thames police court Levine told the magistrate, 'I'm filled with horror that police officers should attempt to swear away my life. What has been stated has been a tissue of falsehoods. I hold a prominent position in the civil service and I know how to behave myself.' It was entirely the wrong approach. The magistrate, Mr Dickinson, snapped:

There are not three officers in the service who hold better positions for good character, yet it was alleged by the prisoners that they had committed an unprovoked attack on them. I am not able to accept that.

He was also not able to accept from Levine's solicitor that his client was 'a well-behaved, inoffensive man', and he sentenced Levine to one month's imprisonment, with a forty-shilling fine for Rose who, for good measure, was bound over for six months to be of good behaviour.

★ ★ ★

A month later, Thomas Keith was driving his employer's van containing eleven chests and four half-chests of tea, valued at £97, along Great Prescott Street, when he became aware that his tailboard was down and a chest of tea was missing. He ran up the street and saw a light van driven by George Avey draw away from a gateway, pulled the flaps of the van apart and saw the chest of tea. He caught hold of the pony's head to stop it and Avey picked up the chest of tea, threw it into the road and said, 'Now you've got your chest of tea – now, go.' Avey jumped down and pushed Keith away and another man struck him. Avey then drove away, and when Keith returned to his van, it had vanished. The man who had stolen the chest of tea from Keith's van was William Murray, and the whole scene had been witnessed by a gatekeeper in nearby Mansell Street.

The van was found, minus its load, three hours later, in Oxford Street, Mile End by police, who reported, 'There was only tea-dust at the bottom of the van.'

By the time Murray was arrested, four days after the theft, and Avey surrendered himself to Wensley four days after that, of the tea there was no trace. There were no confessions either, although both men were positively identified. Avey stated that at the material time he was at work; his employer said that he was not. Murray claimed he was in the West End at the time of the theft and that numerous witnesses who were with him had promised to say so in court; unfortunately, they failed to materialize.

Both having been found guilty, Wensley told the court that Avey had five previous convictions and was 'an associate of thieves'; he was sentenced to five years' penal servitude, and Murray to twelve months' hard labour.

While Wensley was waiting for Avey to surrender he had been occupied in keeping observation with Detective Girdler in response to a request from Godfrey Phillips & Sons, tobacconists of Commercial Street, who had been experiencing losses of tobacco for some considerable time. Two days before Avey's arrest, they saw two dustmen, John Petley, aged forty-eight and Robert Hall, aged thirty-one, enter the rear of the premises and remove what appeared to be refuse but turned out to be three pounds of tobacco, which was loaded into the front of the van and put thence into the dustmen's pockets. It resulted in hard labour: one month for Petley and six weeks for Hall.

★ ★ ★

There followed two killings, both completely representative of the East End. In the first, alcohol played a prominent part, and both were carried out by persons who were themselves characteristic of the social inadequates of the area.

The marriage of William and Elizabeth Jane Abel was doomed, more or less from the start. Mrs Abel soon acquired a drink problem and was prone to attack her husband on occasions when she had had too much; she was regarded as a bad-tempered and a very drunken woman. On the evening of 22 February 1902 the couple had been out together, and after they returned to their flat on the second floor of 115 Cable Street at about 6.30 pm, one of the other occupants of the house, Mrs Mary Harold, heard the sound of an argument coming from their room and the sound of smashing crockery. William Abel, aged twenty-nine, a coal carman, saw Mrs Harold and showed her a cut and bleeding head and elbow. She offered to bathe the wounds but he refused, telling her, 'I wish I was dead.' He then left. It was later that Mrs Harold discovered the lifeless body of Mrs Abel.

Wensley arrived at about 9.00 pm, together with Detective Inspector Divall and the police surgeon, Dr Thomas Jones. There was smashed crockery in the couple's room. Dr Jones examined the body and found a wound on the chin; further examination revealed that death had been caused by Mrs Abel's head striking the floor with great force.

Wensley and Detective Sergeant Thornell were waiting for Abel when he returned home at midnight, drunk. Told he would be arrested for the murder of his wife, Abel replied, 'She kicked up a row with me because I hadn't been to work and threw the sugar basin and saucer at me, cutting my head. I pushed her away and went out. That's all I know.'

It did not seem the strongest evidence upon which to proffer a charge of murder, but the magistrate, Mr Dickinson, at Thames Police court obviously thought there was enough. Asked if he wished to say anything, Abel replied, 'Only this. I wish to say I am innocent of the charge against me.' On being told he would be remanded, he asked, 'Can I have bail?' but Mr Dickinson replied, 'Oh, no!'

The Coroner's Court agreed with the views of Mr Dickinson; Abel was committed on a charge of murder to the Old Bailey, where he was defended by Edward Abinger, of whom more later. Abel's defence was that his wife had come home drunk, called him names and hit him with a cup on the elbow and a sugar bowl on the head; he shoved her away, she fell over and Abel walked out. As he did so, she called him a filthy name as he went downstairs; he did not believe his wife was dead and he had not intended to hurt her.

Abinger called the two doctors who had examined and carried out post mortems on Mrs Abel, and it seems strange that neither was asked if there was alcohol in her stomach, to substantiate Abel's claim that she was drunk at the time of her death. Perhaps the jury assumed that there was, because they duly acquitted Abel of murder.

★ ★ ★

The death of any child is distressing, but that of two-year-old Emily Tucker on 15 March 1902 was horrifying in its brutality.

Emily lived with her mother, Matilda Tucker, at 15 Little Pearl Street, Spitalfields, where for the last five months of the child's life her mother's companion had been William George Burley. There is little doubt that Burley had what would nowadays be referred to as 'issues', because on one occasion he said to the child's mother, 'Lil, hasn't she got fine eyes? I could kill her but I love her too much.'

On the night of the murder, the couple had quarrelled and separated. Percy Hughes, aged thirteen, who lived in the same house, later saw Burley holding the naked child underneath a cold water tap, and when Mrs Tucker returned home she found her child dead, with terrible injuries to the head, vagina and anus. Nearby was an iron bar; it had previously been used as a poker and it was bloodstained.

When Burley later returned, Percy's mother, Eileen Hughes, told him that Mrs Tucker had rushed the child to hospital. Burley attempted to leave and Mrs Hughes grabbed hold of him, saying, 'You wait here till the police come', but he threw her to the ground and ran out into the street. Mrs Hughes followed, shouting 'Murder', and Burley was arrested by a passing constable.

Interviewed by Wensley, Burley told him, 'I don't care a fuck. You can hang me now if you like but if I get the chance, I'm not going to get the rope round my head and dance on nothing.' He later admitted that his name was not, as he previously had stated, 'Arthur Thompson' and that he had killed Emily 'because the kid had made a mess'.

At the Old Bailey, Burley's defence was, 'I strongly deny striking it on the head or any other part of its body, barring its arse.' It would appear that the jury found this explanation acceptable, because Burley was cleared of murder, found guilty of manslaughter and sentenced to five years' penal servitude.

★ ★ ★

For several years prior to 1902 the East End had been terrorized by a gang of thugs led by twenty-eight-year-old John Bonn, who also used the names McCarthy and George Marriott. He had been convicted at the Great Midlothian Sessions five years previously, and invariably carried a loaded revolver. His second-in-command was James Brooks, aged twenty, who had been convicted at Clerkenwell, three years previously; he, too, carried a revolver. Other gang members were James Edwards, aged thirty-three, who had also been convicted at Clerkenwell two years previously, and Harry Sharper, aged eighteen, convicted the previous year.

Their way of working was simple and uncomplicated: they demanded money from shopkeepers, bookmakers and stallholders, and if the money was not forthcoming, inflicted extreme violence upon their victims.

Myer Edgar was a bookmaker who had been targeted by the gang; initially, he had paid up, but in January 1902 in the King's Arms public house he was introduced to a local tough named

Thomas Tamplin, who had convictions for assaults and robberies. At the end of February, Bonn & Co issued their usual demand to Edgar, who refused to pay; instead, he spoke to Tamplin, who paid Sharper a visit, taking with him an iron bar. Since Bonn headed 'a gang of about twelve murderers', as Edgar later colourfully described the organization, it was rather unwise for one man to take on the group. Tamplin should have been aware that this piece of *lèse-majesté* would not go unnoticed or unpunished.

On 5 March Edgar was playing billiards in the Black Bull public house, Old Montague Street, together with his brother David and some friends, when the door opened and the gang walked in. Sharper said, 'What did you send Tamplin round to me for?' and Edgar replied, 'I know nothing about it.'

Sharper punched him in the face, Bonn said, 'Go on, do him in', and Sharper, picking up a billiard cue from the table, cracked Edgar over the head with it. Brooks pulled out a knife, saying, 'Come out of the way, and I'll kill him', although he was prevented from doing so by a gang member. The gang acted like a pack of wild animals; several of them, including Edwards, beat Edgar (and anyone else who got in the way) with billiard cues. Bonn produced a chopper, saying, 'Come out of the way, I'll finish him', and with that he struck Edgar three times over the head. As Edgar fell to the ground, Bonn picked up a water jug, which he smashed on his head. Most of the clientele had already fled; the gang left, too, but they were not finished for the evening.

Within an hour the six-handed gang entered The King's Arms, Whitechapel Road, where they correctly guessed they would find Thomas Tamplin. Bonn hit Tamplin with a chair, Brooks used an iron bar on him and the police were called. Police Constable 243 'H' Major Jones arrived and arrested Bonn, who told him, 'Let go of me, I'll have your fucking life, you bastard', and punched him on the jaw. PC Jones drew his truncheon and hit Bonn once on the arm, then on the head, whereupon Brooks grabbed PC Jones by the collar, saying, 'Come on Jack, have a fucking go for it.' Brooks, too, was arrested and taken to Leman Street police station, where Wensley was acquainted with the circumstances of the incidents.

Almost immediately afterwards, Sharper walked into the police station and with unbelievable arrogance told Wensley, 'I am come here to see they get fair play.' Upon being charged with the two assaults, Sharper replied, 'It served them right, I wish we had given them more.'

That left Edwards. It also meant that Tamplin and perhaps one or two associates were able to take a suitable revenge on 8 March, including the use of an iron bar. On that date Wensley and Gill were in the Whitechapel Road when they saw Edwards in a cab; Wensley shouted at the cab to stop, but Edwards told the driver to whip up the horse. Wensley chased the cab and, grabbing the horse's bridle, forced it to stop. Told he would be arrested, Edwards replied, 'Yes, that's right. Look what they've done to me tonight; I mean to put some of them through it.' He was relieved of an iron bar, which he stated he had taken from Tamplin, and when charged he replied, 'I was there but I didn't put a hand on either of them.'

Tamplin was not eager to assist the prosecution, but fortunately Edgar was, and the four men appeared at the Old Bailey before the Common Serjeant on 7 April 1902 where they pleaded not guilty to wounding with intent.

Their extortion enterprise had not been a huge financial success, because only one of them – Bonn – was able to afford a defence counsel. Their defence was that there had been a quarrel and that the witnesses were committing perjury; this did them no good at all, and they were all found guilty.

Wensley told the court:

> I have known the prisoners for years. Bonn is one of the most brutal and cowardly ruffians I have ever met – he was the pioneer of a very desperate gang of blackmailers in the East End of London who went about demanding money from small tradesmen. When money was not forthcoming they wrecked the shop and carried away whatever they could lay their hands on. Brooks was the second-in-command of the gang. Both he and Bonn always carried about with them loaded revolvers. Sharper was 'the king of the purse bouncers' – people who did 'the purse trick'.[9] Edwards was mixed up with the stabbing of a man to death last October. Nobody could imagine the terror that the gang inspired in the neighbourhood, even among their own class.

The judge declared that the prisoners had been found guilty of 'an outrageous and combined assault' and that their characters were of the worst; he sentenced Bonn, Sharper and Brooks to five years' penal servitude and Edwards, who, he believed, had not taken so active a part in the assault, to four years.

---

9   Purse bouncing: a scam in which three half-crowns (7s 6d) were purported to be put into a purse and sold at a knock-down price, only for the dupe to later discover that the purse contained three pennies instead.

This may have been misplaced clemency because, leaning over the edge of the dock and looking at the police officers, Edwards said, 'When I come out, I'll settle one of them.' The judge immediately ordered Edwards to be returned to the dock and told him:

> The court will consider whether the threats which you have uttered against the witnesses ought to be considered as a reason for increasing the sentence that would otherwise stand against you. Your case will be adjourned for the present.

Edwards replied, 'Well, look at this scar on my face, which was caused by the police. Didn't they ought to be punished for that?'

At the close of the sitting, Edwards was brought up to the dock again, the judge telling him that on consideration he regarded Edwards' earlier outburst as 'an idle threat' and that the sentence of four years' penal servitude would stand.

Why did Edwards blame the police for his scar? Is it possible that Thomas Tamplin, after extracting his own brand of justice and having caused Edwards to be sent to the London Hospital, informed Wensley of his whereabouts so that he could be arrested?

It was nonsense, of course.

# CHAPTER 9

# Gangsters from Eastern Europe

For a decade from the 1890s onwards turf wars were fought in the East End between two rival, predominantly Russian, gangs, the Bessarabians and the Odessians. The Bessarabians took their name from the region in southern Russia which borders Romania; they had drifted from country to country before finally ending up on the streets of Whitechapel. The Odessians were named after the port of Odessa on the Black Sea.

Detective Ben Leeson claimed that he went undercover to penetrate and disrupt the gangs, although unless he spoke fluent and colloquial Russian, Polish, Romanian, Greek, Tartar and the various gypsy dialects which made up the lingua franca used by the gang members, he may have experienced certain difficulties in being accepted as one of their own. Having the appearance of an English music hall artiste would not have helped;[10] a good detective Leeson may have been, but he was one blessed with a fanciful imagination, and it is more likely that his 'undercover' activities simply consisted of keeping the gang members under observation.

The gang's prey were the foreign shopkeepers and tradesmen of the area, from whom they demanded payment, and they were merciless in their retribution when faced with refusal. Stalls and shops were wrecked and their occupiers beaten up. Matters were not helped by their victims' refusal to prosecute, either through distrust of the police or fear of reprisals, or both. The Bessarabians – also known as the Bessarabian Tigers or Fighters, or the 'Stop-at-nothing Gang' – roamed the streets in groups thirty to forty strong and were utterly unscrupulous and terrifying fighters, who used a variety of weapons: guns, knives and broken bottles. One of their more unpleasant tricks was to approach the family of a girl soon to be married and threaten to destroy her reputation by spreading false rumours regarding her virtue, unless the father of the bride paid up. Invariably, he did.

When the proprietor of the Odessa Café, a man named Weinstein, refused to pay the Bessarabians protection money, they attacked him with an axe and he fought back with an iron bar. Tit-

---

10 See the photograph of Leeson on p.4 of the plates section.

for-tat operations were frequent: the Odessians lured a Bessarabian named Perkoff into an alley and cut off one of his ears with a razor; in response, the Bessarabians wrecked a coffee stall which was under Odessian protection.

On 3 July 1902 Wensley must have thought he had made a breakthrough in smashing up the gangs. Three members of the Bessarabians – Max Moses, a twenty-two-year-old pugilist who boxed under the ring name of Kid McCoy, Joseph Weinstein and Barnett Brozishewski, aged thirty – attacked a former Russian police officer named Philip Garalovitch, knocked him to the ground and stole £6, his watch, umbrella and hat. When his companion, a man named Rosenberg, tried to intervene, he, too, was assaulted by Moses. Wensley arrested them all and charged them with robbery with violence. When they appeared at Thames police court, Garalovitch told the magistrate that Weinstein had approached him and said, 'Hello, you gave me two years' imprisonment in Russia.' Garalovitch replied, 'I only did my duty', and was then attacked. It was sufficient for the three men to be remanded in custody for a week; it was also sufficient time for some exceedingly dirty business to be transacted, with the result that by their next appearance Garalovitch had beaten a hasty retreat to South Africa, Moses was fined £3 (or one month's imprisonment in default) for the assault on Rosenberg and the other two men were discharged.

Wensley was furious, and the three Bessarabians were triumphant; by now, they must have felt that they could walk on water, but when they put it to the test, three months later, Wensley was ready for them, and witnesses who might have been reluctant to come forward in the past now did so, undoubtedly, on this occasion, at Wensley's prompting.

★ ★ ★

On 4 October at about 2.30 pm, one of the Bessarabians, Samuel Oreman – also known as Monge – went to a cookshop in Church Lane and there he met Cooksey Lewis and Henry Brodovitz. There had been bad blood between the men and – as was later recounted through an interpreter – Oreman told Lewis, 'I want you for a fight.' Lewis stated that he did not wish to fight and Brodovitz intervened, saying, 'If you fight him, I will take his part.' Oreman replied, 'I don't want to fight you, and if you take his part I will watch you and kill you.' He then left the shop and walked off with some other men, including Max Moses.

Several hours later, Police Constable 145 'H' Arthur Pryor was on duty at the York Minster Music Hall in Philpot Street.

There had been trouble there the previous week, and now crowds of Bessarabians were in Commercial Road, asking where the Odessians were likely to be. It appeared that they found out, because Max Moses, who was sitting in the sixpenny seats with Oreman, said to PC Pryor, 'I expect a bit of a fight here tonight from the mob that was here last Saturday night.'

The officer was not aware of any trouble the previous week, since he had not then been on duty and, furthermore, he did not know Moses, whom he mistook for one of the hall officials. He therefore replied, 'All right. If any of them come in here, will you show me who they are?'

Two brothers, Hyman and Israel Colman, accompanied Henry Brodovitz to the Music Hall, but before they could pay the entrance fee, Moses, Oreman and Brozishewski walked down the stairs and attacked them. The fight spilled out into the street, and approximately fifteen men ran into Varden Street; another group of men, probably fifty or sixty in number, ran up from Newark Street, and when the two groups met in the middle of Varden Street, a pitched battle broke out, the numbers swelling until they reached two hundred.

PC Pryor left the music hall and attempted to disperse the fighting crowd; Brozishewski aimed a punch at him and Pryor hit him with his truncheon. He heard cries of 'Murder!' from the crowd and then a shout of 'Let's out him!' which he took to mean that they intended murder. As the former soldier later told an Old Bailey jury, 'I have seen a good deal of fighting in the East End on Saturday nights – I would rather be in South Africa [the Boer War] than a fight like this one, where I was not sure of my back.'

Simon Tanenbaum went into Varden Street and saw Oreman holding Brodovitz; both Oreman and Moses were brandishing knives, and he was hit by a bottle thrown by Brozishewski which made a half-inch deep cut on his temple. He also heard someone say, 'You have stabbed me'.

Simon Krovesky was cut on the back of the head with a knife wielded by Moses and asked him, 'What have you against me?' Oreman and Brozishewski were nearby, and the latter hit Krovesky hard on the jaw. Dr Charles Grant, the divisional surgeon later examined the wound on Krovesky's jaw but, as he told the Old Bailey jury, 'It was of no gravity.'

Solomon Shamos witnessed the fighting in Philpot Street, saw Oreman holding Brodovitz, who cried out (according to the interpreter, who translated quite literally instead of colloquially, with unintentionally hilarious results), 'Oh, you have given me a blow – Max, you gave me a blow.' Shamos then saw Brodovitz run into the White Hart public house.

Joseph Haimovitch heard Moses say, in English, 'It is done.' He also saw Brodovitz lying on the floor of the public bar, as did Henry Charles Grose, who had been playing bagatelle in the White Hart. Brodovitz had been surrounded by a number of people who had come in from the street. One of them was Max Moses, who pushed past Grose and picked up a knuckleduster from the floor close to Brodovitz and said, 'I'll give you India rubber mob', an expression that Grose had never heard before – it is likely to have meant that Brodovitz had suggested that the gang of which Moses was a member was pliant rather than hard and inflexible. Grose heard the licensee say, 'Come on, old chap, we can't have you lying here; you will have to get outside,' but Brodovitz replied, 'I can't – I'm stabbed.'

Moses met Brozishewski in the street, and they and some others walked off. When Inspector John Pickett arrived, Grose told him what he had seen and accompanied him to Back Church Lane, where on the corner were about twenty of the gang. With great presence of mind Grose grabbed hold of Brozishewski; the rest took to their heels, and Inspector Pickett carried out the arrest. 'This is what I get through trying to take a knife off a man,' complained Brozishewski, holding up a hand swathed in bandages, and was taken to Arbour Square police station.

When Samuel Cohen, an interpreter, told Brozishewski that he would be charged with maliciously wounding both Tanenbaum and Krovesky, he replied, 'Are you sure I have had a bottle in my possession? I did knock Krovesky about, but not Tanenbaum.' Since Cohen had not mentioned the existence of a bottle, this was regarded as a classic slip-up.

Brodovitz was still alive when Dr Edward Ambrose arrived at the White Hart, but he died six or seven minutes later. The wound in his chest, which also penetrated the pericardium and liver, was six inches deep and, as Dr Ambrose observed, 'terrible force must have been used'.

The following day, at 33 Wharfedale Road, King's Cross, Wensley arrested Max Moses for murder. He responded, 'I was there but I didn't kill him.' Later, he told Wensley, 'Last night I was with some pals at the York Minster Music Hall. Someone told me the Bessarabian Mob was outside; I went outside, someone threw a bottle at me, I had a fight and went away. One of my pals is in the hospital; the row was all over me.' And then, possibly to display the power he held over a rival gang, he added, 'If that man hadn't died, £15 would have squared it.'

It was not until 2.00 am on 13 October that Oreman arrived at Leman Street police station and said, 'I want to give myself up; the boys say the police want me about the fight the other night. I'm Sam – they call me Monge.'

The following day, all three prisoners were formally charged with murder, as well as with wounding Tanenbaum and Krovesky. Moses made no reply, Oreman said, 'I reported myself after hearing that I was wanted concerning this murder' and Brozishewski said, 'I know nothing at all about it. I had a fight with Krovesky but I don't know anything at all about the murder.'

★ ★ ★

Wensley had no intention of letting witnesses to the case be terrorized, so he had a discreet word with the magistrate at Thames police court, Mr Mead, who stated quite unequivocally that anyone attempting to intimidate witnesses would be sent to prison. Woolf Selvitzky and Marks Lipman duly took up this challenge, and for punching Marks Mieland and saying, 'My pal is in trouble through you,' both were sentenced on 1 November to two months' hard labour. Still the magistrate's dictum had not been heeded; the following week, Woolf Kigesky and Joe Zelkowitz who had tried to extort money for the prisoners' defence from Morris Goldberg, each received one month's hard labour.

The prisoners were committed on a charge of wilful murder on the Coroner's inquisition to the Old Bailey, where on 24 November 1902 they appeared before Mr Justice Bigham. Edward Abinger defended and, true to form, as it will be later explained, became emotionally involved with his clients; he brought a number of witnesses to say that it had been Brodovitz who had been the aggressor and Moses the intended victim.

These witnesses' testimony was as colourful (and in part, probably just as untruthful) as several of the prosecution witnesses had been. Abraham Neimann stated that he saw 'a mob of fifty people' (at the police court, he had said there were twenty or twenty-five), including Cooksey Lewis holding an iron bar and, Neimann said, dancing, proclaiming 'Tonight, I will be happy – there will be a joyful event.' (During cross-examination he decided that Lewis was holding a knife rather than an iron bar – 'that', he said, 'was another man'.) The Colman brothers were there, Israel holding a chisel and Hyman a knife. The latter said, 'Where is Monge and where is Max? Tonight will be the end of them.' He also saw Krovesky with a knife in his hand, and they, with several others, ran towards the music hall.

Krovesky was also present with Brodovitz and eight other men earlier in the day at the Union Restaurant, when, according to a customer, George Green, Brodovitz demanded to know the whereabouts of Max Moses, saying, 'If I get hold of him, they're be nothing left of him.'

At the music hall, before the performance, Harris Shalinsky and his friend Isadore Shor were having a drink in the bar when Hyman Colman told Shalinsky, 'Harry, we're going to have a fight, don't mix up, go home because there will be murder.'

Shalinsky asked, 'Why, murder? What do you mean?'

To this, Colman replied, 'Don't ask questions, take my advice and go home.'

When Lewis Miller gave evidence, he informed the jury that he was currently serving four months' imprisonment for keeping a gambling house, although the real reason for his conviction was because he was telling the truth about what he had seen. Having cleared the decks for some remarkable evidence, he said that on the night of the murder, at about 7.00 pm, Brodovitz walked into his restaurant and demanded to know the whereabouts of Max Moses.

'What do you want him for?' asked Miller, noticing a thick iron bar up his sleeve.

Brodovitz replied, 'I want to kill him.'

Telling him that Moses had gone to the music hall, Miller said that Brodovitz went outside and addressed a sixty-strong crowd. Krovesky was there, holding a bottle, as were Hyman Colman, Shamos and Tanenbaum, and Cooksey was holding an iron poker 'three-quarters of a yard long'. Having apprised the mob of Moses' whereabouts, Brodovitz told them, 'Come along, and we'll kill him there.'

This was corroborated, in part, by Max Weir, who had been convicted with Miller. He had seen Brodovitz with the iron bar up his sleeve ('the bottom was showing'), and as the crowd gathered, it divided into two parties, one group outside the music hall, the other in Varden Street. Brozishewski was struck on the head with a bottle wielded by Krovesky, another man ran up holding a knife, and when Brozishewski tried to disarm him, his own hand was cut. Twenty men rushed Moses – Brodovitz, iron bar in hand, was one of them – and Moses was kicked on the ground. The gambling charge against Weir, for which he was currently serving fourteen days' imprisonment, he told the court, was of course a trumped-up one.

The testimony of Morris Goldsmith – again, given via an interpreter – was even more thrilling. He had seen Brodovitz running down the street brandishing an iron bar and said to him, 'Where are you running with that piece of iron in your hand? You may kill somebody with this iron.' To this, Brodovitz replied, 'I am going to kill him. I have a good number of people with me.' Goldsmith, who of course, had no idea whom Brodovitz wished to kill, followed the mob into Varden Street and Turner Street, where he saw Moses. 'Max, you had better run away, you can see all the people have weapons and irons,' he told him; but since Moses was on the ground being kicked by a number of people, this advice was not particularly helpful. Krovesky was one who was kicking Moses, as were Hyman Colman and his brother Israel, although, according to Goldsmith, Israel was kneeling on him and kicking him at the same time. The jury doubtless pondered the physical difficulties that this must have entailed.

Louis Latinsky, Hyman Clainowitz and Abraham Steinberg also gave evidence, but although every witness for the defence had differing views on who did what to whom, one thing was clear: none of them had seen any of the three prisoners carrying weapons, and although some had heard of the Bessarabians, they were unable to say who were members of the gang; certainly, they themselves were not.

Abinger did his very best to show that his clients were the victims in this case – he had acquired slightly more private witnesses for the defence than the prosecution had – but after a two-day trial, although the jury acquitted the prisoners of murder, they convicted them of manslaughter.

Wensley told the judge that Moses was a pugilist but for years had been getting his living as a bully, and that the other two prisoners were 'associates of bad characters'. The judge adopted the jury's recommendation of mercy for Brozishewski and sentenced him to six months' hard labour. The others, however, were sentenced to penal servitude, Oreman to five years and Moses to ten.

Almost immediately, cracks appeared in the Bessarabian organization. With the ringleaders in prison, the gang broke up and dispersed, but this was only a temporary respite. There was plenty of room for more gangs to flourish – and they did.

Great Scotland Yard, where
Wensley was sworn in as
Constable ...

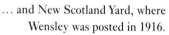

... and New Scotland Yard, where
Wensley was posted in 1916.

Kennington Lane police station.

Whitechapel, at the time of Wensley's arrival.

Leman Street police station.

Arbour Square police station.

# Some of Wensley's 'H' Division contemporaries

DDI Edmund Reid.

DDI Stephen White.

D/Sgt. William Thick.

D/Sgt. William Brogden.

DDI Tom Divall.

D/Sgt. Ben Leeson.

Sir Melville Macnaghten CB, KPM.

Arthur Harding – Wensley's nemesis.

The Old Bailey.

Detectives in disguise.

# The Houndsditch victims and their murderers

Jacob Peters.

George Gardstein.

Yourka Dubof.

Memorial to the murdered police officers.

Max Smoller.

Nina Vassilleva.

# The Anarchists at 59 Grove Street

Fritz Svaars.

Peter Piatkov.

Sara Trassjonsky.

Luba Milstein.

Winston Churchill directing operations at Sidney Street.

(L–R) Det. Insp. Fred Wensley, Chief Det. Insp. John McCarthy, Chief Constable (CID) the Hon. Trevor Bingham, Ass. Commissioner Sir Melville Macnaghten, Superintendent Patrick Quinn (Special Branch).

# The Judge and the Houndsditch conspirators

Mr Justice Grantham.

Karl Hoffman.

John Rosen.

Osip Federoff.

# The Murder at Clapham Common

Stinie Morrison at South-Western police court.
The police constable's facial expression bears
mute testimony to his thoughts on Morrison's
theatrical pose.

Leon Beron – victim.

Preliminary proceedings at South-Western police court; the magistrate is The Hon. John de Grey.

# Judge, barristers and defendant in the Morrison trial

Mr Justice Darling.

Sir Richard Muir KC.

Edward Abinger.

Morrison – convicted.

(L-R) Standing – Chief Inspectors Elias Bower, Alfred Ward, Tom Divall, Fred Wensley, Charles Collins. Seated – Albert Lawrence, John McCarthy, Superintendent Frank Froest, Henry Collins, Frederick Thomas.

Ass. Commissioner Sir Basil Thomson.

Sir Bernard Spilsbury.

# CHAPTER 10

# Overlook Nothing!

During his relentless pursuit of criminals Wensley never stopped learning not only the ways, the haunts and the associates of the miscreants of Whitechapel, but also their cunning defences. One ploy used by Samuel Bowman he never forgot.

During the night of 10 April 1902 George Rush awoke at 222 Whitechapel Road to discover a man ransacking the drawers in his bedroom. 'What are you doing here?' shouted Rush, and the man ran out of the room. Two purses had been stolen, containing £1 0s 10d, plus a bunch of keys and a police whistle. Police were called, and a search of the area revealed a distinctive looking button, found at the rear of the premises.

Four days later, Wensley was on patrol in Charles Street when he saw Samuel Bowman, who he knew to be a prolific burglar. He also noticed that a button was missing on Bowman's waistcoat and that the other buttons completely matched the one which Wensley had in his possession. 'I'm not one of those chaps,' responded Bowman indignantly to Wensley's accusation of burglary, but a search revealed that he was in possession of the keys and whistle, which were identified by Mr Rush.

Because it had been dark, Mr Rush could not identify the intruder; but even without identification or a confession, the case against Bowman seemed pretty watertight, and Wensley's enquiries revealed that the button had been missing from Bowman's waistcoat since the night of the burglary. So Bowman was committed for trial to the Clerkenwell Sessions, only to reveal that the missing button's shank was still attached to his waistcoat – and the button which Wensley produced had its shank intact. Therefore, it was put to the jury, the button produced by the prosecution could not possibly have previously adorned Bowman's waistcoat. Except of course that it had; Bowman had induced a friend to bring in a broken shank whilst he was on remand in prison and had sewed it into position. But it was sufficient for the jury to acquit, and Wensley learnt a bitter lesson: take possession of *all* the evidence in future – especially waistcoats – and leave no room for argument.

This specially applied when eighteen-year-old William George Perrin stole 112 lbs of tea from his employers, Messrs Donaldson, and took it to Cherry Tree Court, where it was handed to Henry Delafuente, his brother Abraham and Robert Hill. The transaction was observed by a clerk, James Panton, and he called Police Constable 474 'H' Bertrand Roberts, who rather gormlessly asked Abraham if anything had been brought into his yard. 'No,' he replied, 'but if it has, it's gone through the boozer.' He was referring to the Cherry Tree Court public house, so PC Roberts made enquiries in there; by the time he returned, there was a large fire burning in the Delafuentes' fireplace. Wood which bore a suspicious resemblance to parts of a tea chest was ablaze. PC Roberts' ten-minute absence had given Henry Delafuente and Hill sufficient time to load the tea into a sack and wheel it away on a barrow. This was witnessed by Thomas Griffiths, coincidentally employed as a carman by Donaldson. The unsuspecting PC Roberts collected his witness, Mr Panton, and wandered off to the police station with him.

Speed was of the essence, so Wensley and his men rushed to Cherry Tree Court and arrested the Delafuente brothers. Abraham told him, 'All right, you've got to prove it. I had some tea in my overcoat pocket which fell to the floor. The tea has gone, we have done you and all your bloody cleverness, do what you like.'

Henry stated, 'I know there was a chest of tea brought in. I wasn't here; I can prove I was in my father's house. Abie bought a pound of tea and the tea you see lying about the floor dropped from his pocket.'

Wensley looked on the ground; there was about 2 lbs of tea there, rather a large amount for anybody to put in their pocket, and Abraham's overcoat pocket certainly revealed no traces of tea. Next, Wensley examined the fireplace, which was a large one and capable, in his opinion, of burning a large packing case; it contained melted lead and iron banding of the type used to bind a tea chest. Enquiries were made in the pub; Alice Dalby, the landlady, was able to say that no chest of tea had been taken through the pub at the material time. What was more, Wensley instructed Detective Charlie Smith to measure the width of the doors; no chest of tea could have passed through them. There were hammers and iron implements in the yard, and Wensley estimated that it would have taken about two minutes for an experienced workman such as Abraham to have broken up the tea chest.

Perrin and Robert Hill were also arrested, and the Delafuente brothers and Perrin were positively identified by James Panton, as was Hill, after Panton had first mistakenly touched the wrong man (in cross-examination he denied that Wensley had told him, 'Have another go').

It was Hill who received a good character reference; he entered into recognisances to be of good behaviour at the Old Bailey. But not so Perrin, who had been convicted at Thames police court a year previously – he was sentenced to twelve months' hard labour, as was Henry Delafuente. Abraham, with two previous convictions, was sent to penal servitude for five years.

If it wasn't tea, it was coffee. Henry Reiners and William Chapman were two carmen who took delivery of nine bags of coffee beans from Victoria Docks to deliver to a warehouse; but by the time they arrived, some of the bags were torn and there was a discrepancy in the weight of 96 lbs.

Wensley heard of the coffee's ultimate destination; he, Divall and other officers kept observation from a covered wagon on Henry Lawrence's shop at 39 Gault Street and they saw the two carmen draw up in a van and take a very full sack into the shop. After the men left, Gill stayed behind and Divall and Wensley overtook Reiners' and Chapman's van and brought them back to the shop. Meanwhile, Gill had seen Henry Lawrence's brother John leave the shop, carrying the sack; asked what was in it, John replied, 'I don't know, I'm going to take it to the stables.' Both men returned to the shop and when asked what was in the sack, Henry replied, 'Food for the horses, that's all.' If so, it was exotic fodder, since the sack contained the missing 96 lbs of coffee, valued at £3 12s 0d.

At the Old Bailey John was given the benefit of the doubt (even though there is a big difference between the smell of hay and of the coffee which he had carried for thirty-five yards) and he was discharged; the two carmen pleaded guilty to stealing the coffee and were sent to hard labour, Chapman to four months and Reiners to six. However, although Henry Lawrence had no previous convictions, for his first offence he was sentenced to three years' penal servitude.

It was a busy day for Wensley and Gill; as well as carrying out observation on the coffee thieves, later the same day they made time to carry out a further observation on two other carmen, David McGuire and William Venn. This was purely because of their suspicious behaviour, but on stopping and questioning them in Royal Mint Street it was revealed that the men had stolen eighteen sacks of coke from their employer in the Wandsworth Road, and both were sentenced to three months' hard labour.

For every crime committed it seemed Wensley had informants who would point him in the right direction. Six days after Charles Gilby had stolen coffee essence, wax and india-rubber shoes valued at £85 from his employer, Wensley and Detective Sergeant Gould went to a stable in Fox's Lane, Hackney and recovered the bulk of the property; more of the shoes were found at Gilby's address and the rest with his brother-in-law and his landlord.

It was the same story with Joseph Flitcher, a thirty-four-year-old dealer from Prince Street, Deptford, whom Wensley arrested for being in possession of 303 pelts valued at £100. They had been stolen from Finsbury, and Wensley, who had charged Flitcher with both the break-in and receiving, informed Greenwich police court that Flitcher had told him he had bought the skins for £45. Possibly Flitcher was more receiver than thief, although the going rate would have been less than half that sum.

It was not all stealing and receiving, nor was it always Wensley's information which brought about arrests; on 25 September 1902 George Pride, then a detective sergeant on 'P' Division, was in pursuit of a man and a woman known to be counterfeiting coins, in this particular case florins, or two-shilling pieces. Because the address was on 'H' Division, at 107 Wentworth Street, Spitalfields, Wensley accompanied Pride, and they saw the shadows of a man and woman behind the blinds of a second-floor room. Both left the scene to obtain assistance; a mistake, because when they returned, fifteen minutes later, only the woman, Harriet Summers, was there – the man was missing.

However, Summers was surrounded by incriminating evidence: underneath the window a mould for florins, which was still hot, a spoon with hot metal in it, a saucepan with molten metal in it, a fire burning in the grate, sixteen counterfeit florins wrapped in paper, and a quantity of plaster of Paris and antimony, ingredients used for coining.

Referring to her absent companion, Summers told Wensley, 'He only came here today; this is the first time I have seen him doing this sort of thing,' and added, 'You would not have found me here if I'd known you were coming.' At the Old Bailey Summers was sentenced to six months' hard labour, which was quite lenient; coiners, or 'smashers' as they were often known, were almost invariably sent to penal servitude.

★ ★ ★

Of the three men planning to break into the living quarters of the Leighhoy public house in Hanbury Street during the early hours of 22 May 1902, Charles Wilson was certainly the most dangerous. True, Daniel Morrissy had eleven convictions recorded against him and Francis Fitzwater had fourteen, including terms of penal servitude in respect of which he still had 255 days to serve. Charles Wilson had just six previous convictions, modest by comparison, with 263 days yet to serve; but what made him the most dangerous of the three was that he was armed with a fully loaded revolver.

Disturbed by Police Constable 325 'H' James Hawkins, the men walked off. Hawkins engaged the group in conversation as they walked along, playing for time until he could meet up with other officers who would provide assistance. Suddenly he spotted Police Constable 332 'H' Henry Lewis, as did Wilson, who drew the revolver from his pocket, said, 'You won't follow us any further, you fucker', and fired. The bullet struck a button on PC Hawkins' greatcoat, the three men turned and ran, and PC Hawkins shouted to PC Lewis, 'Stop the man in the trilby hat!' (this was Wilson); the officers then chased him through the streets. Police Constable 472 'H' George Clay joined in the hunt and Wilson fired again, hitting Clay in the hand. The chase continued, with PC Clay blowing his whistle. Then Wilson stopped, aimed the revolver at PC Lewis' face and said, 'If you touch me, I'll shoot you stone dead.' With that, he fired; the bullet struck Lewis between his chest and his belt, and as Wilson turned to run, Lewis drew his truncheon and during a fierce struggle hit Wilson once between the eyes and then again across the forehead. En route to the police station, Wilson again became violent and was 'sticked' once more.

Meanwhile, Police Constable 286 'H' John Muclock heard the sound of a police whistle blowing and saw Fitzwater running; he struggled as he was caught, but as PC Muclock told him, 'If you don't come with me, I'll take my truncheon out and knock you down', and the pure, reasoned logic of this statement was enough for Fitzwater to comply. The following afternoon, Morrissy was seen in the Whitechapel Road and arrested. 'I admit I was there but I didn't shoot at the police,' he said.

Wensley was at the police court when he saw Wilson. 'I wish the revolver had been bigger,' he said. 'I would have shot them stone dead. When I come out, I'll make no mistake; I'll kill the whole bloody lot of them.' Wilson's forehead was covered in sticking plaster, and Wensley suggested, 'He was a little bit hurt when he said that.'

There was no real defence; two of the prisoners told the jury at the Old Bailey that they had no intention of breaking into the public house but would probably have done it some other time when they had the appropriate tools with them. Regarding the offence of shooting at the police officers, Wilson said that it was the sort of gun that could be purchased in any toy shop for two or three shillings. He defiantly stated, 'There is not sufficient strength in the bullets to go through clothes; the revolver should be tested'.

It was the wrong kind of mitigation; all three men were sentenced to eighteen months' hard labour for the attempted burglary, and Wilson received ten years' penal servitude, to be served concurrently.

\* \* \*

When James McNally (said by Wensley to be 'one of the cleverest van thieves') stole a horse and van containing butter, eggs and bacon, valued at £230, it was clear that due to the perishable nature of the commodities they would have to be disposed of as soon as possible. Wensley, of course, knew just where to go: to a stable at 82 Ford Road, Bethnal Green, rented by Charles Burton. There he saw Burton and McNally; when they left, Wensley entered the stable and under a tarpaulin found the entire consignment. He then hid until, hours later, the two men, together with Robert Leigh, returned. McNally was heard to say, 'You'll find it all right, Bob, won't he, Charlie?'

Burton agreed, saying, 'It's some good stuff, real Danish.'

'Yes, it looks good stuff.' said Leigh. 'Come on, Charlie, let's have a look at it.'

It was at this point that Wensley made his presence known, whereupon Leigh said, 'Very well, you've got us and we'll give you no trouble.' This was not entirely correct; he later escaped from custody and vanished.

Burton's evidence that 'a strange man' named Matthews had rented part of his stable, and that it must have been he who had deposited the property, did not hold water, and they were found guilty. Tom Divall told the court that Burton's stable had been a rendezvous for the exchange of stolen property for years, as did Wensley, and Burton was sentenced to twenty-one months' hard labour; McNally, with two previous convictions, was sentenced to three years' penal servitude.

\* \* \*

By 1903 police numbers in the capital had risen to 16,517, and Wensley got the year off to a rolling start with a couple of first-rate arrests.

When he saw Jane Lewis, who was carrying a parcel and strolling along Commercial Street, Stepney on 7 January 1903, together with Julius Joslovitch, there was nothing suspicious in the way that they were conducting themselves that would normally have compelled Wensley to stop and question them. Thirty-five-year-old Joslovitch appeared respectable enough, as befitted a diamond dealer, whilst Lewis looked downright stunning, dressed in a three-quarter length sealskin coat, valued conservatively at £150. However, as Wensley later told the magistrate at Thames police court, when he did stop them it was because he was in possession of information, details of which he did not wish to disclose but which suggested that 'he was on the fringe of an important matter'. This seemed to be the case, because Lewis – who refused to give her address and occupation – said she had no idea what was contained in the parcel, and her companion stated that Lewis had asked him to carry it but he had refused. Therefore they were arrested on a charge of 'unlawful possession' and taken to the police station.

There it quickly appeared that something was very wrong indeed. Inside the parcel were a silver-backed hairbrush and two sable collarettes, valued at eighteen guineas, the property of Messrs Turner & Co, Birmingham and which had been shoplifted by two women. Lewis was also wearing a gold watch which had been stolen from a lady's maid the previous July. In the pocket of the sealskin coat was a silver purse, for which she was unable to provide an acceptable origin.

Both the prisoners were Russian, and it transpired that Lewis' real name was Konopbaki – she was described as being 'an expert shoplifter'. Twenty-five-year-old Lewis visited provincial towns to ply her trade and would send the stolen goods by rail to her receiver, who, it was strongly suspected, was Julius Joslovitch, particularly on the occasion when she had been sentenced to fifteen months' hard labour at the age of nineteen for shoplifting. In 1899 she had been sentenced to one month's imprisonment for attempted pickpocketing, and then her travels took her firstly to Paris, then Brussels, where she received a sentence of three years' penal servitude and was expelled from the country. Back home in England, and the day following the shoplifting expedition in Birmingham, she was arrested in Manchester, again for shoplifting. After two weeks on remand, and with the authorities unaware of her true identity, she was fined and released.

Now, she promised to take all of the responsibility, as long as Joslovitch was released. Unfortunately, her escort had problems of his own. Amongst the large quantity of jewellery in his possession there was a watch, later identified as having been stolen from a lady in Hyde Park the previous June. And when his home address at Hanbury Street was searched, there was found a sable muff, stolen from the shop belonging to Joseph Fordred, Birmingham.

Both were committed to the Clerkenwell Sessions for trial. Lewis was sentenced to eighteen months' hard labour, and when

Joslovitch was sentenced to three years' penal servitude, he cried loudly and his two daughters in the back of the court became hysterical and, according to a press report, 'shrieked in a frantic manner', with one of them fainting into the arms of a police officer.

Perhaps they found comfort in being handed, by order of the court, the items of jewellery which had been found in their father's possession and which were unable to be identified as stolen property. They were worth £200 – or at 2014 value, £20,000.

★ ★ ★

Thieves used many different and often novel ways to carry out thefts. On 3 February 1903 in Bethnal Green, a rather gormless carman was induced to send a telegram for 'a gentleman', for which he was rewarded with 2s 6d. The thieves could well afford it, because when the carman returned, his horse, van, harness and a load of leather, valued at £385, were gone. Two weeks later saw Wensley keeping observation in the Holloway area, and when he saw Robert Woolbright, Frank Day and Frederick Taylor, he followed them to some stables at Annetta Road, Holloway. Woolbright tried to disclaim all knowledge of the stables, but unfortunately a search revealed the stable key in his pocket and there was found the whole consignment of leather.

Messrs Lavington Brothers Ltd of Whitechapel were very much up-to-date in 1903 because they had their own private telephone wire connecting their office to another; so when the line suddenly went dead, John Wilcox, the manager, thought it was being repaired. Crossing Tower Hill, he saw John W. Briggs coiling a quantity of telephone wire, which Mr Wilcox recognized as belonging to his company. Briggs said that he and his mate had been given the job of taking the wire down; his 'mate' turned out to be his father, who informed Mr Wilcox that his name was 'Baker' and that he was working for Messrs G.A. Edwards & Co of Fore Street. However, upon checking with this company, Mr Wilcox discovered that this was not the case.

Two days later, Wensley and Detective Sergeant Sam Lee were making enquiries about the case in the Old Kent Road, saw Briggs Jr and asked him if his name was, in fact, Briggs. 'You've made a mistake,' he replied. 'I know no one of that name.' Upon being arrested, Briggs broke free and fled for a mile before running into a stable in Chatham Road, where he concealed his hat and coat in a van, rolled up his sleeves and with bare-faced effrontery told his panting pursuers, 'I've only just come out of my house.' However, on his way to the police station, he admitted, 'I've been drawn into this; my father wanted the wire for a job.' Arrested in turn, John Briggs Sr stated, 'I'm very sorry but I was driven to it by want.' None of this impressed the magistrate at Thames police court, who told them, 'It was a most impudent robbery' (as indeed it was) and sentenced father and son to six months' hard labour.

There was often unconscious humour to be found in prisoners' replies and the absurd circumstances in which they found themselves.

After a horse and van containing sixteen boxes of butter, valued at £100, was stolen from Aberdeen Wharf, Wensley's information led him and Tom Divall to 93 St. Leonard's Street, where they saw Henry Young and Albert Beilby, plus fourteen of the boxes of butter in the cellar. Young said that Beilby had had two men bring the butter round and admitted that he had sold two boxes to his former partner for 36s 0d.

On his way to the police station, Young morosely complained, 'This is what they do – bring it to you, pretend to do you a turn, then get someone to put you away!'

The prize for the utmost audacity surely went to David Lazarus and Robert Wallace, who Wensley, Lee and Dessent saw entering a house in Cable Street carrying two parcels. They imprudently left the front door ajar, and Wensley took this opportunity to surreptitiously enter the house and take up a position to see and hear what transpired.

Lazarus opened the parcels, which contained thirty silver watches, and told the occupier, 'There you are – you can see what they are – ten quid the lot.'

The occupier asked, 'Are they all right?'

Wallace told him, 'This is the first time we've had a deal with you. If you have them, you've got a bargain, but don't sell them in London.'

Lazarus added, 'Go on, have them. We can do you a bit of good later.'

This was the moment when Wensley and the others walked into the room. 'We want to know whose watches these are,' said Wensley.

As quick as a flash, Lazarus replied, 'They're not ours. This man [pointing to the occupier] asked us to buy them.'

'Yes, we were just going to pay for them,' agreed Wallace, and added virtuously, 'but I'm glad we didn't.'

Aghast, the occupier told the officers, 'What do you think of that? I know them. They met me in a public house and asked if I wanted to buy any watches. I said I didn't mind if they were all right and it suited me. They just brought them in and I was asking the price.'

After due deliberation, Wensley & Co decided to disbelieve Lazarus' and Wallace's story of intending to buy the watches. For one thing, they had seen the two men bring them into the house; for another, the total amount of money they possessed was tuppence.

# CHAPTER 11

# Conmen & Screwsmen

Lazarus' and Wallace's cheek was undeniable, but it was as nothing compared to that of David Weinstone (a Russian) and Rosen Soulman (a Romanian), whose fraudulent scheme compelled Wensley to work undercover.

These two were part of an eight-man team who travelled Europe purporting to be acting on behalf of Russian officials secretly disposing of gold dust from mines in Siberia. They would produce a genuine gold nugget to show the dupe, then test it with aqua fortis (nitric acid) to prove it was genuine; once the deal was struck, brass filings would be substituted for the gold.

Soulman met a fellow Romanian known as John Marks – his real name was Mark Zakeria – and suggested that he induce his employer, who he knew to be wealthy, to purchase some 'gold dust'. But Marks went to Arbour Square police station and told Ben Leeson, and a plan was devised. The following day, Marks told Soulman that his employer wanted to see a sample of the gold; Soulman duly produced a genuine gold nugget, and a few days later Marks reported back to Soulman, telling him that his master had tested the nugget and now wanted to know all of the particulars. Soulman told Marks that his employer would have to go to Germany for the gold, which would be well below market price, but that he (Soulman) would pay all the expenses.

This, of course was out of the question, so Wensley turned the tables right around; on his instructions, Marks went to see Weinstone and told him that his employer would have nothing to do with the scheme, since it was quite obviously a swindle. The bait and hook was swallowed by the two fraudsters; Soulman insisted to Marks that the scheme was perfectly genuine and that he wanted to meet his employer.

Posing as Marks' employer, Wensley now took an opulent rented house in Camberwell, and when he was introduced to Soulman (who used the name Kaplin) it was clear that Wensley had taken him in completely.

'I've tested that nugget of gold you let Marks have,' said Wensley, 'and I'm satisfied it's pure gold. What's the quantity you want to sell and is the bulk up to sample?'

'There is about 90 lbs,' replied Soulman. 'It is all virgin gold, the same as the nugget I gave Marks to show you, but before entering into business I want to ask you a question: can you keep a secret?'

'Yes,' replied Wensley. 'I have done so.'

Soulman nodded his head in approval. 'I can see you are a business man,' he said. 'I will tell you a great secret and if you keep it, we will make you very rich. There is an officer in a very high position in the Russian army and his position enables him to get large quantities of raw gold from the Russian mines across the frontier, two or three times a year. The gentleman who used to purchase it is dead, he died worth a lot of money; we now have to find another buyer.'

'Do you mean the gold is stolen?' asked Wensley.

'I am surprised you should ask me such a question,' was the reply, 'but there, you Englishmen are all alike, you are not clever, you are too straightforward to be clever, we foreigners know the world best.'

'There may be a great deal of truth in what you say,' replied Wensley, 'but I want to know my position.'

'Of course, it is what you would call stolen,' said Soulman, 'but the police here cannot touch you. The risk is getting it over the frontier and would mean terrible punishment if they caught us there.'

'What do you want for it?' asked Wensley.

He was then told, 'We have always had 25 per cent below the market value.'

'That is a lot more than I should give,' responded Wensley, and the haggling commenced. It was eventually agreed that the gold would be sold at 35 per cent below market value, at £3 5s 0d per ounce or £39 per pound. In this way, Soulman would receive 25 per cent and the Russian officer (Weinstone) and Wensley 35 per cent each, leaving 5 per cent for working expenses.

'That's more reasonable,' remarked Wensley. 'How much do you propose to bring, and what are the facilities you intend to offer me to see that the bulk is up to sample? How many do you wish to be present at the transaction and what do you propose about payment?'

Soulman laughed. 'You really are more clever than I thought you were; I like dealing with clever men. I shall bring about 90 lbs and shall bring everything you want, both to test the gold and to weigh it. You can have Marks to look after your interests, and my principal, the Russian officer, will come with me, because although he has got confidence in me, I should hardly like to ask him to trust me with such a large quantity, and he would not come alone because he would expect me to look after his interests and do the work.' It was agreed that Wensley would pay £2,285 for the 90 lbs of gold.

With that, the men parted, Soulman stating that he would communicate through Marks and that he would arrange a date for the transaction and let Wensley know it two or three days beforehand, in order that he could get together the money, which he would prefer to be in gold.

Soulman and Marks left together, with Soulman saying that he was satisfied now that he had met Marks' 'master' and that he would send a telegram to the Russian officer the following day. Several days later, Soulman handed Marks a telegram to show to Wensley which purported to come from a town in Russia, saying that the price agreed by Wensley and Soulman was acceptable to the officer.

But when Marks saw Soulman a few days later, he stated – on Wensley's instructions – that he (Wensley) had decided to have nothing to do with the scheme, since it must be a swindle. But the bait been swallowed by a particularly greedy pair of fish, and Wensley's now stating that he wished to withdraw from the transaction after matters had progressed so far prompted Soulman to take desperate measures; the double-cross turned into a triple-cross.

'Can you keep a secret?' Soulman asked Marks, and after he admitted that he could, Soulman explained that what he was trying to sell Wensley was not gold at all but brass filings.

Marks gave every indication of being shocked, saying, 'You're trying to do me as well.'

Soulman told him, 'Never mind that, if we succeed in getting the money, we shall have equal shares.'

Soulman was appealing to Marks' greed and it appeared to work; Marks agreed to assure his 'employer' that everything was all right. A day or two later, Soulman showed Marks a telegram in German, saying, 'Left Russia for England', and a week later Marks met Weinstone at his house at 33 Maidman Street, Bow. There he saw Soulman filling a bag with brass filings – he had engaged a man to file up the brass at 2s 8d per pound – and it was agreed that the transaction would take place the following evening at 9.00 pm.

This was the plan: after getting the money (which naturally would be in equal shares) Soulman would ask Wensley if Marks could show him the way to the bus. Once out of the house, the three men would go straight to Euston, then to Manchester and thence to Berlin, where further business would be awaiting them, or so they said. It is debatable how far Marks would have accompanied them on their journey.

On 27 June – one month after Marks had first been approached – Burdett Road, Bow had sufficient police officers to keep observation on Marks and Soulman, who left Maidman Street, with Soulman, carrying a black bag, and travelled to the Great Eastern Hotel. Weinstone was there, wearing a silk top hat and looking every inch a Russian army officer in mufti, and after a few drinks they set off in a cab to go to Wensley's 'home' in Camberwell.

The officers waited until the cab turned into Christian Street before they stopped it and arrested the men. Under Soulman's waistcoat were two pads filled with brass filings; there was another in his overcoat pocket and two more in the black bag he was carrying, together with a mass of paraphernalia designed to prove that the brass filings were genuine gold. Two similar bags of filings were found under Weinstone's shirt and two more in a bag. The filings were weighed and amounted to 72 lbs avoirdupois or 90 lbs troy; they were all tested and proved to be brass.

Seeing Wensley in the charge room, his real identity revealed, was the final straw.

When charged, Weinstone said, 'It was brass filings I had on me; I had it for gold dust. He [indicating Soulman] brought it to my house and I helped to load it up. You can only charge us with an attempt, we have not got anything yet.'

Soulman's response was, 'Well, you have only got me for an attempt, I had not got the money. I first learnt how to do it in Minsk, the law is different in this country to what it is in other countries, that is why I wanted to get the buyer into another country.' He added, 'I hope you will be merciful.'

It appeared the fraudsters had already prepared their defence, but at the Old Bailey on 23 July 1903 Mr Justice Lawrence sent them both to hard labour; Weinstone for twelve months and Soulman for eighteen.

* * *

The public have always been enchanted by the idea of the 'gentleman crook' – someone like Leslie Charteris' fictional character, 'The Saint', or E.W. Hornung's creation, 'Raffles, the Amateur Cracksman', both of whom could be relied upon to skilfully break and enter a country house, make off with the jewels from the safe and simultaneously cock a cheeky snook at the law. In fact, very few such people exist in real life and those that do seldom succeed in keeping their ill-gotten gains. One such person was Robert Graham, and it was inevitable that he and Wensley should meet in a professional capacity.

★ ★ ★

Graham's real name was Arthur Brook, and he was born in 1871 in Leeds. His criminal career began at the early age of nine, when for stealing money he was sentenced to five years' in Adel Reformatory in Leeds. Released in November 1885, he remained at liberty until March 1886, when he was sentenced to three months' hard labour for stealing a pair of boots. This was quickly followed by nine months' imprisonment for a jewel robbery, and in December 1888, for breaking into a jeweller's shop, he received fifteen months' hard labour. Released in May 1891, he broke into two shops, stole jewellery and was sentenced to twelve months' imprisonment. He was released in June 1892, when he took the name William Pollard and was involved in a robbery at a shop; astonishingly, he was sentenced to just seven days' imprisonment. Now calling himself William Crichton, in 1893 he assaulted a police constable and was sentenced to one month's imprisonment. In April 1894 he was arrested as a suspected person and again assaulted the arresting officer; this time he was sentenced to five months' imprisonment.

Following his release, Graham, having learnt from past experiences, now exhibited a great deal of skill and cunning – he was strongly suspected of a number of jewel robberies (and had accumulated a great deal of wealth) but he remained at liberty for the longest period of his career. He was an expert and agile burglar, spending time and money planning his coups and crossing roofs until he reached his objective, before removing tiles and breaking in. Matters came to a temporary halt in 1899, when Graham broke into a jeweller's shop in Shrewsbury, passed the loot out to an associate and returned home to London before the break-in had even been discovered. Unfortunately, it was whilst he was en route across the Shrewsbury roof-tops that his hat blew off, and this led to his arrest and a five-year sentence of penal servitude, followed by seven years' police supervision.

However, he received a considerable reduction of his sentence after he restrained a demented prisoner who had run amuck with a chisel, attacking a warder. This led to Graham being released on 6 December 1902.

It was whilst serving that sentence that he met up with Henry Moffatt, aged thirty-five, another who, like Graham, suffered from an identity crisis, being variously known as Henry Seymour, Henry Edward, Maxwell Moffatt, Edward M. Moffatt and Henry

Palmer. Born in Glasgow in 1879, Moffatt at the age of seventeen was sentenced to three months' hard labour for stealing from a public house. A year later, he received another twelve months' hard labour at the Old Bailey, this time for stealing jewellery, and on 2 May 1899 at the North London Sessions he got twenty months' hard labour for stealing a scarf pin. Hardly had he been released when on 9 January 1901 he appeared at Cardiff Quarter Sessions for housebreaking, asked for a theft at a hotel in St Mary Street, Cardiff to be taken into consideration and was sentenced to three years' penal servitude. On his release, on 15 April 1903, his friend Graham was waiting for him.

★ ★ ★

On 8 June 1903 both men travelled to Cardiff. They stayed at the Glamorgan Restaurant, Barry Dock, and later purchased a brace and bit from Henry Ash, a pawnbroker, at 2 Constellation Street, Cardiff. The following night, they broke into a jeweller's shop at 48 Queen Street, Cardiff; entry was effected by forcing the building's skylight and then drilling down into the jeweller's shop from an unoccupied room above it. The following morning, the owner of the shop, Henry Crouch, discovered the burglary and found jewellery cases strewn all over the shop floor; gold and other valuable items valued at between £900 and £1,000 had been stolen.

Detective Inspector Rankin of the Cardiff Police made a number of enquiries very quickly and decided that it was in London that the men responsible would be found. There were only a select few thieves who were capable of such a slick job, and the commissioner had already issued a special notice in respect of Graham and Moffatt, outlining their expertise and informing his officers that both men invariably carried firearms, which they were quite prepared to use. Inspector Rankin made contact with Wensley, who knew both men and also discovered that at the time of the break-in at Cardiff the men were not in their usual London haunts. However, speed was of the utmost importance, to find them before the property could be disposed of, and on the morning of 11 June observation was kept on one of Moffatt's usual haunts, The Ship and Blue Bowl public house in Shoreditch. When Moffatt arrived he was seized and after a short-lived resistance taken to the police station, where a search revealed a gold watch and a gold sovereign purse containing five sovereigns, the property of Henry Crouch.

Some extremely promising information must have come into Wensley's possession very quickly, because it now led him and his men to 31 Compton Road, Islington – Mrs Graham would later say that she had only rented the room that morning. Graham unsuccessfully tried to make a swift exit through the bedroom window, and in the bedroom was found a kitbag. Inside it was a grey suit, a file, a chisel, ten skeleton keys and a set of jeweller's scales. 'A good workman,' said Graham modestly, 'always carries his own tools.' Two flannel shirts were also in the bag; wrapped inside one of them was a diamond pendant, also the property of Mr Crouch. 'I bought it on Friday and gave £20 for it,' claimed Graham.

The two men appeared at Cardiff Quarter Sessions before Mr Recorder B. Francis-Williams KC. They were expensively defended, but then again Graham could certainly afford it; his bank balance was extremely healthy, and he kept his own carriage to drive around London. In addition – and at the last moment – Moffatt changed his plea to one of guilty; he also pleaded guilty to breaking into another shop the same night, just along the road from Mr Crouch's premises at 66 Queen Street, and stealing a suit and an overcoat valued at £4 14s 6d, the property of a Thomas Palmer.

Therefore, Graham's defence now rested on his own skilful testimony, plus a little help and a witness whom it would be difficult to contradict.

It appeared that Graham's marriage was less than satisfactory – he had discovered that his wife Jennie had received some passionate letters from a sailor named Shiel, whose ship, he believed, was berthed at Barry, in Wales. Therefore, he said, when he happened to meet his friend Moffatt, whom he had known for four or five weeks, having met him in New York – 'and one other place', Graham told the court, but he refused to say where – and discovered that Moffatt was going to visit his sister who lived in Llanishen, Cardiff, the two men decided to travel together. They caught the train from Paddington, had a meal with Moffatt's sister, then travelled to Barry Docks, where Graham was unable to discover the whereabouts of the amorous Mr Shiel; they then stayed overnight at the Glamorgan Restaurant. On 9 June they travelled to Cardiff, where Graham purchased the brace and bit for his brother, who 'was an amateur carpenter', before departing on the 10.35 pm train to London, leaving Moffatt in Cardiff. Before he left, he and Moffatt agreed to meet later at The Bell public house, since Graham wished to borrow Moffatt's kitbag. He had, of course, no idea that Moffatt intended to break into one shop in his absence, let alone two.

On 10 June they met in The Bell, where Moffatt introduced him to a certain Ben Hymes, who was described as a diamond merchant and who produced a number of rings, plus a diamond pendant, for which Graham paid £20.

'You say you bought the pendant from a respectable diamond merchant?' Graham was asked in cross-examination, to which he wittily replied, 'Yes, but he couldn't have been very respectable if he had sold a stolen article', which caused some merriment in court.

The pendant, said Graham, was tossed into Moffatt's borrowed kitbag – it was not, he stated, wrapped in a shirt, and everything else in the bag, of course, belonged to Moffatt, including the burglar's kit. He also denied making the aforementioned highly incriminating remark about his alleged ownership of the tools.

It was a good defence. If he had indeed caught the late train from Cardiff, he could not possibly have taken part in the jeweller's shop break-in. Moffatt had, of course – he had already admitted it – and he had obviously sold some if not all of the proceeds to this mysterious Ben Hymes, from whom he, Graham, had in good faith unknowingly purchased stolen property. What he needed now was someone who had seen him in London early on the morning of 10 June.

This someone was Mr J. W. Carr, an insurance clerk, who unwillingly told the court that on that morning he had seen Graham walking down the steps at Baker Street station and wished him, 'Good morning'. Unfortunately, Carr did not make a good impression when he asked the Recorder if he could give his name and address in private. 'Certainly not!' was the reply. 'You have come here as a witness and you must give your name and address.'

Mr Carr stated that he did not want his fellow clerks to know that he was 'mixed up in a case of this sort', but told the Recorder, 'All right, sir, I have no objection.'

'I don't care whether you object or not,' retorted the Recorder, but it was later disclosed that Carr knew Graham because he had previously lodged in his house and had come only at Mrs Graham's insistence. 'He came to give evidence,' the Recorder later accurately told the jury, 'with very great reluctance.'

Jennie Graham was next in the witness box – she was 'stylishly dressed', commented a newspaper report – and she sorrowfully told the court that she and her husband had been living 'most unhappily' for some time, thanks to the attentions of the enamoured sailor. On the morning of 10 June she had received a note from her husband asking to meet that evening for a reconciliation; they had spent the night in the Canonbury Hotel and the following day had hired rooms at Compton Road, which was where she had first seen the kitbag.

But Mrs Graham started to lose credibility after it was revealed that she had served fourteen days' imprisonment for receiving a silk handkerchief and, later, three months' hard labour for a shopbreaking in Northumberland. 'I think it is very unfair to me that this should be brought against me,' she told prosecution counsel. 'I have been getting my own living for the last eight years.'

Indeed she had; she owned several houses, the rents of which provided her with an income of £7–£8 per week, a very creditable sum when one considers that at that time the minimum weekly wage was twenty-one shillings. It begged the question, why, unless she and her husband were trying to keep out of the clutches of the law, did she need to rent rooms at Compton Road?

On 27 October that year, *Raffles, the Amateur Cracksman*, commenced a long run at the Princess Theatre, New York. Unfortunately, neither Moffatt nor Graham were able to attend the star-studded first night; they had just commenced long runs of their own – sentences of seven years' penal servitude.

★ ★ ★

It had been a busy time for Wensley. During the evening of 10 June, in his guise as a wealthy business man, he had met Soulman to finalise the bogus gold transaction. The following day, he had carried out the arrest of Moffatt, and on the day following that, 12 June 1903, he was promoted to detective sergeant (first-class).

# CHAPTER 12

# Murders – Pointless & Squalid

There are detectives who never bother with mundane cases, saying that they are waiting for 'The Big Job' to come along. Wensley was not of that breed; he knew full well that small jobs can turn into big ones, and that even if they don't, small ones can be rewarding because (a) prisoners can be turned into informants, and (b) commendations aren't awarded to detectives for sitting on their arses.

So it was in the case of twenty-six-year-old Gladys Lyall, who was erroneously thought to be the wife of Albert Stores; although she was not his partner in marriage, she was certainly his partner in crime. Both were employed by James Farley to manage his bootmaker's shop at 298 Hoe Street, Walthamstow; what Mr Farley did not know was that the couple were liberally helping themselves to his stock.

Two days before Christmas 1903, Lyall took a quantity of Mr Farley's boots to Mrs Symons, a wardrobe dealer in Bethnal Green, asking her to look after them for Stores, who was going into business; and for this service, Mrs Symons could keep half the boots.

On Boxing Day, Stores and another man were obliged to drop the two parcels containing boots they had stolen from the shop when they were spotted by a patrolling constable. Having made good his escape, Stores decided to bluff matters out and told Mr Farley that there had been a burglary at the shop.

The offence had taken place on 'J' Division, but Wensley had received information of a sufficiently high standard to keep Stores and Lyall under observation, and on New Year's Eve he followed them to Mrs Symons' shop and arrested them both. Lyall blamed Stores and begged him to tell the truth, and the forty-three pairs of boots, and one pair apiece of gaiters and spats, valued together at £140, were recovered. The magistrate at Stratford police court sentenced Stores to a well-merited three months' hard labour; Lyall was bound over – a leniency she probably did not deserve; and a commendation was given to Wensley, which he had quite properly earned.

Two days later, Wensley made his next appearance at Thames police court with a rather more distasteful prisoner.

Jacob Bietz, a Russian blacksmith, had arrived in England on 26 November 1903 but only regarded this country as a jumping-off point, since he wished to live in the United States. He explained his plight to Hyman Karowsky, who told him he could provide a solution to his problem. Bietz sent home for 37 roubles, and when the money arrived, Karowsky accompanied him to a money changer, who converted the currency into £3 17s 6d; this sum was then handed over to Karowsky to purchase a ticket on Bietz's behalf for a passage to America – which he failed to do.

When Bietz and other defrauded immigrants went to Karowsky's home at Market Buildings, Shadwell and caught him in the act of moving his furniture, they realized that no tickets were likely to be forthcoming. They called the police, and Wensley arrested Karowsky. He was charged with two specimen cases of obtaining money by fraud, and Wensley told the court that it was believed that there had been thirty or forty such victims, sufficient for the magistrate, Mr Dickinson, to thunder, 'These poor foreigners landed here in a helpless condition and were pounced on by bloodsuckers who robbed them of their all.' He sentenced Karowsky to six months' hard labour on each charge, to run consecutively.

\* \* \*

With promotion came more responsibility, so whilst Wensley still tended to the 'bread and butter' crimes, he also dealt with more killings, of which there was no shortage in Whitechapel. Drink normally played a part in the crimes, as did jealousy, insanity and greed – all of the killings were squalid.

Dennis McCarthy was twenty years of age when he killed Rose McCarthy (no relation), and it appeared inevitable, right from the start of his life, that it would end in tragedy. When he was four he was knocked down in an accident, sustained a badly cut head and suffered from headaches thereafter. He started work when he was ten and worked in a tarpaulin factory; his employer stated that he possessed 'not the highest order of intelligence'. McCarthy's grandfather was insane and died in the asylum at Colney Hatch; his uncle had been treated for mental illness on three occasions and was an alcoholic.

McCarthy was a teetotaller, until the evening of 28 September when he became quite stupendously drunk and stabbed Rose McCarthy several times in the throat, severing her carotid artery and her jugular vein. Immediately, his clothes saturated with blood, he went up to Police Constable 256 'H' William Parnell and said, 'Guv'nor, take me to the police station, I have stabbed a young woman with a knife.' PC Parnell was joined by another officer, and McCarthy said, 'I done it in a fit of temper, and directly I done it, I ran to you gentleman. I saw her drinking in a public house with several other women and as I thought I ought to have her company, I called her outside and when she came outside I stabbed her with the knife and I shall have to suffer for it.'

He was seen by Wensley, but there was little else that he could add to his confession. When he was charged, McCarthy replied, 'I understand.' Seven witnesses were called for the defence at the Old Bailey, and fortunately for the clearly inadequate Dennis McCarthy he was cleared of murder, convicted of manslaughter and sentenced (less fortunately) to fifteen years' penal servitude.

The poor McCarthys – both victim and perpetrator – had been involved in a grubby killing, but for sheer senselessness the circumstances of the death of John Arthur Williams, a twenty-two-year-old private with the 2nd Grenadier Guards put that case in the shade.

On Boxing Day 1903 Williams had gone on a pub crawl and, almost paralytically drunk, had ended up at a party at 23 Little Pearl Street, where thirteen or fourteen people had gathered. Williams had no contribution to make to the general festivities; he passed out on a bed which was already occupied by a woman and two other men. Then a drunken woman entered the house and was promptly ejected. This provoked a group of some twenty or more hooligans to arrive, armed with belts, sticks and pokers. In the ensuing drunken mêlée Williams was hit over the head with a belt by John Long, a twenty-year-old newsvendor, who also used an iron bar which resulted in an indentation in his skull three-quarters of an inch deep and two inches long, and caused his death.

The drunken woman, explained Wensley to the Coroner's Court, was unable to be present, due to the fact that she was serving seven days' imprisonment; but in returning a verdict of manslaughter and committing Long for trial, the jury also commended Wensley on the way he had presented the case.

It is clear that James Valentine Curry was a kind, caring father to his two boys aged four and six, but he was epileptic, and this, coupled with the anxiety caused by being out of work for two weeks, and the presence of a very strange wife who not only nagged him, falsely accused him of adulterous affairs and tended to follow him everywhere, was enough to push him over the edge. On the evening of 20 January 1904 he strangled and stabbed his two children to death at their home at 49 Gibraltar Walk, then immediately gave himself up to the police. By the time Wensley conveyed him to Worship Street police court Curry was raving, and although the jury at the Old Bailey found him guilty, they also found him to be insane, and he was detained during His Majesty's pleasure.

Epilepsy also featured in the case of John Colman, a thirty-three-year-old former soldier with the Durham Light Infantry, who purchased a revolver since he intended to travel to Tasmania. As well as suffering from epilepsy, he had had sunstroke as a boy and during his army service had been hospitalized on three occasions as a result of malaria. Over a period of months he had been consorting with a number of prostitutes, including one named Hulda Poppie, who lived in a brothel at 5 Artichoke Hill; and three days after purchasing the revolver, Colman proceeded to get staggeringly drunk together with Poppie and another 'unfortunate'. When he came to believe – rightly or wrongly – that some of his money had been stolen, he shot Poppie dead, and when another occupant of the house, Martha Powell, tried to intervene, he also shot her in the neck; she, fortunately, survived.

As Colman accurately told Wensley, 'I have been doing nothing for the past six months, only acting the bloody fool.' Although Richard Muir prosecuted, Colman was defended by leading and junior counsel and he was found guilty of manslaughter. Colman received a good character from the police, the jury recommended mercy on account of the circumstances of the crime and the Recorder of London sentenced him to fifteen years' penal servitude.

★ ★ ★

The next case was rather different: there were a number of reluctant witnesses, a false witness, an eleventh-hour confession (similarly false), an extremely dodgy solicitor, an uncertain juryman, the discovery of a mound of treasure and a great deal of circumstantial evidence. The case attracted just the type of publicity which would propel Wensley straight into the limelight once more.

Miss Emily Farmer was just over sixty; a short, dumpy little woman, she lived alone in rooms above 478 Commercial Road, Stepney, from where she ran a newsagent's and tobacconist's business. She had a fad; in the afternoons she would often adorn herself with jewellery: four or five gold rings, some with stones, a long gold watch chain around her neck, a pair of gold pince-nez with a small gold chain attached and a gold and silver watch. And then, having exhibited her finery, she would put her prized possessions away, no one knew where. But what was known in the area was that Miss Farmer possessed these items; in fact, on one occasion she had been attacked and coshed in her shop, but she screamed and her attacker fled.

She would rise at 5.45 am to take delivery of newspapers, although on the morning of 12 October 1904 she kept the deliveryman, Charles Gillham, waiting for eleven minutes before opening the door. Gillham then left – he noticed the time of 5.57 am on the clock opposite the premises – but, perhaps because he was now late for the rest of his deliveries, if there was anyone in the vicinity he failed to notice them.

It was the same clock that showed 6.33 am when eleven-year-old Harry Wiggins, Miss Farmer's errand boy, arrived at the shop and noticed that, unusually, the front door was open. He saw his employer's false teeth in front of the counter and one of her shoes underneath it; but although he called out 'Miss Farmer!' three or four times, there was no reply. Harry and several other callers at the shop became alarmed at Miss Farmer's absence, and the police were called; Police Constable 111 'H' James Hooper arrived and, together with Cecilia Baker, who lived next door, went upstairs. There, face-down on the bed, was the lifeless body of Emily Farmer, her hands tied behind her back; a rag which had been thrust into her mouth had caused asphyxiation.

Wensley and Divall then arrived. Miss Farmer's everyday pair of pince-nez were found broken, and her bedroom had been ransacked. Of her gold pince-nez or any of her other jewellery there was no trace; it was reasonable to assume that those items, together with any money in the shop, had been taken by the murderers – it was thought right from the start that there must have been more than one assailant, to carry the corpulent Miss Farmer up the stairs and to bind and subdue her.

No one in the vicinity, it appeared, had seen or heard anything. There were a number of false leads. A young boy named Thomas Mitchell told the police – and the coroner – that at the time of the murder he had seen a man aged about thirty leave the shop saying, 'I shall not wait any longer', before getting on to a tramcar. He later admitted that this was a pack of lies.

Three men who had been hanging about in the area prior to the murder were brought in and questioned. The press heard about the arrests; instantly, this became headline news, and the placards proclaimed, 'Whitechapel murder – three men detained!'

However, two of the men were released – the third man was wanted elsewhere for being a convict on licence and failing to report to police, but apart from his negligence in doing so, he was as innocent as the first two. But the fact that the men had been released was not communicated to the press, and as the days passed they demanded to know when the suspects would be appearing before the magistrate. And then, this happened.

At one o'clock in the morning, the weary detectives Divall and Wensley wished each other 'goodnight' outside Divall's house at Carlton Square, with Divall adding, 'And I hope some luck will turn up before daybreak!'

Soon after, there was a knock on the door; answering it, Divall saw a man, whom he described as 'a strange fellow' and who told him, 'Those men you're detaining are perfectly innocent.' If the man was to be believed, Divall guessed he must have had a good idea as to who the real perpetrators might be. In fact, the man was the workmate of a reluctant witness, eighteen-year-old Robert Rae, a fish-curer who worked nights from 10.00 pm to 5.30 am. On the morning of the murder, Rae had seen two men come out of Miss Farmer's shop. He did not know their names, nor had he ever spoken to them; but he had seen them in the neighbourhood since 1902 and he knew that, singly and together, they visited Commercial Road. They were Conrad Donovan, aged thirty-four (who also used the names Rotten, Wade and Joseph Potter) and his half-brother, Charles Wade, aged twenty-two. They were well known to the police as being a pair of violent bullies; both were singularly unintelligent but extremely cunning.

Next, even more reluctantly, came forward a twenty-year-old painter named Richard Barnes. He had seen Donovan and Wade talking outside Miss Farmer's shop, between 10.00 and 11.00 pm the night before the murder; he also saw them the following morning by the shop, prior to the newspaper delivery. But Mr Barnes, who was also a Sunday School teacher, did not offer this information immediately; he discussed it with his parents, and his elderly mother, who suffered from heart disease, begged him not to get involved – her husband had previously been the victim of a street robbery in which he was badly beaten, and Barnes himself had been afraid to give evidence because he lived in 'a rough neighbourhood'.

Three days after the murder, on Saturday 15 October, Detective Sergeant Sam Lee, together with Detective Harry Worsfold, kept observation on 587 Commercial Road, where Wade's parents lived. At 11.40 am they saw Wade and a woman enter the house; thirty-five minutes later, the woman appeared in the doorway, with Wade standing behind her. She looked up and down the street and she must have seen something which she regarded as suspicious, because she motioned Wade to go back and shut the door. Shortly afterwards, she came to the door again and beckoned to Wade, who rushed out of the house, ran across the road and leapt on to a tram travelling in the direction of Limehouse. Lee followed on another tram, but as they reached Limehouse Town Hall, traffic obscured

Lee's view and Wade vanished. Meanwhile, Worsfold followed the woman after she left Wade's parents' house, and she led him to 83 Grosvenor Street.

It had been the intention to arrest Wade and Donovan simultaneously, to stop any possibility of them interfering with witnesses. However, whilst the officers had a feasible address for Wade, they had none for Donovan, and they were all physically exhausted from their non-stop investigations of the past few days. Therefore, they decided to cut their losses; at 6.00 am on the Sunday morning Wensley and his men burst into the Grosvenor Street address, where they found Wade and his woman companion of the previous day and arrested him. As Divall later recounted, 'He turned very pale and trembled'. Now, the officers went straight to 587 Commercial Road and kicked the front door right off its hinges. Donovan was not there, but it is more than possible that the occupants were helpful because by 8.30 am Wensley and his men had arrived at 17 Church Row, Limehouse. A detective entered through a kitchen window and opened the front door to the other officers, who put their shoulders to a bedroom door, behind which they found Donovan in bed with a woman; he, too, was arrested.

At Arbour Square police station Donovan was told, 'I've brought you here on suspicion of being concerned with Wade, detained for the wilful murder of Miss Farmer between 6.00 and 8.00 am on the twelfth instant.'

To this, Donovan replied, 'You've done a bloody fine thing this time. I'll do my utmost to disprove it. This is a bloody nice thing, ain't it?'

When they were put up for identification, Rae unhesitatingly picked out both men, and Donovan – he was the more ebullient of the two – told Detective Thomas Smart, 'Of course the fucking boy knows me; he used to live in the same street as me for about two years.' Donovan was quite right; Rae had lived at 44 Old Church Road and Donovan at no. 100 – hence Rae's reluctance to give evidence.

Both men were committed to the Old Bailey from the coroner's inquest to stand their trial before Mr Justice Grantham. It was not a strong case: neither man had said anything to incriminate himself, there were no fingerprints, and no stolen property had been found in their possession. But there were the identifications, plus some interesting circumstantial evidence. Victor Newton Farmer, Miss Farmer's nephew, gave evidence that he had been in his aunt's shop some nine months prior to the murder, when Wade had entered and, after Miss Farmer had gone into her parlour, had asked, 'Is she any relation to you?'

Farmer replied, 'I'm her nephew.'

After Wade asked if Miss Farmer lived alone, he said to her nephew, 'She ought not to, ought she?' and Farmer agreed that she should not.

It was following that incident that Miss Farmer had been attacked; it was strongly suspected that Wade was responsible, but Miss Farmer could not (or would not) identify him. The next time Victor Farmer saw Wade was when he stepped out of a cab at the inquest.

Edwin Avenall, the licensee of the Royal Duchess public house, almost directly opposite Miss Farmer's shop, saw the two prisoners outside the premises for several days prior to the murder; and James Brootan, the landlord at Grosvenor Street, told the jury that on the night before the murder, Wade's wife had asked him to knock on their door at 5.10 am the following morning and, an hour later, had heard the sound of a man's boots as he descended the stairs. He told the jury that he had never known his lodger of the past four weeks rise so early.

Neither prisoner gave evidence, but after a trial lasting three days there was a sufficiency of evidence from the prosecution to find them both guilty of murder on 21 November. Both were scheduled to hang on 13 December.

Right from the beginning, the case had attracted a lot of publicity, and explicit details of the murder were recorded in the popular press. This prompted James Fitzpatrick, a noted East End pickpocket, to approach a police officer outside Worthing Town Hall and tell him, 'I want to give myself up. I cannot rest anywhere.' He then made a detailed written statement confessing to the murder, saying that he and another man (who, he said, was 'well-known to Inspector Divall') had strangled Miss Farmer and stolen 37s 6d in cash.

He was brought back to London on the eve of the execution, and the now Assistant Commissioner (Crime), Sir Melville Macnaughten, was so agitated at the news that he left a function and turned up at Arbour Square in full evening dress. He need not have worried; there was some brisk questioning and Fitzpatrick admitted that his 'confession' was based on details he had read in the newspapers and he had hoped to do Wade and Donovan 'a good turn'.

So the two half-brothers went off to the scaffold at Pentonville prison, with Donovan belatedly declaring that they had not really meant to kill Miss Farmer. Henry Pierrepoint, with the assistance of William Billington, consigned the charmless pair to oblivion.

A few months after the trial, Divall was approached in the street by one of the jurymen, who stated it had been touch-and-go as to whether they should convict the prisoners. He told Divall that had the prisoners gone into the witness box and told their side of the case, they might well have acquitted them; when they declined to do so, this, said the juryman, made the rest of the jury doubt their innocence.

There were two other matters. Remember young Thomas Mitchell, who concocted the fanciful story of seeing a man leaving the shop on the morning of the murder? He was visited at home by a Mr Harnett, a solicitor for the defence, who asked him, 'Did you see a gentleman come out of Miss Farmer's shop and jump on a tramcar?' Thomas replied, 'No', and Harnett told him, 'You silly little goose, why don't you say so and the men will walk out of the dock, free.'

This led to some very severe questioning by Mr Justice Grantham, and although Harnett agreed he had been to the Mitchell home, he denied much of what was said. The judge suggested that Harnett had told Thomas' mother, 'I've come from Coroner Baxter', and this Harnett strenuously denied, saying, 'No, my Lord, I never said anything of the kind.' Mrs Mitchell was then called, and stated on oath that that was exactly what Harnett had said. The judge was quite plainly furious and informed Harnett that he would be sending the papers to the Law Society.

And the other matter was that workmen engaged in repairing Miss Farmer's premises discovered a tin box under the floorboards. In it were Miss Farmer's rings, watch and chain, bracelets and a great deal more jewellery, including diamond earrings, worth a great deal of money.

Donovan and Wade had missed out on an absolute treasure trove; and if they had stolen any money, it could not have been a great deal. Four days after the murder, when Wensley searched Wade, he had nothing in his pockets; as regards Donovan, his worldly worth amounted to no more than 4s 11½d.

★ ★ ★

But whilst Wensley was waiting for Miss Farmer's murderers to make their appearance at the Old Bailey, he had been doing what he did best: catching thieves (and their receiver) in the act by surveillance in a variety of disguises and using a covered van.

On the afternoon of 3 November Wensley and his men were in their van in the Whitechapel Road when they saw twenty-eight-year-old Esther Joab and Matilda Greenberg, aged twenty-three, board an omnibus; and because they had received information as to the pair's larcenous intentions, they whipped up their horse and followed them. The women got off at Holborn Bars and went into Messrs Samuel Lewis, a draper's company. There Joab purchased four yards of material, and they stole thirty-four and a half yards of silk, valued at £6 16s 6d, the loss of which was not noticed until the following day. Detective Sergeant Sam Lee had noticed that Greenberg was carrying a parcel; the women went into a public house, and when they emerged the parcel she was carrying had increased in size. Boarding a bus to Bayswater, they deposited the parcel in the cloakroom at Queen's Road tube station before they entered the drapery department of Messrs Whiteleys Ltd.

They left Whiteleys with fifty-five yards of satin valued at £9, the loss of which was not discovered until later; however, from his vantage point, Wensley knew that something was amiss, because Greenberg had suddenly appeared to put on a considerable amount of weight. Joab walked in front of her, in an effort to conceal Greenberg's expanded girth. The women returned to the tube station, and when they emerged the parcel which Greenberg was carrying was much larger than the one previously seen.

Once more the women boarded a bus, this time getting off at Berwick Street in Soho, where they approached fifty-year-old Rebecca Hollander. Detective Frederick Gooding was close enough to hear Greenberg say, 'Good evening, we have some silk here, can you do with it?'

Hollander replied, 'What is it? How much do you want?'

Joab said, 'Four pounds', and Greenberg urged her, 'You take it.'

With that, Joab handed over the parcel, which Hollander slipped under her apron, Greenberg telling her, 'We'll go up.'

Then the two thieves walked in to 13 Berwick Street, going up to the third room on the first floor; Wensley and Lee followed them in, concealing themselves in the second room.

Meanwhile, Hollander walked up and down the street, looking all about her, before eventually entering 13 Berwick Street and joining the other two women, thoughtfully leaving the door of the third room open. There followed a conversation in Yiddish, and then something seemed to attract Hollander's attention, because she stopped undoing the parcel and entered the room where the officers were. However, due to the darkness of the room – it was now 6.30 pm – she failed to notice them and returned to the third room, followed by Wensley and Lee. Joab turned and saw Wensley, there was a rapid conversation with the other women in Yiddish and she cried, 'Oh, Mr Wensley, we'll plead guilty, don't let us go for trial!' Perhaps unnecessarily, Wensley later told the Old Bailey, 'She knows me, as I'm in the Whitechapel District.'

Greenberg dropped the ticket to the roll of silk and told Lee, 'I shall plead guilty.'

Although Hollander tried to leave, Lee told her, 'You can't leave the room, as you've received the property.'

Hollander replied, 'I have not paid for it.'

However, on the way to the police station, Hollander patted Detective Sergeant Ben Leeson's hand, telling him, 'Don't be too hard on me on account of my poor husband. I'm obliged to do a little, to keep us both going.'

At the Old Bailey, Joab stated that she had paid for the four yards of silk at Lewis' shop and that when Greenberg showed her the parcel of silk she had stolen from the same shop she (Joab) was horrified and entreated her to take it back. However, Greenberg refused, and they went into Whiteleys where, as far as she was concerned, nothing was stolen. Neither was there any incriminating conversation in Berwick Street; Hollander concurred, and also stated that the only reason she had tried to leave the room was to see how her stall was getting on.

Hollander was defended by a barrister who unwisely and sarcastically asked Wensley if he was in the habit of entering houses unasked, when doors were left open. 'I do, if I'm following people of the prisoners' class,' he replied, and when Gooding was asked about his appearance, he replied, 'I was looking very rough at the time.' It led the jury to believe that the officers' scruffy appearance was necessary to prevent them being recognized by two persistent thieves who were well known to them, and the three women were found guilty.

However, what was not revealed during the trial was that when Joab was searched by the matron at the police station, currency and jewellery were found down the leg of one of her stockings; and a second surprise search revealed a diamond ring.

Hollander, said to be 'a well-known receiver', was sentenced to three years and six months' penal servitude, as was Joab – 'a notorious shoplifter'. Greenberg, described as 'a Continental shoplifter', had also exhibited her expertise in the Home Counties, sending her ill-gotten gains by rail to a receiver in London. On a previous occasion when Wensley had arrested her, the judge at her trial described her as being 'a kind of felonious commercial traveller'. On this occasion, she received three years' penal servitude.

★ ★ ★

As well as being keen to roll up his sleeves and get stuck in to policing the streets, Wensley was more than happy to provide assistance to brother officers when it was thought that evidence was lacking in a case. This happened on 26 November 1904, when officers from the City of London police had followed and arrested father and son Bario and Mark Davis, Daniel Sacker, Eli Leman and Moses Blackcowsky, for breaking and entering a warehouse.

They denied knowing each other, so Wensley and his men were called. 'I know all the prisoners,' Wensley told the Old Bailey jury, and went on to say he had seen them on and off, over a period of three to four months, in the neighbourhood of Commercial Road. In fact, he stated, he had seen them the night before their arrest, outside Shapiro's Restaurant, about ten minutes' walk away from the scene of the breaking. This was vehemently denied by the prisoners, but Wensley's evidence was corroborated by Detective Alfred Pye.

Daniel Sacker was acquitted, but Leman and Blackcowsky, who whined their innocence, both had previous convictions (one of Blackcowsky's was in the name of Beaszon), as did the Davis father-and-son team, who had previously been sentenced to two years' imprisonment in Dublin for conspiracy to break into houses. All of the gang received two years on this occasion, this time with hard labour.

★ ★ ★

By 7 December 1905 Wensley had spent just over ten years in the Criminal Investigation Department, and now he was promoted to detective inspector. After almost eighteen years' total service, Wensley had made it – he was now 'the Guv'nor'.

# CHAPTER 13

# The Guv'nor

The press made rather a pig's ear of reporting Wensley's promotion; they recorded that Wensley was replacing Divall as the local inspector, with Divall being transferred to 'J' Division. Because Wensley had been promoted to the rank of detective inspector (second class), as opposed to local inspector, he did not in fact succeed Divall. Instead, he replaced George Albert Godley as detective inspector; and Godley, who had been Abberline's right-hand man during the hunt for Jack the Ripper, with twenty-eight years' service was transferred to 'K' Division to replace the pensioned-off inspector there.

It was true that Divall was transferred to 'J' Division at that time, but as the newspaper remarked, 'He would continue to serve in the neighbourhood'; and for some inexplicable reason, he did.

However, Wensley now consolidated his own men in place: Detective Hunt was promoted to detective sergeant (third class) in place of Richardson, who was advanced to detective sergeant (second class). Lee ('a big, quick-witted man, with enormous hands') now took Wensley's place as detective sergeant (first class), thereby becoming the senior sergeant on the division; he later died in office with the rank of divisional detective inspector.

★ ★ ★

In 1906, the Home Secretary, Herbert Gladstone, set up an enquiry into the conduct of Metropolitan Police officers with regard to disreputable behaviour occurring on the streets of London. It began with a certain Mme Eva D'Angely, who at around midnight on 24 April 1906 was arrested in Regent Street for soliciting prostitution; the case was thrown out at Marlborough Street police court by the magistrate, Mr Denman, when René D'Angely gave evidence that he was the prisoner's husband and that she had merely been waiting for him. Mr Denman made his decision after Sub-Divisional Inspector McKay informed him that he believed the D'Angelys to be a respectable couple. There was a tremendous uproar in the press and in Parliament, amidst a number of allegations of police harassment, bribery and corruption, and this led to the appointment of a Royal Commission, which invited anybody with complaints about police conduct within the previous four years to air their grievances. The Commission received 300 letters alleging police misconduct, with witnesses eager to give evidence of wrongdoing.

Unfortunately, Mme and M D'Angely were not amongst them. Leaving a trail of unpaid debts behind them, they had already fled to Paris, where the police already knew her as a prostitute by the name of Eva Clavell and him, whose real name was Soubiger, as her pimp. Mlle Clavell had already provided M Soubiger with rich pickings by plying her trade in Algiers; now she was doing so again in Paris, using the name Dutiel.

So two people who had committed perjury in an English court wisely refused to attend the Royal Commission, who, incredibly, had not only offered to pay their fare but in fact were deciding whether or not the police should be forced to apologise to this charmless couple.

Of the 300 allegations, just nineteen were found to fall within the Commission's terms of reference, and one of them was made by a vicious, vindictive and unscrupulous character named Arthur Harding.

Harding – he was also known as Tressadern or Tresidern – had been born in 1886 in the Old Nichol, one of the more deprived parts of Bethnal Green. Aged fourteen, he was bound over for possessing a revolver and disorderly conduct, and two years later he received his first custodial sentence, of twelve months' hard labour for larceny. Besides being the leader of a gang of tearaways, Harding was a barrack-room lawyer; he had acquired a thin veneer of education, read law books and – by his own account – had managed to get himself acquitted on twenty-seven occasions. A committee known as the Police and Public Vigilance Society had been set up in Gower Street, WC1, under the auspices of a man named James Timewell, who instructed Earl Russell to act on their behalf before the Royal Commission, which was sitting at the Guildhall, Broad Sanctuary, Westminster. The peer described Timewell as 'a fanatic ... prepared always to believe anything he was told against the police and to resent with some indignation the demand for proof which a lawyer always makes'.

Harding must have thought that the meeting with Timewell was providential; he had a loathing for the police in general and Wensley in particular. However, the Commission decided against hearing details of all his acquittals and restricted themselves to hearing just one case, which they did on 2/3 December 1906. Harding had been arrested on 6 September 1906 for assaulting Police Constable Carr, who had with some difficulty arrested Charles Callaghan, one of Harding's gang, and who, with other officers, was taking him to the station. As they were passing a public house in Slater Street, Harding punched PC Carr in the ear, saying, 'You're not taking him.' Harding was part of a crowd who surged around the officers; a bottle was thrown, there were shouts of 'Let 'em have it' and 'Go for 'em', and someone was heard to shout, 'If he had his shooter here, he'd stop some of their fun'. The assault was witnessed by PCs Ashford and Philbey, who informed the Commission, 'There was nearly always an attempt to free a prisoner.' PC Deller assisted in Callaghan's arrest and stated that Harding approached him and said, 'Let him go; I'll take him home.' This is still a commonly used ploy by gang leaders; it arrogantly demonstrates their power over the police to their followers and saves the guilty party from arrest. It did not work, however, on this occasion, because PC Deller told him, 'He's in our hands, now.'

In his memoirs Harding described PC Carr's evidence to the commission as 'a failure, very incoherent ... suffering from mental strain', but of course, Harding only provided half the picture. Carr did experience difficulties giving evidence, so much so that one of the commissioners, Mr C.A. Whitmore, asked if he was unwell. PC Carr replied that he was feeling very dazed as the result of receiving a punch six days previously in exactly the same place as Harding had struck him and was currently placed on the sick list. So when Harding stated that the officer was 'permitted to resign', once again he was telling his readers what he wanted them to believe. PC Carr was in fact medically discharged as the result of being injured on duty.

The assault case against Harding had been dismissed at court. The magistrate, Mr Cluer, was called and told the Commission he had dismissed the case because he was doubtful of Harding's guilt. How this benefited Harding it is difficult to say, although he 'found witnesses' in other cases against the police. This included an assault on a man by PC Ashford (which had occurred one month prior to the assault on PC Carr), for which the officer was subsequently sentenced to nine months' hard labour.

But it was Wensley that Harding was after, and in the witness box Sir Eldon Bankes KC for the police said, 'In his examination in chief, Harding suggested that you said to him, "Well, Harding, we will have you for another offence".'

Wensley replied, 'I said nothing of the kind.'

'Is that absolutely untrue?' asked Sir Eldon.

Wensley confirmed, 'Absolutely untrue.'

'Did you not say something of the kind to him?' asked Earl Russell.

Wensley replied, 'No.'

The Chairman, Sir David Brynmor Jones, asked him, 'Had you been acquainted with Harding before?'

'I had seen him,' Wensley replied. 'I knew him by repute.'

'That is not an answer to my question,' persisted Sir David. 'Had you known Harding before?'

Wensley replied, 'Yes.'

'Personally?'

'Personally.'

It was a poor performance by Wensley, in which he appeared to give – certainly in the latter part of his evidence, at any event – answers which seemed evasive and needed to be dragged out of him. In fact, he had known Harding at least as early as 1902, when the latter had been arrested by Detective Sergeant Jack 'Jew Boy' Stevens after being implicated in a railway swindle, although after a week's remand the charge had been dismissed by the magistrate.

In addition, Wensley told the Commission that after Harding and members of his gang had been arrested for a series of larcenies, Harding had said to him, 'Mr Wensley, I want you to stop here and see I get a fair show.' Wensley obliged him, and when Harding was not identified he told Wensley, 'I am satisfied; thanks very much for stopping.'

So why Wensley prevaricated is inexplicable; he knew that Harding was up to his armpits in criminality and in addition had wanted to pin the blame for a string of robberies on him, something he had been unable to do because of a lack of evidence – but in an enquiry of this nature, this would not have precluded him from saying so.

William Southey, who had two shops in the area, was certainly not so reticent when giving evidence to the Commission. He described the modus operandi of Harding's thirty-strong gang in great detail, explaining that they communicated between themselves using sign language when they were about to rob a passer-by. Mr Southey stated that when he informed members of the public about Harding's activities, Harding returned and threw a lighted paper underneath his stall, intending to set fire to paper stored there; and he also informed the Commission of the time when Harding's gang threw a man through his shop window. Stating that 'Harding is the captain of the gang and has been for many, many years', Mr Southey referred to Harding's serving a prison sentence for street robbery, saying to general laughter in the room, 'When he was doing twenty months, it was paradise.'

Mr Southey's evidence was corroborated by Mr Gillender, a seller of leather in Bethnal Green, who informed the Commission that Harding and his gang specialized in stealing watches from passers-by, and also by Frank Rayner, a Brick Lane publican, who stated he had seen Harding 'kick a man's head in'. When one of the gang was fined, said Mr Rayner, the others terrorized the neighbourhood for subscriptions to pay the fine; if the money was not given voluntarily, it was forced out of people.

The nineteen cases were scrupulously investigated, and the Commission sat on sixty-four occasions over a period of eleven months. It resulted in nine officers being found guilty of misconduct; some were sent to prison, and four more officers who had made errors of judgement were disciplined. In spite of this, the Commission's report, published in 1908, ruled that, 'The Metropolitan Police are entitled to the confidence of all classes of the community'. Harding, naturally, described the proceedings as 'a whitewash'; and he later claimed in a whining monologue, 'The weak, the poor and oppressed of the land have always been without the means to fight against injustice.'

So although Wensley (and several other officers) were completely exonerated, neither he nor Harding emerged from the enquiry with any great credit – Harding especially, because he had been exposed as the leader of a gang of hooligans who systematically carried out street robberies and protection rackets. 'After the publicity of the Royal Commission,' wrote Harding, 'I knew the police would strain every inch to get me convicted for some offence ... the police officer I feared most was the CID Inspector in charge of 'H' Division – DDI F. Wensley ... He was not the kind of man one wants as an enemy ... He never forgot or forgave.'

Harding was right. Wensley was not a man to be crossed, let alone publicly vilified, as he would soon find out. In April 1908 Harding was arrested once more by Detective Sergeant Stevens in Church Row for being a suspected person, after Stevens had kept him under observation and seen him drop a purse by his side. This time, the magistrate, Mr Cluer, did not give him the benefit of the doubt; as an habitual criminal, Harding was sentenced to twelve months' imprisonment. But that was just a salutary slap on the wrist; Wensley had not finished with him, not by any means, as later events would prove.

★ ★ ★

Notwithstanding the Royal Commission, in 1906 police conditions had improved sufficiently for officers to restrict their duties to thirteen days per fortnight and to enjoy ten days' annual leave.

However, to thoroughly spoil Wensley and his officers' New Year celebrations, David Marks, Louis Cohen and Morris Kron broke into a warehouse via the cellar at 16 Great Alie Street, Whitechapel and stole cutlery valued at £79 14s 0d. Wensley and his men caught up with them at midnight in the back room on the second floor of 32 Plough Street Buildings, where Wensley – recognizing the voice of the occupier, Morris Winterman – heard him say, 'I'll give you £5 for the lot', whereupon the officers made their presence known.

With the property all intact, Kron told Wensley, 'I'll tell you the truth. We three [indicating Marks and Cohen] did the job and he [Winterman] was just buying.'

The newly promoted Sergeant Lee arrested Marks, who said, 'Give me a chance; you've got me properly, this time.'

Arriving at the police station, Cohen said, 'I shall plead guilty', and Winterman asked Ben Leeson, 'Can't you make it all right for me? I was only looking at the stuff.'

Whether Leeson could 'make it all right' is debatable, but the fact was that the following week at Thames police court, Winterman was discharged; the others were committed for trial at the North London Sessions.

Thirty-seven-year-old Lewis Calib described himself as a tailor, but he was also the leader of a gang of burglars; in 1903 he had been sentenced to fifteen months' imprisonment in Cardiff for possessing housebreaking implements by night. Marks Smeller, aged twenty-six, also stated that he was a tailor, although he had been convicted with a thirty-two-year-old bootmaker named Lewis Jacobs, who, in 1898 had been sentenced to three years' penal servitude for burglary and inflicting grievous bodily harm with intent.

On 7 July 1906, those men, together with Jacob Bloom, a forty-two-year-old traveller and Soloman Lipshitz, a cook aged twenty-eight, broke into a Stepney warehouse, where they stole 49,950 squirrel tails and 428 marmot skins, valued together at £800.

Informants told Wensley the names of the men they had seen keeping watch on the premises in the week prior to the break-in; and also suggested that observation at a certain time on a certain day on a barber's shop in High Street, Stratford would be fruitful.

After hours of waiting there, Wensley, together with other officers including Tom Divall, saw a horse and van pull up outside the shop. Lewis Girtler, a forty-six-year-old furrier, and the others got down and prepared to go into the premises. Suddenly, the horse took fright and reared up, one of the gang recognized the detectives and shouted a warning and the gang fled. However, at least the stolen furs were recovered intact at the shop, and the miscreants were later rounded up and arrested.

At the North London Sessions the men were found guilty, and it was revealed that bribes had been offered to some of the witnesses, including £200 to Divall, 'if he would omit some of his evidence'.

Bloom, Wensley told the court, was 'the worst of the lot' and the only member of his family not to have undergone penal servitude.

'Surely that is to his credit?' asked Mr Elliott, the barrister for Lewis Girtler, to the general amusement of the court; but matters became slightly less entertaining after Wensley stated that Mr Elliott's client had long been suspected of receiving stolen property 'on an extensive scale' and was believed to have been involved in receiving the proceeds of fourteen burglaries, with a total value of £1,200.

Bloom told the court, 'I swear by the King of England, I'm innocent', and many members of the public gallery wept (they were described in the press as being 'foreigners') when he was sentenced to twenty-three months' hard labour. Girtler, too, was sentenced to hard labour (twenty-one months) – as were Smeller (eighteen months) and Lipshitz (fifteen months) – and ordered to pay £20 prosecution costs. The ringleaders, Calib and Jacobs, were sent to penal servitude, three and a half years for the former, three years for the latter, to be followed with two years' police supervision.

In a particularly flowery commendation, the chairman of the Sessions, Mr Richard Loveland-Loveland KC, DL, JP, told the court:

> I wish the names of the officers in this case to go before the commissioner because I think they had a very difficult case. They managed remarkably well. Inspectors of eminence they are in the detective force and I think great credit is due to one and all of them for having brought these men to justice.

It was a commendation echoed by both the petty and the grand jury – and by the commissioner.

★ ★ ★

William Filler was a twenty-four-year-old carman who vanished on 7 November 1906 after his employers sent him to a warehouse at the London & India Docks to pick up a consignment of forty-two chests and four half chests of tea, valued at £230. His horse and van – minus its load – was later found in Stepney Green.

By the following morning, Wensley's informants had done their work. First, he and his men descended upon an address in

West Street, Stepney; there, they arrested Filler, George Smith, a sixty-one-year-old hawker[11], James Herbert, sixty-three and also a hawker and James Beechenow, a thirty-nine-year-old harness maker. They also recovered thirteen chests of the stolen tea. In a nearby stable they found eight more chests of tea, four half chests and a chest which had been partly emptied, plus two lots of tea in packages. Then on to Master Street, Stepney, where two more chests of tea were seized – so too were Martin Dacey, a forty-eight-year-old dealer, who was arrested in bed, and William Lawrence, a twenty-eight-year-old hawker.

Some stables in Whiston Street were rented by a cooper[12] named John Jones, aged twenty-four, and this was Wensley's next port of call. Whilst Wensley was there, James Thompson, a dealer aged thirty-four, arrived with a pony and cart containing five chests of tea. Jones told Wensley, 'You've got me on a piece of toast. I was a fool. I should have got very little out of it.'

The last address visited by Wensley was occupied by William Hiller, a thirty-one-year-old carman. The circumstances of his arrest caused great amusement at the Clerkenwell Sessions, because when Wensley knocked on the door, Hiller stuck his head out of the window and shouted, 'Police! Police! There are burglars at the back!' Unfortunately for Hiller, there were also ten sacks of tea in the premises, about which he explained to the officers, 'I was only minding it until a buyer could be found.'

The chairman handed out sentences of hard labour – Thomson (twenty-three months), Smith (eighteen months), Hiller (sixteen months), Beechenow (twelve months) and Dacey (nine months). A rather harsher view – probably because of their previous convictions – was taken of Herbert and Dacey, who received sentences of penal servitude of five years and four years respectively. William Filler, the thief who started the whole business, was fortunate to receive a six-month sentence, and Jones, who made the rather incriminating statement, must have been ecstatic to have been acquitted.

In the space of twenty hours Wensley had roped in the entire gang and recovered practically all of the stolen property; the grand jury specially commended Wensley and his men 'for their clever capture', and the chairman of the sessions told the court that he had 'great pleasure in endorsing it'.

★ ★ ★

---

11 Street seller.
12 Cask or barrel maker.

At thirty-six years of age, Charles Croney was what might be described as an industrious 'coiner'. Aged twenty-three, he had been sentenced to seven years' penal servitude for possessing a mould, and scarcely had he been released before he was sentenced to a further seven years at the Old Bailey on 2 April 1900 for possessing counterfeit coins. At the time of his arrest on 16 January 1907 he was on licence, the remainder of his sentence not expiring until November of that year.

Croney's crony was a twenty-eight-year-old flower seller named Mary Ann Sullivan – also known as Williams – who had left her husband three months previously and was suspected of previously associating with persons in the trade of uttering counterfeit coins.

Both were in a furnished room at 14 Margaret Place, Bethnal Green, when Wensley hammered on the door; he heard Sullivan call out, 'Shut up! Who's there?' whereupon Wensley burst the door open. Croney made for the window, but Wensley stopped him and took three counterfeit sixpences from his hand. The room was full of counterfeiting equipment, and Wensley found seventeen more counterfeit sixpences, whilst Inspector Frank Knell discovered a mould containing a hot sixpence which Sullivan had concealed under her apron, plus three more counterfeit coins.

'This is the first day we've been making it,' said Sullivan, rather unconvincingly, and Croney, foreseeing a dismal future, seized a saucer containing potassium of cyanide and drank it. It must have been a weak solution because, following the administration of an emetic at London Hospital, he was well enough to stand trial at the Old Bailey.

Croney did his unsuccessful best to exonerate Sullivan, telling the court that he had started the counterfeiting operation about half an hour before she came in, followed seconds later by the arrival of the police. But Sullivan was sentenced to six months' hard labour, and, given his previous history, Croney was undoubtedly fortunate to receive just five years' penal servitude.

★ ★ ★

The CID often supervised raids on gambling houses; quite apart from the unlawful nature of the activity, this provided the detectives with intelligence on who was associating with whom.

A room at the back of 41 Kinder Street, St George's was fitted out for gambling, with a quilt hung over the window. The door was opened by Jack Lewis, who had previously served a term of penal servitude for robbery with violence; seeing Wensley, he shouted, 'Police! – You can't come in here!' Despite knocking off Wensley's hat and arming himself with a jemmy, Lewis failed to stop the officers flooding into the room, where they discovered twenty men playing faro.

The banker, Michael Cohen, told Wensley, 'I'm sorry you found me here', and both men were fortunate to be fined.

Three weeks later, a 'strange man' was observed talking through the letterbox of 5 Duncan Street, and whatever he said, it resulted in Abraham Levy opening the door. Then, 'Police, police!' shouted Levy, as Wensley and Gill and their men pushed their way in. There were twenty-three men playing faro, and although three of the gamblers escaped, the banker, Harry Simmons, who snatched up the cash-box was not among them; he and Levy were both sentenced to three months' hard labour.

Wensley with Divall and a large number of officers then hit a gaming house at 8 Langdale Street, Commercial Road, where Alex Chasleberg was the doorkeeper, and in the back room thirty-four men were playing faro, with Joseph Wax as banker and Samuel Alonsky as croupier.

Two days later, Wensley raided 79 Davis Buildings, where he discovered Wax, Alonsky and three other men playing faro. During a second raid of the evening at 1 Assam Street, Chasleberg, together with fifteen other men, was found to be playing faro. Inevitably, fines and sentences of hard labour were handed down.

When Wensley and his men interrupted a game of faro at another gaming house, so great was the rush of players to disassociate themselves from the proceedings that about ten shillings' worth of copper and silver cascaded over the floor. James Wax, the croupier, had two similar convictions and he received a six-month sentence. Twenty-five other men entered into recognizances of £50 each not to frequent gaming houses for the next two years.

What was described as 'the whole of the detective department' accompanied Wensley 'in covered wagons' to raid a restaurant at 165 Commercial Road, where, in two first-floor rooms 'alien Jews' were discovered playing faro. The organizers were fined, and fifty-one of the clientele were bound over not to frequent gambling clubs for the next twenty-one months.

Finally, a club frequented by Germans – Divall described their faces as being 'more like bulldogs than human beings' – had proved impossible to prosecute because of the club's vigilance, so Wensley and Gill disguised themselves in uniforms of the Royal Horse Artillery and mingled with the gamblers. It was intended that, following a blast from Gill's whistle, a pantechnicon-load of police officers would burst in through the door, and with Wensley's and Gill's testimony of the gambling, everyone would be caught red-handed.

Wensley sauntered around the club, his riding crop under his arm, and then Gill sounded his whistle. Instantly there was pandemonium, and Wensley knew he had to preserve the evidence; he flung himself down on the gaming table, trapping the cards and money with his body. But the officers in the pantechnicon had managed to lock themselves in, so one of the Germans picked up Wensley's dropped riding crop and proceeded to thrash him across the buttocks. It took several minutes of whipping – although to Wensley it must have seemed an eternity – before the key to the pantechnicon was found and Wensley was extricated from a very painful encounter. It was his last foray into undercover work; Russians and Romanians he could contend with, but not a German with a face like a bulldog.

But gamblers were pretty small beer compared to the trade in human misery which Wensley dealt with next; and as a result, once more, he was propelled into the newspaper headlines.

★ ★ ★

The city of Buenos Aires in the Argentine had become notorious for the 'white slave' trade. Thousands of Jewish women, many from Poland, Russia and Germany, had arrived there from the 1880s onwards and were pressed into service in the state-run brothels. It caused an affront to the predominantly Catholic Argentinians and the decent majority of the Jewish community, who were appalled that many of the brothels were staffed by Jewish women and that Jewish men acted as their pimps.

When street protests were organized to campaign against the trade, pimps paid the crowd to shout insults in Yiddish and throw missiles at the organizers. Matters became so bad that Samuel Cohen, the secretary of the London-based Jewish Association for the Protection of Girls and Women, visited South America, where he had to establish a home for these women, so great was the traffic.

Wensley had received reports of girls vanishing from their homes in the East End, and he discovered that men were in the habit of seducing these girls, then taking them to Argentina for 'a new life', only for them to discover, too late, that this meant that they were sold into brothels.

Two such girls were Jane Goldbloom, who had yet to reach her eighteenth birthday, and Sarah Levine. They were taken to South America by Louis Gold – his real name, fittingly, was Ratman – a twenty-seven-year-old carpenter and Harry Cohen, a twenty-four-

year-old tailor. It was this charmless pair's intention for the girls
to become 'inmates of a brothel for the purposes of prostitution'.
Gold had originally come to England from Minsk in Russia when
he was fifteen. He had no dependants in England, although he
had a wife who lived in the United States. Cohen was a native
of Warsaw, and both men had, for four or five years, enjoyed a
lucrative trade in exporting girls to Buenos Aires.

Wensley was informed of Gold's and Cohen's precise plans;
he obtained warrants for their arrest and sent a telegram to the
police in Rio de Janeiro. When the SS *Orissa* docked, detectives
boarded the ship, took off the party of four and transferred them
to the steamship *Oravia*. The *Oravia* docked at Liverpool on 1
March 1907, and Wensley and his officers were waiting; Gold –
who had received a letter from Buenos Aires 'offering £100 each
for good-looking girls with long hair' – was found to have tickets in
the names of Louis and Sarah Gold and Henry and Sarah Cohen
in his possession, and both men were arrested. They travelled back
to London by train, and Gold told Wensley, 'I know who has done
this for me; it is a girl who went with me to Buenos Aires. We had
a row.'

Cohen, seeing Gold talking to Wensley, guessed that he was
confessing all of his misdeeds, and in that mistaken belief decided
to put his side of the affair to Detective Sergeant Lee, telling him:

> I shall tell you all about it. I shouldn't have taken Jenny if it
> hadn't been for him. I had no money. He gets his living at
> this. I was a respectable chap when I met him. He asked me
> if I could find a girl to take away and I should do myself a bit
> of good. I was hard up and told him I would. I got Jenny to
> go. I'm sorry now. I will marry her if they let me. How do you
> think I will get on?

The short answer was, not very well. At the Old Bailey, Judge
Lumley Smith, referring to Buenos Aires, remarked, 'It is clear
there is a market there', and sentenced the pair to hard labour,
Gold to fifteen months and Cohen to twelve, and certified them
for expulsion under the Aliens Act. In addition, Wensley's principal
witness was attacked in the street by a man and a woman; both
were sentenced to hard labour, the man to two months, the woman
to one month. The latter told the court, 'I can do that – it won't
kill me.'

★ ★ ★

By 1909 police personnel in the capital had risen steadily; now they numbered 18,657.

Wensley was hard at work liaising with 'C' Division officers when a warehouse at 18 Charing Cross Road was broken into and a large quantity of cloth and silk, valued at £952, was stolen. Enquiries led the West End officers to the thieves; local knowledge resulted in Wensley arresting the receivers, Gershon Warshawsky and Isaac and Benjamin Rosenthal. Wensley described how, upon accusing the Rosenthal brothers of receiving the stolen cloth, they had shrugged their shoulders and shaken their heads, 'in a very emphatic manner'. This led the defence counsel to ask Wensley to demonstrate how this was done; this was a common defence trick (still used nowadays) to humiliate and embarrass a witness, and had nothing whatsoever to do with the case. Wensley was up to that one and he replied, 'I cannot do it as emphatically as they did', adding, 'It belongs to their race.' In an effort to be helpful, he told the jury, 'I should say it went on for a minute or so', which was rather stretching credulity. Whether it did or not, all of the thieves and receivers received varying amounts of hard labour.

But within three weeks Wensley would once more attract the press like a lodestone. It was not a deliberate act; the attention was simply inescapable.

# CHAPTER 14

# Sailors and Prostitutes

Although twenty-three-year-old Morris Reubens described his occupation as 'salesman' and that of his twenty-two-year-old brother Marks as 'costermonger', they were in fact violent pimps. For two or three years prior to their arrest they had lived off the immoral earnings of two prostitutes, Ellen Stevens, aka Brooks (who originally stated that she was twenty-one, but at the Old Bailey deducted three years from her age) and Emily Allen, aged twenty-five. Allen had met Morris when, as she modestly told a jury, 'I was an unfortunate and he protected me against a man who was attacking me.'

Allen and Stevens were in the habit of bringing customers back to their room at 3 Rupert Street. The men – normally drunk – could then be fleeced of their valuables; if there was any resistance they could be subdued by the brothers, taken out into the street and dumped, some way away. That was possibly the plan on the night of 15 March 1909, but it would end in tragedy.

★ ★ ★

Earlier that day, the SS *Dorset*, of the Shire Line, arrived from Australia and berthed at the Victoria Docks; Charles Malcolm McEacharn, the second mate, and William Sproul, the second engineer, left the ship at about 8.30 pm, each with about £5 in cash as well as a number of silver threepenny pieces to hand out to spongers in the dock area.

At about 11.00 pm, after a meal, the men met up with Allen and Stevens; they had a drink, went to the address in Rupert Street and then went out for another drink. It was on this latter occasion that they were seen by Police Constable 75 'H' Henry Simmons, at 12.30 am as they left the Swan public house in Whitechapel High Street and returned to Rupert Street, where they entered room 13. By now, both seamen were very drunk; and since it was their intention to stay the night, McEacharn gave Allen seven shillings and Sproul gave Stevens sixteen shillings. At 1.10 am, the area was being patrolled by Police Constable 323 'H' James MacIntosh, who saw the Reubens brothers standing outside 3 Rupert Street;

Morris knocked on the shutter, the door was opened and both men went inside.

Suddenly, the brothers burst into room 13; without warning or provocation, Morris struck Sproul on the head with a stick bound in hippopotamus hide. But Sproul, at five feet ten, was powerfully built and, drunk or not, he fought back; McEacharn went to his assistance but received several hard blows to the head.

Morris' stick had now broken in two, but Marks produced and opened a pocket knife and with this he frenziedly stabbed Sproul in the face and wrist and then, with a single thrust, two and a half inches deep to the heart. Dr Thomas Jones MRCS would later tell the coroner that 'considerable force must have been used'. Sproul was dying, but as the Reubens brothers dragged him from the room, they were busily rifling through his pockets for whatever they could steal. As he was pulled through the front door Sproul put his hand on it, possibly to try to steady himself, leaving a bloody palm print behind. He staggered across the road, and Morris followed him to steal his gold watch and chain.

The brothers returned to the house, and when Allen saw the broken stick and the knife on the table she cried, 'Oh, Morrie and Mark, what have you done?'

Morris replied, 'That's all right, Emmy, you'll be all right', and told her to go up to Mrs Nutt who lived in room no. 18. Before she did so, Allen closed the knife and threw it behind the gas stove.

At 1.20 am, PC MacIntosh, who had seen the brothers half an hour earlier, discovered Sproul's body in Rupert Street. McEacharn, meanwhile, had staggered off, was found by Inspector John Freeman of 'H' Division in Commercial Road and provided a garbled account of what had happened.

Inspector Freeman went to Rupert Street, arriving at 1.45 am, saw Sproul's lifeless body and immediately took charge of the situation. Seeing the blood on the door of no. 3, he immediately posted constables at the rear of the premises to prevent any escape. He saw some silver threepenny pieces by the body and noticed that Sproul's pockets had been turned inside out. When he later searched the body, he found an empty sovereign purse, 1s 3d in silver and a pipe, but no watch or chain. With the arrival of Chief Inspector George Loughlin both men banged repeatedly on the door of no. 3 and when they got no answer, they forced entry. In room 13 they found Ellen Stevens lying drunk and unconscious on the bed. They then went up to the second landing, where they met Marks Reubens descending the stairs. Asked who he was and if he lived in the premises, Marks replied, 'Yes; what's that to do with you?' and tried to push past. That was unwise, because Freeman prevented him from doing so, and this resulted in Marks collecting a small mark on his cheek which he was later quick to attribute to police brutality.

'I live here,' Marks told the officers, banging on the door of no. 19. But when there was no reply, he banged on the door of no. 20 instead, which prompted the occupier, Morris Premislow, to state, 'I don't know you. You don't live here. I've never seen you before.' Marks was duly arrested. On his way to the station, Marks took a handkerchief from his pocket, pretended to wipe his nose and threw it on the ground. It was picked up by PC Simmons, who was accompanying him and who noticed it was partly wet and bloodstained. 'Oh, that's nothing,' said Marks, 'I've got another one in my pocket.' But he had not; what he did have was 7s 0d in silver and some coppers, plus two keys, one of which fitted the front door of 3 Rupert Street and the other, room 13.

But at 1.30 that morning, Albert Nutt, the occupant of Room 18 on the first floor, had heard a knock on the door; answering it, he saw Emily Allen, who asked if she could come in. Later, Morris Reubens arrived, asking if he could stay for a few minutes since he had 'had a row, downstairs'. Hearing a lot of people in the house, Nutt suspected the worst and told Allen and Morris that they must leave. Morris replied, 'I'm going out, now – I'm going to give myself up.'

Wensley, called from his bed, went straight to Leman Street police station, where he saw that Marks had been detained, and then to Rupert Street, where he saw Sproul's body. He searched room 13 – Stevens was still insensible on the bed – and took possession of Sproul's overcoat, in which there was a bottle of whisky; although he looked for the murder weapon, he was unable to find the knife.

Now Wensley walked in to room 18 and grabbed Morris by the wrist. 'I want you, Reubens,' he said.

Morris replied, 'All right, guv'nor, I was going to give myself up; I don't want to cause these people no trouble. The two girls brought two fellows home tonight and they wouldn't part up; me and my brother had a row with them. They threw a glass at one of the girls and we set about them. I then came up here with my missus.[13] I don't mind telling you, I robbed the fellow lying on the ground over there.' As he said this, he looked out of the window at

---

13 It was quite common for both pimp and prostitute to assume married status, possibly hoping that this brought a degree of respectability into their relationship.

where Sproul's body lay underneath a street gas lamp and added, 'I hope he's not dead; there was only me and my brother there.'

Morris and the two women were taken to the police station. En route, Morris told Detective Henry Rutter, who was accompanying him, 'Just after one o'clock I went home with my young brother. I saw two men in the room with my wife and his young woman; we had a row with the men. I didn't stab him; if he was stabbed, my brother must have done it.'

At the police station, Morris removed from beneath his underpants a gold watch and chain, which had been suspended on hooks, saying, 'This is what you want; I own I robbed him. I did it in the street. I went back indoors and said to my young brother, "I think he'll be all right in a couple of hours" – I left him lying in the street.' And upon searching him, two keys identical to those found in his brother's possession were discovered.

Both prisoners were examined at the police station by Dr Jones, as was the handkerchief retained by PC Simmons from Marks. It was partially wet and had recent blood on it, and the doctor formed the opinion that whoever had used it had had blood on his hands, which were washed and then dried with the handkerchief. Marks' hands were clean, suggesting that water had recently been applied to them; there was no indication that Morris' hands had recently been washed. There was a tap in the backyard of 3 Rupert Street but no towel, hence the wet handkerchief in Marks' possession.

Lionel Tramberg, the licensee of the White Hart public house, Hooper Street, knew both the Reubens brothers and recognized the hippopotamus-hide stick that Morris habitually carried, although when he had last seen it, it was not in its present broken state.

The same morning, Wensley charged the four prisoners with murder, and on the way to Thames police court, Morris said, 'Mr Wensley, do what you can for us. We never meant to murder the man and you don't want to see a couple of young fellows like us topped.'

It may be thought that Wensley acted with almost indecent haste in charging the prisoners, but there was sound reasoning behind his decision. The evidence against Allen for murder was thin, although there was a fairly sound basis to substantiate a charge of robbery with violence. Against Stevens there was no evidence in respect of either charge, since for all of the relevant time she was insensible. But Wensley knew that one or both could assist the prosecution, and unless they had a substantial charge hanging over their heads, there was little chance that they would cooperate. When he escorted Allen to Holloway prison, she provided him with the evidence he required about the whereabouts of the murder weapon; returning to Rupert Street, he searched the gas stove, but without success; then, ripping away a piece of sheet iron nailed to the wall at the back of the stove, he heard something drop. It was the bloodstained knife.

On 22 April at the Old Bailey, before Mr Justice Jelf – he had just concluded the sentencing in the Warshawsky case – Morris Reubens pleaded guilty to robbery with violence but, together with his brother, not guilty to Sproul's murder. Although Allen and Stevens had been indicted for murder on the Coroner's inquisition (and Allen also for robbery with violence), it was decided to use them as prosecution witnesses, as Wensley must have foreseen. Richard Muir led for the prosecution, and Wensley (with a fine sense of the theatrical) had the front door of 3 Rupert Street, adorned with Sproul's blood-print, brought into court; Ellen Stevens, who told the court that she 'came over sillified' and slept until the police awoke her, dutifully identified the murder weapon as belonging to Marks.

But if Wensley's performance was theatrical, the histrionics of the two prisoners put him in the shade. No evidence for the defence was called; instead, throughout the trial, the brothers groaned, burst into tears and had to fortify themselves with smelling salts. When the jury retired to consider their verdict, Morris Reubens was 'in a fainting condition' and Marks was audibly sobbing.

Just twelve minutes later, the jury returned to find both men guilty of murder. Morris threw up his arms. 'Oh, my God! My God!' he cried. He then turned to the jury. 'Is there no recommendation of mercy for me?' he shrieked. 'Won't you have mercy upon me, gentlemen? Please do!' Both men received the death sentence, and Morris turned once more to the jury. 'Is there no recommendation of mercy for me?' he pleaded. Leaning against a warder, he cried, 'Oh, my God! My God!'

Quite obviously, neither the jury nor anybody else in the court was going to say or do anything of a conciliatory nature, and Morris must have realized this, because he then screamed, 'God curse everybody in the court!'

Marks now flung himself to the floor of the dock, shrieking, 'Let me get out of this!' – and as the two men were dragged off to the cells, their screams gradually faded from the court's hearing.

Details of this sensational trial were flashed around the world. With a distinct lack of sympathy, the New Zealand newspaper, the *Marlborough Express*, noted:

So the public saw and heard the last of the two men who may be ranked as belonging to the most despicable class of society – men who live a life of idleness and crime and receive their sustenance from the immoral earnings of women euphemistically termed 'unfortunates'. It may sound brutal to say so, but such creatures are better dead.

Mr Justice Jelf gave the police a tremendous commendation, saying, 'I'm sure the jury will agree that they owe very much to Detective Inspector Wensley and the other police engaged, and considerable credit is due to those who took part in bringing the two men to justice.'

The brothers' appeal failed, and both were executed on 20 May 1909. Their case was later commemorated by a rather macabre present to Wensley, in the form of a glass tumbler, on the bottom of which was an engraving of two men hanging from a scaffold, with the inscription, 'The Brothers Reubens. The Last Drop'.

\* \* \*

Wensley's next murder case also featured a seaman and a prostitute; however, in this case the roles would be reversed, the prostitute being the victim and the seaman the murderer.

Fate had dealt Harold Hall a pretty shabby hand. Born in 1882, Hall and his three brothers had been sent from Strangeways Workhouse to Canada as children. He had become a seaman, and when his ship docked in South Africa, his encounter with a larcenous French lady in a Johannesburg brothel left him £30 the poorer. 'I didn't do anything to her,' he later told Wensley, 'but I made up my mind, if it occurred again, what I would do.' Eventually, he landed at Liverpool on 22 October 1908, having worked his passage on the SS *Thelma* from Spain. Hall was then employed as a paper-sorter by the Salvation Army, in Spa Road, Bermondsey, where a sharp knife with a broken small blade was used for cutting the string in the back of books. When Hall left on 1 July 1909, the knife – which, after continual use, was now quite blunt – went with him.

As Hall and his siblings were travelling west to Canada, so Kate – or Kitty – Ronan and her father were travelling the other way from New York to London, to settle in Fulham. Ronan first entered domestic service but she ended up in Spitalfields, acquired a ponce named Henry Benstead and from room 12 at 11 Millar's Court, Duval Street, industriously went to work for him.

Harold Hall met Ronan in Commercial Street just before midnight on 1 July, and as they returned to her room they were seen by Alfred Wilkins, who was standing outside 17 Duval Street.

What happened next comes from Hall's account: 'I took off my jacket and waistcoat and asked her to light the gas. She said there was none. She then asked me to light a candle. I struck a match and just as I was lighting the candle on the mantelpiece, I turned round sharp and saw she had her hand inside my coat pocket. I said, "Is that your game?" I flew at her in a rage and caught her by the throat and threw her on the bed and held her there. She never spoke. I took out my knife which I opened with my teeth and stuck it in the side of her neck. I then threw the knife on the bed.'

Hall had already booked a bed at the Queen Victoria's Seamen's Rest, Poplar, where he arrived at 1.30 am; having spent the night there, he vanished. As Hall was arriving at the hostel, so Henry Benstead arrived home from a day's drinking to find Ronan's body and ran into the street shouting, 'Someone's cut my Kitty's throat!'

Police were called, and when Percy John Clarke, the divisional surgeon, arrived he came to the conclusion that sexual intercourse had taken place within a couple of hours of his examination and also that death had been caused by strangulation and then by cutting the throat. 'A good deal of force must have been used,' observed the doctor later, 'because the knife is not at all sharp.'

Wensley, who arrived just after 2.00 am, noticed that the girl's left hand was under her hip and that when it was moved a penny fell from it; the inference to Wensley was that she had been in the act of robbing someone. But suspects had he none. Benstead naturally attracted a good deal of police questioning, but his alibi was unshakeable. So the coroner recorded a verdict of 'murder by some person or persons unknown' and the enquiry was scaled down.

But then, over two weeks later, Police Sergeant 14 'A' Sidney Richards, a member of the Bristol Constabulary, was on patrol when he was approached by Harold Hall, who, Sergeant Richards later told an Old Bailey jury, 'appeared to be in great trouble and not to have had much rest for some time, and not much food'. Richards added, 'He was not very tidy. His boots were worn and dilapidated.'

Hall had arrived in Bristol on 14 July and lodged at the Salvation Army, Tower Street. And now, tired and worried, he told Sergeant Richards that he wanted to give himself up for murder. He thought the victim's name was Kate Rooney, but of course it was Kitty Ronan he was referring to. Taken to the police station, he made a full written confession, and when he saw Wensley on 19 July he told him, 'Yes, that is true. I did it and intended when I came here to act like a man and I mean to see it through.'

Taken to London, he was formally charged, and when he saw the murder weapon on the inspector's desk he said, 'That is my knife.'

The trial at the Old Bailey before Mr Justice Coleridge was little more than a formality. Richard Muir prosecuted and Mr H.D. Harben, at the request of the court, defended. An attempt was made to show that Hall had made a bogus confession, but Alfred Wilkins came along to say that he had picked out Hall on an identification parade as being the person he had seen with Ronan (even though, at the time of identification, Wilkins said, 'I had just got up out of a drunken sleep' – and since at the time of his Old Bailey appearance Wilkins was on remand, accused of robbery with violence, he was probably quite happy to have a day out).

Inevitably, Hall was found guilty. He shook his head when asked if he had anything to say, and the judge passed the death sentence.

Yet Hall did not die. Wensley always believed that although there were murderers who thoroughly deserved the death penalty, there were also those who killed because they found themselves the victims of circumstance; and Hall's situation he believed to be one such case. He set out the full facts of the enquiry in a written report and on 3 October he was called to the Home Office to give his views in person. Hall was reprieved and his sentence commuted to one of life imprisonment, but he served little enough of it. At the outbreak of the First World War he was released to join the army and served with distinction in France, being discharged with the rank of sergeant. And twenty years after the murder, when Wensley had just days left to serve before retiring from the Metropolitan Police, he had an unexpected visitor at the Yard. It was Harold Hall, now forty-seven years of age, coming to thank Wensley for giving him his life back.

★ ★ ★

Wensley was a hard man but, as was seen in the Hall case, he could also be a compassionate one.

Thomas and Catherine Stephenson were called from their bed, early in the morning of 20 March 1910, by the screams of their daughter Jane, aged twenty-one and a domestic servant. She was sitting on the seat of the outside lavatory at their home at 131 Tate Street, St George's-in-the-East, with blood on her legs and nightdress and a holding a newborn baby, who was quite dead, wrapped in one of her flannel petticoats. Her parents had no idea that she was pregnant, and Jane, who appeared dazed, kept crying and told her mother that the baby had been born in the lavatory pan; she had pulled it out by its arm and the baby had cried a little.

Dr Jerome Joseph Reidy arrived and noted a serious bruise on the back of the baby's head which could certainly have caused death and was consistent with the child hitting its head on the side of the lavatory pan during delivery. However, inside its mouth was a gaping penetrating wound, and he found that the windpipe had been torn across; these injuries were so serious that they, too, could have caused death. It was possible that the girl's nails could have caused the wounds, but he could not say whether they were inflicted before or after death. Certainly, the doctor conceded, Jane would have been in very great pain and in a state of frenzy.

It was now up to Wensley, who pulled out all the stops. Telling the court that at the direction of the Coroner's inquisition he had been obliged to charge Jane with murder (to which she had replied, 'I understand'), he went on to say that he had made enquiries about her which revealed that she was the daughter of highly respectable parents and indeed, that Jane was highly respectable herself, having left school aged fourteen and been employed in domestic service ever since.

Jane Stephenson was found not guilty of murder, and the court was told that the Grand Jury had ignored a bill for murder but had found one for manslaughter; however, it was not proposed to offer any evidence on that charge, and Jane emerged from court a free woman and a victim only of the circumstances of the era.

Wensley must have been justifiably pleased with the verdict – and with his career at this time; the previous year, the King's Police Medal had been struck, and on 9 November 1909 Wensley was one of thirty-three recipients of the medal presented by King George V at Marlborough House for 'distinguished service'. Hopefully, he then had time for some welcome relaxation, because the Siege of Sidney Street was just around the corner.

# CHAPTER 15

# Anarchy

With terrorism striking right at the heart of England in the twenty-first century, it would profit today's politicians if, instead of fiddling their expenses, performing U-turns, apologising for and telling outright lies about their policies, ruining the economy and inflicting swingeing cuts on the armed and essential services, they looked instead to history and reflected on the mistakes of the past. Because over a century ago England was in the grip of dangerous, subversive anarchists who were imported from Eastern Europe and Russia by the shipload, and little if anything was done to stop them.

Following the assassination of Tsar Alexander II by revolutionaries in 1881, and the pogroms which commenced against the 5,000,000 Jews who then lived in Russia, refugees, including criminals and anarchists, started swarming into England in huge numbers. This caused a certain amount of disquiet but not enough to prompt the Alien Immigration Bill, introduced to Parliament in 1894, to be given a second reading. However, Special Branch was concerned, and this led to the Home Office forming a committee in June 1902 to assess this growing problem; in turn, the following year, a Royal Commission was appointed to deal with the question of the ever-increasing alien population. The Commission's report was published in August 1903 and it revealed that from 1881 to 1901 the number of resident foreigners had increased from 135,000 to 286,000. Out of the 30,000 Russians, Poles and Romanians who had arrived in the country, 8,000 of them had landed in the twelve months prior to June 1902 – and most of them were in London's East End.

It caused a backlash; the British Brothers' League was formed and speakers informed the crowds who attended their meetings, 'Britain should not become the dumping ground for the scum of Europe'. The *Manchester Evening Chronicle* added fuel to the fire in a 1905 editorial which stated that 'the dirty, destitute, diseased, verminous and criminal foreigner who dumps himself on our soil and rates simultaneously, shall be forbidden to land'.

The Aliens Act – in the face of strong opposition – received the Royal Assent on 11 August 1905 and it introduced immigration controls and regulations principally aimed at preventing criminals entering the country and deporting those who slipped through. This was easier said than done, however, because there were many loopholes in the law, and although Aliens Officers, the police and the judiciary were often able to provide compelling evidence for the expulsion of undesirables, these recommendations were not always implemented by the statutory appeal boards. Not much has changed *there*, then.

Just how much this often misplaced lenience and tolerance was abused was brought home to the public in stunning style, early in 1909.

★ ★ ★

What became known as 'The Tottenham Outrage' occurred on 23 January 1909, when two Eastern Europeans, Jacob Lepidus and Paul Hefeld, carried out an armed robbery of £80 in broad daylight at a factory in High Street, Tottenham, North London. During the course of the six-and-a-half mile chase which followed, the two men fired 400 shots, killing a police constable and a ten-year-old boy, as well as wounding twenty-one other people, before turning their weapons on themselves.

These events led to King Edward VII instituting the King's Police Medal, which he bestowed on three of the pursuing constables, who were additionally promoted to sergeant. However, the widow of the murdered police officer received a pension of only £15 per year, and although a public appeal raised £1,055 for her, the money was invested and she was only permitted to receive the annual interest from it.

The British public were initially stunned, then made furious by this incident. The popular press responded with characteristic xenophobia. But then it all died down ... until the events of less than two years later.

★ ★ ★

The City of London, with its own police force, was situated right next door to 'H' Division. Houndsditch is one of the City's main thoroughfares, running diagonally from Aldgate up towards Liverpool Street. About half way along is Cutler Street, and Exchange Buildings is a cul-de-sac which runs off it.

Late in the evening of Friday 16 December 1910, Max Weil, an importer of fancy goods at 120 Houndsditch, heard the sound of sawing and drilling; and since Exchange Buildings backed on to a jeweller's shop, the property of Henry Samuel Harris, situated at 119 Houndsditch, he alerted the beat officer, Police Constable Walter Piper, who made an enquiry at 11 Exchange Buildings, from where the sounds appeared to be emanating, was dissatisfied with the reply he received and sent for assistance. More police officers arrived, including Sergeant Robert Bentley, who knocked on the door and asked if he might look around. He was allowed to enter but was unaware that he was walking into a house full of Russian anarchists. Two shots rang out, fired by Jacob Peters, and Bentley fell to the ground mortally wounded. As the other police officers dashed towards the house, a man appeared in the doorway and sprayed the street with automatic fire; he was followed by a number of other men who similarly opened fire with automatic weapons. In all, twenty-two shots were fired. Four more officers were hit, two of them seriously, and a third, Sergeant Charles Tucker, also shot by Peters, who died instantly. The fourth officer, Police Constable Walter Choat, although badly wounded, grabbed hold of one of the gunmen, George Gardstein, but Peters shot Choat in the back, fatally wounding him. It was the last of eight bullets which had struck Choat.

The armed anarchists, four men and a woman – this was Nina Vassilleva – emerged into Cutler Street. Two of the men, Jacob Peters and Yourka Dubof, were supporting Gardstein, who had been accidentally shot by another anarchist, Max Smoller, who was covering their retreat. As they ran out of Exchange Buildings they almost collided with Isaac Levy, a tobacconist's manager. Two pistols were pointed at Mr Levy, who was warned, 'Don't follow us; don't follow.' They then ran through Harrow Alley, towards Middlesex Street, and disappeared.

Detective Superintendents John Stark and John Ottaway of the City Police led the investigation, and it was quickly established that during the early part of December a foreigner who gave his name as Joe Levi (but who, in fact, was Max Smoller) had rented 11 Exchange Buildings, and that a few days later, a man giving the name of Goldstein – this was another anarchist, Fritz Svaars – had rented no. 9. A day or two prior to the murders, no. 10 had become empty and these premises backed on directly to the jeweller's shop. In the yard of no. 9 was found a cylinder containing oxygen-compressed gas and a collection of burglars tools, and in the house sixty feet of rubber tubing attached to a gas pipe. A hole approximately two feet square had been smashed through the nine-inch thick rear wall to the jeweller's premises, and it was obvious that the intention of the gang – approximately seven in number – had been to break into the shop's safe, where it was usual to keep jewellery overnight valued at £7,000.

Meanwhile, Gardstein, over the space of half an hour, had been dragged for a mile through the streets until the gang reached 59 Grove Street, Whitechapel – no longer in the territory of the City Police but part of the Metropolitan Police's 'H' Division. This was the residence of Fritz Svaars where he lived with his mistress, Luba Milstein, and Gardstein was pulled up the stairs to the first-floor bedroom and laid on the bed. Also present were Sara Rosa Trassjonsky, a hunchbacked Polish Jewess, and the gang's leader, Peter Piatkov, also known as 'Peter the Painter'.

Luba and Sara went in search of a doctor; at 3.30 am they found one, Dr John James Scanlon, who normally practised at 53 Commercial Road but on this occasion was standing in for a Dr Bernstein at his surgery in Whitechapel Road. He was told, 'A man is very bad at 59 Grove Street', and he accompanied the women there; upon examining Gardstein he realized that a bullet had entered his back and was lodged in his chest. He wanted to arrange for Gardstein's removal to the London Hospital, a suggestion which Gardstein rejected. So Dr Scanlon pocketed his ten-shilling fee and went home. Later that morning, he decided to contact Arbour Square police station, and Wensley was informed. He, in turn, contacted Detective Inspector Ernest Thompson of the City police, and the men went directly to Dr Scanlon's surgery. It appeared that Scanlon's biggest fear was that he would be regarded as a police informer by the immigrant community; therefore, Wensley told him to pay a second visit to the house to allay suspicion but, of course, to inform no one of what he had seen.

Dr Scanlon returned to Grove Street at 11.00 am, only to discover that Gardstein had died. Before they disappeared, the occupants of the premises told him that they had no idea of what had occurred. Dr Scanlon had failed to promptly notify the police following his first visit to Grove Street; now, following his second visit, he behaved with unimaginable stupidity. Instead of immediately informing Wensley, he reported this matter to the coroner's officer, and the news was leaked to the press – whether this was by the coroner's officer, the coroner himself or Dr Scanlon, is a matter of conjecture. The doctor then returned to his surgery and informed the detectives, who were understandably incredulous and furious and raced to Grove Street in an effort to outrun the press. Nevertheless, had the very foolish doctor immediately discharged what was quite obviously his professional duty at the time of first seeing Gardstein, the siege of Sidney Street would almost certainly not have occurred.[14]

* * *

---

14 When this was mentioned in Wensley's serialised memoirs in the *Sunday Express* in 1930, it prompted Dr Scanlon to expostulate pompously, 'It is no part of a doctor's duty to be a detective.'

Lizzie Katz, the landlady of 59 Grove Street – inelegantly described by Wensley as 'a fat old Jewess' – was either unwilling or, due to language difficulties, unable to assist Wensley with his enquiries, so he propelled her up the stairs in front of him in order that, in the event of any resistance, it would be Mrs Katz and not him who would be hit by any bullets. Of course, as he later stated, in the event of a hostile reception there was the distinct possibility that he would have been crushed to death by her falling bulk.

But there was no such resistance; and in the bedroom Wensley found the lifeless body of Gardstein – as well as a tweed cap containing twenty-nine cartridges of differing calibres, plus thirty more in Gardstein's coat and trousers. In Gardstein's overcoat – with a bullet-hole in the back, courtesy of the excitable Max Smoller – were fourteen more cartridges. Under the pillow was a fully loaded Dreyse pistol and two more clips of ammunition. In addition, a door key which fitted 9 Exchange Buildings was found, as were instructions for exploding devices by means of electricity, a forged passport in the name of 'Schafshi Khan', a membership card showing allegiance to a Latvian Anarchist Group and correspondence linking Gardstein with other anarchists.

At the same time as Wensley's entry into the bedroom, Detective Sergeant Ben Leeson burst into the second room on that floor and discovered Sara Trassjonsky industriously burning photographs and papers in the fireplace. He grabbed her wrist, and although she informed him, 'Me no understand', she was hauled off to Old Jewry police station, the headquarters of the City Police – but not before she was seen by fourteen-year-old Soloman Abrahams, who had witnessed the shootings from his parents' house at 12 Exchange Buildings. He had been brought to Grove Street by Inspector Thompson, and had provided a rather rough and ready identification of Trassjonsky as the woman he had seen at Exchange Buildings. Since the woman who was present that night was Nina Vassilleva, it was also an inaccurate one.

It is clear that Luba Milstein's brothers, Jack and Nathan, possessed more of a sense of civic responsibility than most of her associates – and this certainly included Dr Scanlon – because on Sunday 18 December they dragged her into Leman Street police station, informing the desk sergeant, 'This is the young woman the police are looking for!' She was then handed over to the City Police. In fact, the description published in the newspapers was a vague one, and it referred to Nina Vassilleva. However, further information was forthcoming.

Nicholas Tomacoff was a young Russian mandolin player who had visited a club in Jubilee Street. Also known as the Anarchists'

Club, it had been opened in 1906; it had a reading room and a library, and music recitals were held there; it was also a centre for anarchy and criminality. Tomacoff knew several of the conspirators involved in the planned break-in at Houndsditch. Now he became an informant – he was boastful and liked to spin out and embroider his information, but essentially he was reliable.

At eight o'clock that evening Wensley and his men went to a tenement at 141 Romford Street, where, after they had knocked on the door, someone extinguished the gas lights, thereby making their entry doubly hazardous. Osip Federoff had been involved in the planned break-in and he was arrested; told of the circumstances of the shootings, he replied, 'Very well. I was not there when they did it.'

The same evening, at 10.30 pm, Wensley and two other officers arrived at 11 Buross Street. The reason was because a tenant there, Nina Vassilleva, had entrusted to Isaac Gordon, her landlord, an incriminating bundle of papers and photographs, and he had promptly taken these items to Arbour Square police station. At Buross Street, Wensley – who had missed John Rosen, another of the break-in conspirators, by ten minutes – saw Nina Vassilleva. She had made an unwise decision to dye her brown hair black, and it now looked extremely odd.

'Do you understand English?' asked Wensley.

'Just a little,' she replied.

'We are police officers and I want to speak with you,' said Wensley. 'Do you understand me?'

'Yes,' replied Vassilleva, 'If you don't speak too quick.'

During the ensuing conversation she told Wensley that she was Russian and a cigarette maker (which was true) and that her name was Lena Vasilev (which was not). She also had a passport in the name of Minna Gristis – this was now in Wensley's possession. She also admitted visiting the Anarchist Club in Jubilee Street.

'Do you know that some police officers were shot at Houndsditch on Friday night?' asked Wensley.

She replied, 'I have heard of it.'

'Some of the men who were engaged in the shooting are said to have been members of that club. Do you know them?'

'Perhaps I do,' replied Vassilleva. 'Perhaps I don't.'

'We have been told that you have been away from home these three weeks, and only came home yesterday,' said Wensley.

Realising the possible implications of the question, Vassilleva replied furiously, 'It's a lie!' adding, 'I have always been here.'

'I am also told that you have some bullets and cartridges here,' said Wensley, untruthfully.

Vassilleva, knowing full well there were none, replied, 'I have not; you can look, gentlemen, if you like.'

Wensley did so. He found no ammunition; what he did see was clothing, some of which was bloodstained and which fitted the description of that worn by the woman at Exchange Buildings – as did Vassilleva. He showed her thirteen photographs which had been contained in the bundle taken to the police station; she identified none of them, including that of her lover, Gardstein, or one of herself. And therefore, after forty-five minutes, and to Vassilleva's total astonishment, Wensley left. He had decided not to arrest her but to have the premises – and her – placed under observation in the hope that she would lead the police to the rest of the wanted murderers. But she did not. The following day, Vassilleva tried to escape to Paris, but due to the number of detectives following her was unable to do so. Should Wensley have taken possession of the bloodstained clothing and arrested her there and then? With hindsight, yes, he should.

*The Times* had certainly had enough of foreign anarchists, and on 19 December, with more than a dash of jingoism, it told its readers:

> Now the British criminal never does a thing like that. Burglars very rarely use firearms at all; a savage delight in the taking of life is the mark of the modern anarchist criminal. We have our own ruffians, but we do not breed that type here and we do not want them.

On Thursday 22 December the City Police offered the enormous reward of £500 for information leading to the arrest of the perpetrators, and on that date Yourka Dubof was arrested by Detective Inspector William Newell of the City Police at 20 Galloway Road, Shepherd's Bush; his response was, 'You make a mistake. I will go with you.'

During the same evening, Wensley and his officers were waiting for Jacob Peters to return to 48 Turner Street; when, at 8.15 pm, he did, he was told by Casimir Pilenas, an interpreter based at Thames Police Court, 'These persons are police officers making enquiries about the Houndsditch murder.'

Peters replied, 'I do not care. I cannot help what my cousin Fritz has done; I know nothing about it.' He was arrested.

On 24 December, Federoff, Peters and Dubof were charged at Bishopsgate police station and Federoff, acting as spokesman for the group, replied, 'We deny all knowledge and we are not guilty.'

On 2 February 1911, John Rosen (who quite rightly told the officers, 'I know you have come to arrest me') was brought in from Well Street, Hackney, and five days later, after considerable surveillance, Vassilleva was finally arrested by Detective Inspector Newell. She denied knowing anybody named Gardstein, Dubof or Peters and denied being at Exchange Buildings on the night of the murders. When she was charged with conspiracy to break and enter and steal the goods of Mr Harris and with being an accessory after the fact to the murder of Tucker by Gardstein, she replied, 'I do not know either of those persons or either of those places. It is a false accusation! Who accuses me? It is all lies!'

The police were aware that Dubof was either married to or was living with a woman, but they were unaware that her name was Betty Gershon. They were equally unaware that she lived at 100 Sidney Street.

★ ★ ★

Just before midnight on Monday 2 January 1911, Superintendent Ottaway received the breakthrough that he had been waiting for. Tomacoff had provided the name of Dubof's wife and her address, where, he said, two of the wanted men would be found. Ottaway contacted Wensley, and they and their men, both City and Metropolitan police officers, went to Sidney Street, where they observed a drab four-storey building.

Sidney Street is a long thoroughfare, stretching between Whitechapel Road and Commercial Road. However, the block of terraced houses which included no. 100 was in the centre of Sidney Street, surrounded by Hawkins Street, Richardson Street and Lindley Street. It was a large area which would need a considerable number of police to contain a very fragile situation; it was not known when the anarchists would try to make a break for it, or in fact, if they were even there. But this was a scenario where no chances could be taken, and therefore plainclothes officers were left in the vicinity to keep observation. However, Wensley knew from bitter experience that it would not take too long for their presence to be detected and in consequence, for the anarchists to be alerted; therefore, a plan would have to be set out to arrest the suspects without delay.

Uniformed officers and detectives were called in, and at 12.45 am Wensley commenced briefing the 200-strong force at Arbour Square police station. He stated that men should be placed in the houses either side of no. 100 in case the gang tried to break through the walls – this technique had already been used at the jeweller's in

Houndsditch – and that marksmen should cover the front and the rear of the premises. The rest of the officers would cover the three streets surrounding the block.

With the house surrounded, Wensley persuaded Mrs Rebecca Fleishman, the landlady of no. 100, to go up to the second floor and tell Mrs Gershon that her husband was unwell and that she required her assistance. Mrs Fleishman reluctantly agreed and knocked on Mrs Gershon's door, but was surprised when Mrs Gershon emerged from the stockroom opposite, saying that she intended to put a penny in the gas meter. She accompanied Mrs Fleishman downstairs but gasped when she saw the front door open; she was promptly seized and carried bodily to the house next door. She denied that anyone was in her room, but when Wensley informed her that he intended to ascend the stairs and, if he were killed, she would hang for murder since she was aware that the two men were in the room, she capitulated. She admitted that a cousin of her husband's and another man were there.

Now, as a matter of urgency, the rest of the occupants of the building had to be removed, and this manoeuvre was carried out, not without difficulty.

By 7.30 that morning dawn had broken, to the accompaniment of a mixture of sleet and rain, and it was decided to make the occupants of the second-floor bedroom aware of the police presence – if, of course, they were not already. Entry to the bedroom via the staircase had already been considered and rejected; it was extremely narrow and turned sharply at the top, and only one officer at a time could have ascended. If that officer's presence had been detected by the anarchists, the consequences for him (and any officer following him) would have been fatal. Therefore, one police officer banged on the still open front door, then pebbles were thrown at the bedroom window, followed by a brick. Immediately there was a volley of shots from the first-floor window, and Sergeant Leeson, who was in an alleyway opposite, cried out, 'Jack, I'm hit!' and collapsed. Wensley pulled open Leeson's shirt and coat, which were covered in blood. 'Mr Wensley, I'm dying,' gasped Leeson. 'They have shot me through the heart. Goodbye. Give my love to the children. Bury me at Putney.'

Over the years, a great deal of supercilious criticism has been levelled at Leeson's emotive choice of words, usually by people who have never encountered real danger in their lives; but Leeson had been seriously wounded and there is little doubt that he did believe he was dying. That was Wensley's perception of the situation, too. He patted Leeson's hand and told him, 'We will be with you to the last.'

A doctor was summoned – a bullet narrowly missed him as he crossed Sidney Street – and after plugging Leeson's wounds stated that he must be taken to hospital, without delay. This was easier said than done, with the anarchists shooting at anything that moved, including a cat which ventured out of a doorway and paid the ultimate price for its impetuosity. The only way was over some outbuildings close to a brewery, and a ladder was placed up to the roof; Leeson, on a stretcher, was dragged up it by Wensley and the doctor on to the roof. They were seen, and the anarchists directed their fire at them; bullets shattered the roof tiles and one grazed the doctor's head. Leeson cried, 'You are taking me into the line of fire, again!' and rolled off the stretcher and over to the wall, where he was helped down. Wensley, however, was now the solitary target of the gunmen and he had to lie full-length in a gutter in an inch of sleet and water, partially shielded by the ridge of the wall. There he lay for thirty minutes, his slightest movement attracting the anarchists' bullets. Then there was a lull in the firing, enabling Wensley to escape from the roof, but rumours had already spread that he was dead. In a special edition of the *Evening News*, the headlines read:

> Detective Inspector Wensley's Gallant End
> Killed while helping a wounded colleague.

In fact, it was believed that Leeson was dead as well, and a team of police officers who wanted to storm the house were only restrained from doing so with great difficulty.

It was clear that the anarchists' weapons – Mausers – were far superior to the Morris-tube rifles which had been issued to the police, and a request was made, via the Deputy Commissioner, Major Frederick Wodehouse, to Winston Churchill, the Home Secretary, for additional armaments. Permission to use troops from the Tower of London was granted, and twenty officers and men arrived from the Scots Guards. The guardsmen delivered volleys of withering fire at the second floor of the house, forcing the gunmen to move down to the first, then to the ground floor, which were similarly subjected to a fusillade. By 11.00 am crowds had gathered, and another sixty police officers had appeared, as had a gunsmith, who distributed shotguns, revolvers and ammunition to the officers. An hour later, Winston Churchill himself arrived to orchestrate the operation. The deputy commissioner also came, as did Sir Melville McNaughton and other Scotland Yard luminaries.

At about one o'clock a flame was seen in a window, and it appeared the occupants had set fire to the premises to facilitate their escape. As the fire gathered momentum, one of the anarchists leant out of a window and was shot through the head. The Fire Brigade was standing by, but Churchill refused to let them extinguish the blaze. 'No, let the buggers burn,' was his comment.

Within a quarter of an hour the flames had broken through the roof, which then collapsed. Only when it was thought that nobody could possibly have survived the conflagration, were the Fire Brigade permitted to turn on their hoses.

One of the dead men was Fritz Svaars; the other was a man who had been known as 'Joseph' or 'Yoska', but whose real identity was almost certainly William Sokoloff. It was said that he had set up the Houndsditch burglary and was wanted for several similar burglaries in the Crimea. It was thought at one stage that Svaars' companion had been 'Peter the Painter', but it is believed that following the Houndsditch murders he fled to Paris.

Meanwhile, King George V sent a message of sympathy to Ben Leeson and the other injured officers and 'earnestly enquired as to their progress'.

★ ★ ★

Opinions, worldwide, were diverse regarding the murders and the siege. Mr E.T.H. Lawes, the Recorder of the Salisbury Quarter Sessions, wondered if the provisions of the Aliens Act ought to be strengthened to prevent alien criminals' entry into the country. He hastily added that he did not wish to see asylum refused to political refugees, but 'there was such a thing as going too far'. A less charitable view was expressed by Father Bernard Vaughan, who stated that foreign undesirables must be stopped from making England 'a spawning ground for breeding vice for foreign exportation'. He added that there was not enough food or work to go round and that 'if any starved, surely it ought not to be members of our own family but the undesirable lawless alien'.

The authorities in St Petersburg were of the opinion that the English police should establish complete surveillance on foreigners, while the French warmly congratulated the British upon their prompt action in Sidney Street and agreed that the Aliens Act should be substantially tightened. Germany was sharply divided in its views: the *Lokal Anzeiger* newspaper criticized the amount of firepower used to subdue a couple of criminals, likening it to 'shooting sparrows with a cannon', and hoped that the incident would lead to the abolition of what it described as 'the foolish right of asylum'. The *Berliner Tageblatt*, together with Vienna's *Neue Freie Presse*, on the other hand, strenuously protested against the concept of restricting the right of asylum which, they stated, 'hitherto has been one of Britain's glories'.

⋆ ⋆ ⋆

The case against the prisoners commenced at the Guildhall Court on 23 January 1911. It was said that Peters, Dubof and Federoff were involved in the police murders, Trassjonsky and Milstein were accessories after the fact and all five had been involved in the attempted break-in. The committal proceedings, which lasted four months, were a complete and utter cock-up. The case for the prosecution was that George Gardstein had shot Bentley, Tucker and Choat; but he had not – this was done by Jacob Peters, currently one of the prisoners in the dock. Luba Millstein's counsel successfully argued that no case existed against his client, and on 21 February she was discharged. Karl Hoffman, who been impolitely lifted from his bed in Cannon Street Road and appeared with the other defendants, charged with conspiracy to break and enter, was similarly discharged. The same applied to Sara Trassjonsky, who was promptly certified as being insane and was detained as a pauper lunatic at Colney Hatch Asylum. Federoff was the next to have the charges against him dismissed.

Eventually, the remaining prisoners were committed to the Old Bailey, to stand their trial on the following indictments: Dubof and Peters – the murder of Charles Tucker. Dubof, Peters and Vassilleva – feloniously harbouring a felon (i.e. Gardstein) who was guilty of murder. Dubof, Peters, Rosen and Vassilleva – conspiring to break and enter the shop of Henry Samuel Harris with intent to steal his goods. The trial commenced on 1 May 1911, before Mr Justice Grantham, aged seventy-five and well-known for having his rulings overturned in the Court of Appeal.

On the first day of the trial, PC Piper and Max Weil gave evidence, and then the judge informed the prosecution that whilst it was assumed that Peters and Dubof were present at the shooting (and possibly fired shots as well), there was no evidence to show that they had committed murder themselves; he therefore directed the jury to find them not guilty of murder. The prosecution now proceeded with the next count, that of being accessories before the fact.

Isaac Levy was an impressive witness for the prosecution; out of a group of fifteen to twenty men on an identification parade he had picked out both Peters and Dubof as the men carrying Gardstein, and had also identified Vassilleva as the woman who had followed them. Incredibly, the judge thought that Vassilleva probably took no part in the shooting and that Peters and Dubof may not have known that murder had been committed. Therefore the prosecution withdrew this charge as well, the judge adding that three men were known to have taken part in the shootings and he believed them to be dead: Gardstein and the two men who had perished at Sidney Street. That left the conspiracy to commit the break-in.

Levy's evidence was the subject of sustained, sneering insults from the defence, and in heated cross-examination Wensley was asked if it was proper for a woman whom he suspected of crime to retain her liberty. It was a supercilious question and an unfortunate one, because it permitted Wensley to reply, 'It depends on the circumstances whether we leave a woman at liberty, to watch if men who are wanted come and see her,' – which tended to point out to the jury that Vassilleva made a habit of associating with known criminals.

The defence for all of the defendants was that the conspirators who intended to break into the jeweller's shop were as follows: George Gardstein, Fritz Svaars, William Sokoloff (all conveniently dead), and Max Smoller and 'Peter the Painter', who had both, it was thought, escaped to Paris after the murders.

Luba Milstein and Karl Hoffman, fresh from being discharged at the Police Court, came along to lie their heads off. Milstein, in a complete turnaround from her previous statement, said that it was Fritz Svaars, William Sokoloff and Max Smoller who had brought Gardstein into 59 Grove Street; and Hoffman, who had previously denied knowing the group, said that Max Smoller had killed Gardstein (true) and that it had been Smoller and Svaars who had carried Gardstein to Grove Street (false).

Next, Dubof was in the witness box, taking the earliest opportunity to inform the court that he was a political refugee, stating that he had never been to Exchange Buildings and producing witnesses to place him elsewhere at the times the offences were carried out. Rosen, too, denied ever being at Exchange Buildings, as did Peters.

Vassilleva had rather more to answer for than offering straight denials; true, she readily jumped on the political refugee bandwagon, but evidence was forthcoming that she had been Gardstein's mistress, that following the murders she had dyed her hair, tried to flee to Paris, had burnt items of clothing and attempted to dispose of incriminating documents. In addition, her thumb and finger prints had been found on two bottles at 11 Exchange Buildings, and she was found guilty of conspiracy to commit breaking and entering. With a recommendation from the jury that she should not be deported, she was sentenced to two years' imprisonment.

There was one further indictment against Dubof, Peters and Vassilleva: that they feloniously harboured, comforted, assisted and maintained George Gardstein knowing him to have with a loaded pistol feloniously shot at Robert Bentley with intent to murder him. Once more, the prosecution threw in the towel.

All the male defendants were acquitted of all charges, but if in the unlikely event that they were at all concerned as to their female accomplice's fate, they need not have troubled themselves. The British legal system came to Nina Vassilleva's assistance five weeks later, when the Court of Appeal overturned her conviction on the grounds of the trial judge's misdirection.

Not one person had been convicted of the murder of three police officers, the serious injuries inflicted on several others or the conspiracy to break into the jeweller's shop. It was a triumphant day for the anarchists and a wretched one for British justice.

★ ★ ★

The three murdered police officers were buried on 23 December 1910 and a service for them was held at St Paul's Cathedral. Within four days, the *Daily Express* had raised £2,000 for the officers' dependants, and posthumous King's Police Medals for gallantry were awarded.

After his enforced retirement, Ben Leeson wrote a book entitled *Lost London: the Memoirs of an East End Detective* (Stanley Paul, 1934); in it he claimed that during a convalescent trip to Australia, who should get into his railway carriage but Peter the Painter. The general consensus of opinion was that Leeson had seriously lost the plot. Additionally, information was given that Peter the Painter was none other than the brother of Casimir Pilenas, the court interpreter; what was more, this was not denied by Pilenas, who stated that his brother died in America in 1914. Others said it was 1916. It is hoped that Pilenas interpreted and translated more accurately and honestly at court than he spoke about his alleged brother.

Jacob Peters later returned to Russia and became deputy head of Lenin's infamous Cheka, the secret police responsible for thousands of cases of torture and murder. Justice, delayed for over twenty years, caught up with him when he came to a sticky end during one of Stalin's purges.

Nina Vassilleva remained in the East End; she died in St Bartholomew's Hospital in 1963.

Luba Millstein and Karl Hoffman went to the United States of America in 1912; he died in 1961, she in 1973.

On 20 June, Wensley was awarded £25 by the Lord Mayor and commended by the Aldermen of the City of London as being one of the officers who:

> worked most extensive hours, with exemplary zeal, for weeks after the murders, incurred considerable personal danger and underwent much hardship for want of food and rest. They also showed great intelligence ... directed the whole investigations into the crimes and are deserving of the highest credit.

So why did the case against the anarchists collapse? On the face of it, there was a sufficiency of evidence to convict them, but remember, this was over 100 years ago and an enormous amount of forensic evidence which would delight any present-day Crime Scene Investigator was then virtually useless. There was no way of linking a suspect to the scene of a crime by firearms, or indeed any other kind of residue. Several of the suspects were identified, but having a worse than useless judge put paid to that. Lastly, was the case put together properly? Did Superintendents Stark and Ottaway have the necessary experience to cobble together the evidence for a triple police murder? Possibly not. Fine detectives they might have been in dealing with the City of London's nefarious activities, but the City was not noted for its high murder rate, certainly not complicated police murders. Nevertheless, the Aldermen handed awards to Stark and Ottaway of £50 and £40 respectively.

Would Wensley have done a better job? He was an inspector at the time but he had solved every murder which he had investigated and he had an unrivalled knowledge of the foreign criminals in that part of London. It is highly likely that he could have presented a case which was copper-bottomed and watertight – but the offence took place within the jurisdiction of the City Police, not the Metropolitan Police's 'H' Division.

## The Big Four

Albert Hawkins.

Arthur Neil.

Francis Carlin.

Fred Wensley.

# The Flying Squad

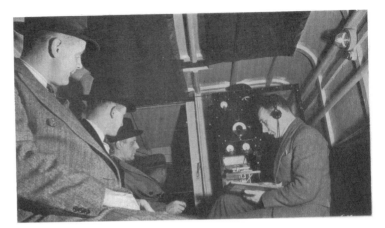

Interior of a Crossley
Tender.

A Crossley Tender.

An Invicta – Wensley's
legacy to the Flying
Squad.

# The Flying Squad

DDI Walter Hambrook.

A 1929 Lea Francis Tourer, capable of speeds of up to 75 mph …

… although often coming off second-best when ramming bandits' heavier vehicles.

A Crossley Tender.

Edith & Percy Thompson – in happier times.

Edward Bywaters.

Mr Justice Shearman.

Major Armstrong – arsenical murderer.

Patrick Mahon – murderer.

Emily Kaye – Mahon's victim.

Mahon's bedroom showing the trunk in which
Miss Kaye's body was hidden.

Sir Bernard Spilsbury carrying out a post mortem.

John Robinson – murderer.

Minnie Bonati – Robinson's victim.

## Exhibits in the Bonati case

The trunk in which Mrs Bonati's body was hidden.

Duster clearly showing the name 'GREYHOUND'.

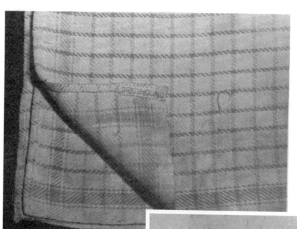

Items wrapped around the dismembered body.

# The first of the 1928 scandals

Ch. Insp. Alfred Collins.

Lilian Wyles.

Sir Leo Money.

Irene Savidge.

# The last of the 1928 scandals

Mrs Kate Meyrick.

George Goddard.

Chief Inspector Cooper.

(L–R): Supt. Brown, Wensley, Hawkins, Carlin.

In Chief Constable's uniform.

'Of all the numerous police officers I have known in my life, he was easily the sternest …'

# The Commissioners during Wensley's service

Sir Charles Warren, 1886–1888.

James Munro, 1888–1890.

Sir Edward Bradford, 1890–1903.

# The Commissioners during Wensley's service

Sir Edward Henry, 1903–1918.

Sir Nevil Macready, 1918–1920.

Sir William Horwood, 1920–1928.

Viscount Byng, 1928–1931.

# CHAPTER 16

# The Man on Clapham Common

On 17 September 1910 a man who had been convicted in the name of Morris Stein was released from Dartmoor Prison. Stein was certainly not his baptismal name – it could have been Alex Petropavloff, but he also called himself Moses Tagger, Morris Steinaud and Stinie Morrison, and he claimed to have been born in both Russia and Australia. It makes little difference; Morrison (as he will be referred to) was utterly incapable of telling the truth and was an habitual criminal. Born in 1879, he arrived in England in 1898 and lost little time in embarking on a career of criminality. In December of that year he was sentenced to one month's hard labour for stealing ledgers, and one month after his release he received another two months' hard labour for being a suspected person. This was followed by six months' hard labour for burglary, and within three months of his release he was found in possession of the proceeds of a break-in at a tobacconist's premises and got fifteen months' hard labour for receiving stolen goods. Within weeks of his release, in July 1901, Morrison was caught breaking into a dwelling house in Wanstead and this time he was sentenced to five years' penal servitude. Released in August 1905, he carried out a string of burglaries and in January 1906 he was stopped in possession of housebreaking implements linked to the burglaries and sentenced to another five years' penal servitude.

He was an unruly prisoner; for attacking a fellow prisoner, Dartmoor's Governor, Sir Basil Thomson (later Assistant Commissioner of the Metropolitan Police), awarded him two days' bread and water. He would later say:

> I saw Stinie Morrison in every mood – defiant and wheedling, sarcastic and murderous – and although we contrived to manage him and keep him clear of open mutiny, I always expected him to commit some act of violence in the prison that would add many years to his sentence.

Sir Basil was not wrong; Morrison later again attacked a fellow inmate in the quarry, also one of the warders, and threatened the Deputy Governor with the assaulted warder's truncheon. For this he was sentenced to three months in chains on a diet of bread and water, plus a 'bashing' – twenty strokes of the cat-o'-nine-tails.

When Morrison was released, he was described as being 'afflicted by this institutionalised brutality'; although, from a more robust viewpoint, it was certainly no more than he deserved. As a convict on licence, which would not expire until March 1912, Morrison reported to Leman Street police station once a month. After a short spell working in a bakery in South London, Morrison returned to the East End and lost no time in returning to criminality; he also acquired a revolver and ammunition.

★ ★ ★

On 1 January 1911 at 8.10 am Police Constable 863 'W' Joseph Mumford from Cavendish Road police station was patrolling Bishop's Walk, an asphalted pathway from Clapham Common's bandstand to Clapham Junction, when he found the lifeless body of a man lying on its back in some bushes. The corpse was dressed in a greatcoat with an astrakhan collar, and a black handkerchief was laid over the dead man's face.

The pathologist, Dr Frederick Freyberger, later examined the body and saw that the man had received several heavy blows to the head with a blunt instrument and that his face had been slashed with a knife, five times on the right-hand side and two on the left, leaving 'S' shaped scars. A further horseshoe-shaped wound on his forehead could have been caused by a jemmy. He had also been stabbed in the chest three times, but this had occurred after death. Altogether, he had sustained eighteen wounds. In his pockets were a few items, which included a rent book.

Divisional Detective Inspector Alfred Ward took charge of the case and was initially unable to identify the corpse, although he thought the man was Jewish. After speaking to Sir Melville Macnaughten, Ward approached Wensley. He showed him the rent book, and from its contents and its owner's description, Wensley realized the victim was Leon Beron.

Beron was a forty-seven-year-old widower. Born on 17 April 1863 in Guvalki, Poland, he was a Jew who had spent much of his life in Paris and had arrived in England in 1894, with his father, two brothers and a sister. He owned and let nine properties in Russell Court, St George's-in-the-East, Stepney, but the rents he collected amounted to no more than ten shillings per week. He paid two shillings per week for his room above a fruit shop, situated at 133 Jubilee Street, Stepney, but nevertheless appeared to be a man of substance; he wore a large gold watch and chain from which hung a five-guinea piece, and he was said to carry twenty sovereigns on his person, this being the case on the night of the murder. It is also possible that he was a receiver of stolen goods.

With Beron's identity established, Ward discovered that a Mrs Nellie Deitch had seen him with an unknown man early on New Year's Day, and from her description – the stranger was over six feet tall and dressed in a long overcoat and a broad-brimmed hat – Wensley realized he had seen this individual before, reporting as a 'ticket of leave' man. He sent for the convict register and discovered that the man was Morrison, released from penal servitude just over three months previously. Morrison had lived in Whitechapel but had moved to Lavender Hill, ten minutes away from Clapham Common. He had been working in a bakery but had moved without permission on 10 November, so was now liable to arrest for failing to comply with the terms of his release. There was insufficient evidence to circulate Morrison for murder – there was nothing to say that he had been the man seen with Beron, let alone was a murderer – but there was enough to order his arrest for failing to reside at his address. In addition, Wensley had discovered from his enquiries that Morrison was alleged to carry a pistol, so he was circulated as wanted in *Confidential Informations*, dated 6 January 1911, as follows:

> *Wanted for Petty Offences.*
> *CO (CSO) Licence holder Morris Stein,*
> *office No. 141,701 for failing to reside*
> *at his registered address. Caution: Carries*
> *firearms and may attempt to use them.*

Morrison had left his East End address at 91 Newark Street on New Year's Day, telling his landlady, Mrs Zimmerman, that he was going to Paris, but was due to call back for his laundry. Detectives kept the house under observation until he returned on 8 January 1911. He was then followed to Cohen's restaurant at 27 Fieldgate Street by Detectives Harry Jefferies from 'H' Division and James Bellinger from 'W' Division, and Wensley was sent for.

What happened next was inaccurately told, following Wensley's retirement, in an American newspaper, which reported that Wensley strolled into the restaurant and casually remarked, 'I want to see you when you've finished your meal'; fifteen minutes later, apparently, the two men strolled off to the police station, 'chatting as if the murder charge was the least thing in their minds'. Unfortunately, this was typical press hyperbole and bore not the slightest resemblance to what actually occurred.

Wensley knew exactly how dangerous Morrison was and he was taking no chances whatsoever. Taking two more officers – Detective Sergeants William Brogden and Henry Dessent – to supplement the first two, the door was thrown open, Morrison was seized and Wensley arrested him with the words, 'Stein, I want you.'

Brogden felt Morrison's back pocket to search for the firearm, causing the latter to cry, 'Don't go putting anything in my pockets!'

Brogden told him, 'You hear what the inspector said to you. You will have to come with me.'

'All right,' Morrison replied, 'I will come.'

On the way to the police station, far from 'chatting casually', Morrison became infuriated when a large crowd gathered, gawping at him and causing him to snap, 'Have another look!' To Wensley he shouted, 'You've made a big blunder. This isn't the first one but it's the biggest blunder you've ever made!' At the police station, Morrison was searched and was found to have two £5 notes, £4 in gold and 5s 6d in change.

Wensley asked him, 'What is your name and where have you been residing?'

Morrison replied, 'You know my name. I am living at 4 Whitfield Street, West. I picked up with a girl a week ago and have been living with her since at York Road, Westminster. I did not go home last night as I lost the last train, so I stopped with Mrs Cinnamon at 32, in the buildings, James Street.'

During the whole time from Morrison's arrest to his detention in the police station no one had mentioned the word 'murder'. He was left in charge of two constables from 10.30 am onwards, and suddenly said, 'I want to make a confession; will you take it down?' This was reported to Inspector Roderick McKenzie, to whom Morrison said, 'I want to speak to Mr Wensley. I have a confession to make. This is a serious matter and I want to clear myself.'

When Wensley arrived, he said, 'I understand you want to see me to make a voluntary statement.'

Morrison told him, 'I see you have accused me of a serious crime – you have accused me of murder.'

'I have done nothing of the kind,' replied Wensley.

But Morrison persisted, 'You told me you wanted me for a serious crime, and that it was murder, and I want to make a voluntary statement.'

'I'm expecting Inspector Ward here, who is dealing with this matter, very shortly,' replied Wensley, 'and if you have no objection, I would prefer him to take your statement.'

Morrison agreed.

When Ward arrived, Wensley introduced him to the prisoner, who said, 'I understand I am detained here on a very serious charge – murder, I am told – and I desire to make a voluntary statement.'

'Very well,' replied Ward. 'Perhaps you will tell us verbally what it is; we shall understand it and then we can write it down correctly.'

In fact, the statement, which was typed rather than written, read as follows:

I have sent for Divisional Detective Ward and Wensley and desire to make a voluntary statement in consequence of my having been arrested this morning under the suspicion of murder – Mr Wensley having told me this. I am an Australian, born in Sydney, brought up in England. I am a confectioner and baker, and now a traveller in common jewellery. During the month of September I obtained a situation as a journeyman baker at 213 Lavender Hill. I should think I was there about ten weeks altogether. I was sleeping there during the whole of that time. I left on my own accord, having saved up about £4. I then commenced to travel in cheap jewellery. I went to reside at No. 5 Grove Street, E., and remained there for two weeks. I bought the cheap jewellery from various persons; you will find the receipt for some of it in my bag. On leaving Grove Street I went to reside at No. 91 Newark Street. I remained there until last Sunday, the 1st, and then went to live with a girl named Florrie at 116 York Road, and have continued to live with her up to the present time. Last night, I stayed with a friend named Mrs Cinnamon, who lives in a building off Grove Street – the number is 32, and is next to a grocer's shop – as I was too late to return to my lodgings. This is my voluntary statement and all I wish to say.

This statement, which Morrison signed as being correct, had of course nothing to do with a murder, Beron's or anybody else's, nor did it provide him with an alibi. Far from it being the 'confession' which he mentioned to the uniform officers, he did not incriminate himself in any way. He was at pains to stress that Wensley had accused him of murder, something which Wensley and all of the other arresting officers denied.

A visit was paid to 116 York Road, Lambeth; the occupier was Florrie Dellow, a lady estranged from her husband and with two convictions for prostitution. The premises were searched and tucked inside a man's hatband a cloakroom ticket was discovered which would result in an interesting find. The evidence was starting to mount up – circumstantial it might have been, but there was a lot of it. Beron and Morrison had been seen together by people in a restaurant on the night before the murder; others had seen them in the street in the early hours of the following morning. Cab drivers were traced, and detectives timed the cab runs they had made. Morrison had pawned a watch and chain two days before Christmas, but he had over £14 in his possession when he was arrested.

Later that day, Brogden noticed what appeared to be bloodstains on Morrison's shirt collar, tie and cuff, and took possession of his clothing. The following morning, Ward told Morrison the reason for seizing his clothing, to which he replied, 'That is not blood at all; that is mud that I got yesterday.' In fact, it was blood, although it was extremely unlikely that a dresser as fastidious as Morrison would have been wearing the same shirt a week after the murder.

But in the meantime, Ward had not been idle; he had interviewed a number of those people who claimed to have seen Beron and Morrison together, both on New Year's Eve and New Year's Day, and Morrison was identified by nine of them. Taken to Brixton police station, Morrison was charged with Beron's murder and replied, 'All I can say is that it is a lie.'

Morrison's initial court appearance was at South-West London Police Court, Lavender Hill, before the magistrate, the Honourable John de Grey. Amongst the witnesses called to provide a sufficiency of evidence to commit the accused for trial was Eva Flitterman, sixteen years of age and not the sharpest knife in the drawer. Described as a tailoress, she had met Morrison on New Year's Day, at which time he was wearing a watch, chain and fob suspiciously like Beron's. He had changed a £4 cheque for half-sovereigns and given Eva two sovereigns to buy a dress. Morrison had asked her to spend the night with him; she had demurred and had artfully replied, 'If you will marry me, I shall stay with you forever', but it appeared that Morrison was not willing to make such a commitment. During cross-examination Eva became hopelessly muddled and admitted that she had made a mistake about the description of the watch.

The second witness was Sam Rosen, a youth of highly dubious character, who initially said that he had seen Morrison and Beron together at the junction of Whitechapel Road and Brick Lane at 1.30 in the morning of New Year's Day, but later admitted that he had gone to bed two hours previously. He also said that Soloman Beron, the dead man's brother, had threatened him with violence if he retracted his evidence. Neither Rosen nor Flitterman were called as witnesses at the trial. An application made by the defence that they be prosecuted for perjury was rejected by the Director of Public Prosecutions.

Max Frank – a receiver of stolen goods who had been arrested for that offence on four previous occasions – was one of many witnesses called to the inquest; he had changed gold for two five pound notes for Morrison on New Year's Day. He also admitted that Morrison already had £15–20 in gold in his possession. The coroner's jury spent just five minutes before deciding that Beron had been murdered and Morrison was responsible.

★ ★ ★

The trial started at the Old Bailey on 6 March 1911, before Mr Justice Darling. Morrison, standing in the dock, hand on hip, replied to the indictment with the words, 'My Lord, if I was standing before the Almighty, I could give but one answer: I am not guilty.' He remained standing for the whole of the trial, striking a pose that his admirers might have seen as scornful and defiant, but to anybody else would have appeared the performance of a rather ridiculous thespian.

The prosecution was led by the very experienced Richard Muir and the defence by Edward Abinger, who might be impolitely described as 'an Old Bailey hack', very much in the mould of John Mortimer's 'Rumpole of the Bailey'. Unfortunately, Abinger possessed little of the fictional barrister's charm or, indeed, his ability. He tended to get emotionally involved with those he represented, was staggeringly rude and thought the best way to get the truth from witnesses was to bellow, sneer and jeer at them. It had in the past led him into conflict with his legal counterparts and with judges; it would certainly do so on this occasion.

The prosecution was able to prove that Morrison had been associating with Beron for some time and that the last occasion had been on New Year's Eve, when they dined at the Warsaw Restaurant, 32 Osborn Street, Whitechapel. Alec Snelwar, the owner, saw them together between 9.00 and 11.45 pm, when they left together. In addition, he told the court that he had previously seen Morrison with a revolver.

A waiter, Joe Mintz, said Morrison had collected a long brown-paper parcel which he had left with him during that evening. Morrison had told Snelwar's ten-year-old daughter Becky that it contained a flute, but when Mintz handed it to Morrison as he and Beron left, it felt, he said, like an iron bar. In cross-examination Mintz admitted that he had previously tried to hang himself. The judge warned Abinger that in producing this matter of attempted suicide, which was then an attempt to commit a felony, he risked bringing Morrison's bad character into the proceedings. Abinger said that he did so to show that the witness might be *non compos mentis*, but the judge ruled that this would have been a question for the court that tried him.

Henry Hermilin, a furrier who knew Beron, saw him and Morrison leave the restaurant between 11.45 pm and midnight. Another waiter, sixteen-year-old Jack Taw, also saw them leave at that time, said he had seen Morrison with a pistol and that he had seen him and Beron at the corner of Church Lane the next morning at a quarter to two.

Jacob Weissberg, a butcher, was with his friend Israel Zaltzman and stated he saw the two men in the Commercial Road at 11.30 pm and that he later saw them in Whitechapel Road at 12.45 am. The latter part of this evidence was corroborated by Mr Zaltzman, although he claimed to have previously seen them in the Commercial Road at 7.30–8.00 pm.

Mrs Nellie Deitch had known Beron for twelve years, and it had been Beron and Morrison she had seen at 2.00 am in the Commercial Road. But she came in for some bruising cross-examination from Abinger, who accused her of being a brothel keeper. Lizzie Holmes, Dolly Nevy, Lena Hall and Becky Blue were brought into court, and amidst shouts of 'Liar!' Mrs Deitch denied knowing them or that she had received money from them for using rooms at her house for the purposes of prostitution. She duly screeched, 'Liar!' back at them. It all rather backfired on Abinger, because it almost certainly appeared to the jury that he was asking these questions quite gratuitously to blacken her character, rather than concentrating on the accuracy of her identification.

A cab driver, Edward Hayman, said he had picked up the two men at two o'clock on the morning of New Year's Day in Sidney Street and driven them to Lavender Hill; he was subjected to some brisk cross-examination by Abinger, and there were some legal arguments between counsel and judge, but Hayman insisted, 'I picked the prisoner out without any hesitation. I have no doubt whatsoever that he is my fare.'

Alfred Stephens, another cab driver, described picking up Morrison alone at Clapham Common at just after 2.30 am and said he had asked to be taken to Kennington Church. 'It was the prisoner,' said Mr Stephens. 'I am quite sure.'

Alfred Castling, a third cab driver, explained how he had picked up two men at Kennington Church at about 3.30 am on New Year's morning and taken them to Seven Sisters Road. The second man was shorter than the first and spoke in a foreign language; the other man did not, and paid the fare. Mr Castling picked out Morrison as being the fare payer on an identification parade.

Thomas Green, a clerk at St Mary's Station, Whitechapel, accepted a parcel at 11.00 am on New Year's Day from a man who gave the name 'Banman'; he identified Morrison as being that man. Harold Cockfield, also a clerk at the station, received the counterfoil which had been handed to Morrison, from Detective Sergeant Richard Nursey of 'W' Division a week later. When the parcel was opened, it contained a towel, a fully loaded revolver and a box containing 44 cartridges.

Wensley and the other officers who had been present at the arrest all denied that Morrison had been told that he was arrested for murder. The 'S' shaped scars – also referred to as the 'f'-shapes seen on either side of a violin – which had been cut into Beron's face were picked up by journalists, who deduced that the scars stood for 'Szpieg' or 'Spic', meaning 'Spy'. The reasons for this were because Beron was an Eastern European Jew, he had lived in Jubilee Street close to Anarchist Club, the Houndsditch murders had occurred two weeks prior to Beron's murder and the siege of Sidney Street had just started. England was in the grip of Russian anarchist fever, and when Wensley admitted that he knew Beron, it was easy to suggest that it was Beron who had pointed Wensley in the direction of the wanted men at 100 Sidney Street. Therefore, it was assumed that Beron had been killed in revenge for being a police informer; however, this was not true.

It was now Morrison's turn to give evidence. After describing the addresses he had lived at since September 1910, he told the courtroom that on or about 28 November he had received in the post a miraculous windfall of £20, in English currency, from his mother in Russia. Over the next few days he purchased a watch and clothing costing a total of £17 0s 5½d, leaving him just under £3. However, he was also earning approximately £2 per week selling common jewellery, and he was able to pay seven or eight shillings for a revolver and ammunition, which he intended to sell on. On 1 December he left a club with £35, having won at faro, and on 23 December, deciding that the watch he had bought as a result of his mother's beneficence had been an impulse purchase, he pawned it for £4 10s 0d and purchased a lady's watch instead for £1 10s 0d. Therefore, he told the jury, on 23 December he had no need of money since he was in possession of almost £30.

Morrison admitted he knew Beron but only as 'the Landlord'. On the morning of 31 December, Morrison stated, he had had breakfast at Snelwar's, and because the waiter, Mintz, was being slow at bringing his breakfast, Morrison, making an unpleasant reference to Mintz's failed suicide attempt, called out, 'What are you doing down there – are you trying to hang yourself, again?'

Mintz brought him his breakfast but warned him, 'If I ever get the chance to get it out of you, I will', and this, Morrison told the court, was what he was doing now. This was a reference to the flute which he had purchased that morning and had wrapped in a parcel which Mintz had kept for him but had said it felt as though it contained an iron bar.

Morrison told the court that he had spent New Year's Eve selling imitation jewellery and that he had dined at the Warsaw Restaurant at eight o'clock. Between 8.45 and 11.10 pm he had visited the Shoreditch Empire of Varieties and recalled that one of the acts was two children acting as man and wife and a man purporting to be a Scot. He was in part supported in this by sixteen-year-old Jane Brodsky and her sister Esther, who stated they had seen the shows provided by Gertie Gitana, Harry Champion and Harry Lauder and also that they had been in the same row of the stalls as Morrison. 'I swear that I saw Morrison there on the night of 31 December!' Jane dramatically told the Old Bailey jury, adding passionately, 'Nobody can deny my own eyes!' She said that she had not admitted to the police that she had seen Morrison on the Saturday night, but that was because they were bullying her and she had objected to the way in which Wensley had spoken to her. She had made a statement to Morrison's lawyers, and when Ward asked her when and where she had seen Morrison before the Monday, she replied it was no concern of his. Perhaps Morrison had advised her to say this, because he admitted that she had visited him on remand at Brixton prison, 'four or five times'. She had also sworn that she had paid one shilling for her seat at the door.

Unfortunately, Hector Munro, the manager of the theatre, was called and was able to say that no such acts as described by Morrison had been performed on the evening of 31 December. In addition, Munro told the court that Jane Brodsky's tale of paying one shilling at the door for her and her sister's seats simply could not be true. All of the seats had been sold out, and in any event the price for admission to the stalls had been raised that night from one shilling to one shilling and sixpence.

The exceedingly cocky Brodsky sisters – especially Jane, whom Morrison described as being 'as innocent a girl as ever there was in the world' – could have thanked their lucky stars that they were not charged with perjury.

Morrison said he returned to Snelwar's, where he saw Beron, had a cup of tea, collected his 'flute' and left alone at approximately 11.45 pm to return home to Newark Street. On the way he had seen Beron, together with an unknown and very tall, well dressed man, standing on the corner of Sidney Street, and Beron had called out, '*Bonsoir, monsieur!*' Morrison then entered Newark Street and went straight to bed.

This was confirmed by Maurice and Annie Zimmerman, who said that Morrison could not have left the house without their knowledge, since the front door had such a noisy bolt that it regularly woke the household. However, it was pointed out that Morrison, being an experienced burglar, could have left by a window. Esther Grose, the Zimmermans' next-door neighbour, testified that she had seen Morrison return home at midnight, go inside the house and not re-emerge. She appeared to get rather confused during Muir's cross-examination and requested an interpreter; since, up till then, she had managed perfectly well without one, this application was refused.

Morrison then launched into a long and often confusing explanation of what he did and where he went from 1 January up until the time of his arrest; before moving in with Florrie Dellow, he left the revolver at the railway station because he did not want it to frighten her, and the day before his arrest he had had a nose bleed that would have accounted for the spots of blood on his shirt. In fact, he was prone to nosebleeds; he called Herbert Raggert and William Cunningham, warders from Brixton prison, to say that whilst on remand he had suffered two nosebleeds and, in a state of excitement, demanded that a record be made of the occurrences.

In describing his arrest, he told the court that Wensley had told him, 'Stinie, I want you for murder', that he beseeched the detectives not to put anything in his pockets and that Wensley had said at the police station, 'You will be detained at present, but you will be charged with murder when Inspector Ward comes.'

But when Morrison was cross-examined about the purchases allegedly made on 30 November, Abinger intervened and asked Muir to what issue the questions were directed; Muir replied that it was to determine if, on 1 January, Morrison was in possession of money stolen during the robbery and murder of Beron. Abinger objected on the grounds that this was prejudicing his client, but as the judge pointed out, this was permissible as a result of introducing evidence of bad character in respect of Joe Mintz and Nellie Deitch.

With each word, Morrison dug a deeper grave for himself. He exaggerated and lied consistently. He had, he said, regular correspondence from his mother in Russia; but he had kept none of the letters and refused to give her address. The cloakroom ticket in the false name was put in the lining of his hat because 'it was just as good as putting it in my pocket'. He knew that at the time of making his statement he was wanted for Beron's murder because Wensley had told him so, and he made the statement for the purpose of clearing himself – but Ward 'put a different face on it' and although he read and signed it, 'I did not think at the time'. Everything the police had said was lies. It was high time for a dramatic claim:

> If Inspector Wensley did not charge me or say that I am wanted for murder in that restaurant, and if the detective whom I now know is Detective Inspector [*sic*] Brogden did not while walking along say to me that I am wanted for murder and if Inspector Wensley did not say again in the police station that I will be charged with murder, may my innocence never be proved.

Now came the matter of his previous convictions, which, Morrison astonishingly told the court, 'were for no crimes whatsoever'. He cherry-picked the detail. He had never served two months' hard labour for being a suspected person. He knew nothing about the stolen property found in his room but nevertheless had been sentenced to fifteen months' imprisonment. It was true that he had been sentenced to five years' penal servitude and when he was released he started a job in a baker's, but 'the police hounded me out of there'. Although he had been arrested in possession of housebreaking implements, a jemmy was not amongst them. He had never had a jemmy in his life. If he had possessed a jemmy it must have been very small. Now he remembered; it was a chisel. The last two crimes he had committed were because he had been hounded by the police, who had bullied and worried him.

All through his evidence Morrison used the phrase 'for the simple reason' when providing an explanation, to give the impression that the person asking the question was a fool for even asking it. With his poses, theatrical sighs and occasional tearful outbursts, it was not the type of evidence that would endear him to a jury.

Both prosecution and defence summed up the evidence, and a very hostile affair it was, with counsel and the judge interrupting each other.

There was a measure of excitement when Soloman Beron, the dead man's brother, crept into court. During proceedings at the police court he had pointed at Morrison and declared, 'He is my brother's murderer!' Abinger had not only suggested that Soloman might have been responsible for his brother's murder; he had also sneered and laughed outright when Soloman gave evidence.

Soloman, quite clearly unhinged, now made straight for Abinger, shouting, 'When are you going to stop?' and aimed a punch at him; it took three police officers to drag him away, and he was later committed to Colney Hatch Asylum.

Abinger, having regained his composure, suggested that Beron had given information to the police in respect of the Houndsditch murders; he did not, he stated, claim that Beron was a criminal.

'You know, Mr Abinger,' said the judge, wearily, 'that is the worst of these indefinite suggestions. It assumes that he might have given information about something, as I understand it, some organized society because he had belonged to it himself. There is the S you know, which means "spic" which is "spy".'

Muir pointed out that Wensley had continually denied that Beron had given him information about the Houndsditch murders, and that there was not a shred of evidence to suggest that Beron was an anarchist. 'But supposing he was?' mused Muir. 'Supposing this was a murder for revenge directed by the Houndsditch murderers. Who were the Houndsditch murderers?' In answer to his own question, he stated, 'Russian burglars'.

This was what Abinger definitely did not want to hear. All through the case, he had played upon the scars on Beron's face to suggest his murder was an act of revenge – but now that Muir had told the jury that the men responsible for the Houndsditch murders were Russian burglars – as indeed they were – it dovetailed rather neatly into Morrison also being a Russian burglar – as indeed he was, and he had the convictions to prove it.

Whatever the reasons for Beron's scars, it was not because he had given information to Wensley about the whereabouts of the anarchists at Sidney Street – Nicholas Tomacoff had been the informant – and now Abinger's plan had badly backfired. It tied Morrison in to the anarchists, although it was highly likely that he had no connection with them or the Houndsditch burglary.

'I object to this!' bellowed a white-faced Abinger. 'What evidence is there before the court to justify my friend that the perpetrators were Russian burglars?'

'It is a notorious fact,' murmured Muir.

But the judge ruled against him, saying, 'It is a purely spurious objection for Mr Abinger to take, as he has himself, whenever it has suited his own purpose, referred to the Sidney Street affair and all about it with considerable freedom and even mentioned the names of people who he says are connected with it, although there is no evidence that they are.' He concluded by telling Muir, 'You must not say they were Russians or that they were burglars.'

'No,' agreed Muir, but then added for the jury's information, 'Their names, gentlemen, were Fritz Svaars and some other similar sounding names.' This may have been a trifle underhand, but compared to some of the strokes Abinger had pulled, Muir was a model of rectitude.

And all would have been well, had Abinger had the sense to shut his mouth, now that the judge had ruled in his favour. But he did not.

'My friend was trying to associate my client with it and that is what I am objecting to.' Abinger persisted. 'He never put a question to him about it when he was in the witness box.'

Mr Justice Darling had just about run out of patience. 'Mr Abinger,' he said, 'I have ruled, very, very strictly in your favour. You yourself used this topic whenever it suited you; the moment it does not, you get up and object, and I have upheld your objection.'

The very last witness of the day was Police Constable 45 'H' Stephen Dart. He had been called because Morrison had told the court that he had purchased the flute on the morning of 31 December at a street market in Whitechapel and had indicated from a plan that he had purchased at it at the third or fourth stall. However, PC Dart was able to tell the court that he was on traffic duty in Whitechapel's High Street between 8 am and 12.00 noon that day, and that because there was a hay market in the street, no stalls were allowed.

That concluded the eighth day of the trial. In fairness, matters looked pretty bad for Morrison. This was partly due to his ridiculous antics in the witness box, of course; but Abinger had to shoulder a lot of the blame as well, due to the reckless way he had conducted his client's defence. But as the court rose, Abinger had no idea that, overnight, a lifeline in the form of a letter marked 'Confidential' and postmarked 'London, E. 8.15 am, Mar. 14th, 1911' from a serving police officer from 'H' Division wishing to give evidence for the defence, would be dropped into his lap. Nobody knew.

★ ★ ★

Police Constable 86 'H' George Greaves was thirty-six years of age and unmarried, and on the morning of Morrison's arrest he was on duty at Leman Street police station. At best, Greaves could be described as eccentric; at worst, he was a notorious and mentally unstable troublemaker who, six years after joining the Force in 1903, had been disciplined for making unfounded statements regarding a sergeant's behaviour. He had tried to enlist the help of John Syme, an outspoken and mentally unbalanced former police inspector, who had been dismissed for insubordination the previous year, had been prosecuted at Bow Street Police Court for threatening to murder the King and who, four months after the Morrison trial, would be sentenced to six months' imprisonment for threatening to murder his former sub-divisional inspector.

During the hunt for the Houndsditch murders, Greaves had bombarded Wensley with information as to the perpetrators. He sent six or seven letters a day which were utter gibberish, and eventually Wensley had him reprimanded and told to desist. And that might well have been the reason why Greaves now wrote to Abinger at four o'clock in the morning, to tell him that, far from not informing Morrison that he had been arrested for murder, the arresting officers had said exactly that.

Abinger received the letter when he returned to his chambers. If he had reflected on its contents a little more calmly, he would have realized that, if true, it meant that five police officers had perjured themselves – although it would have made little and probably no difference to his client's innocence or guilt. If he had possessed even a modicum of common sense, he would have turned up at court the following day, seen the judge in his chambers, together with Muir, explained that evidence crucial to the case had been brought to his attention and asked for an adjournment. Greaves could then have been summonsed, a statement taken by Abinger's instructing solicitor in the presence of a representative from the Director of Public Prosecution's office, and Greaves would have given evidence. But Abinger's normally excitable disposition had now advanced to a state of near-hysteria and, believing he had Morrison's acquittal in the palm of his hand, he rushed out that evening, saw the Attorney General, then the Commissioner of Police, Sir Edward Henry Bt GCVO, KCB, CSI at his home and threatened that if he was obstructed, he would go directly to the Home Secretary, Winston Churchill.

Sir Edward quietened the trembling Abinger with the offer of a drink and a sandwich and contacted Sir Melville Macnaghten, who met Abinger at Leman Street police station; Greaves was summonsed and a statement, written down by Sir Melville, was duly obtained.

The following morning, Abinger made an application to call further evidence, and the judge, who was fully aware of the nature of the application – he had already rebuked Abinger in his chambers for obtaining the statement instead of his solicitor – allowed it. It is also fairly certain that both Muir and Wensley were aware of Greaves' bombshell, since Macnaughten would have undoubtedly marked their cards.

What Greaves had to say was this: on the morning that Morrison had been arrested, he, Greaves, had been 'on reserve'; in other words, in the communications room, which was situated close to the charge room. He heard Brogden say, 'Why don't you sit down?' and Morrison reply, 'What am I brought here for?' Brogden then said, 'I told you before. You are brought here on a serious charge, on suspicion of murder.'

Having seen a report in a newspaper in which it was denied that murder was mentioned at the time of Morrison's arrest, Greaves felt it was his duty to inform Abinger, with 'the object of giving fair play to Morrison'.

But Greaves fared very badly under scathing cross-examination from Muir. He had not reported this serious inconsistency in the evidence to anyone at the police station because 'there was no time to go through such formalities' and because he wanted his name kept out of it. Greaves further stated that he was 'not absolutely certain that it was of importance to the accused'; and when Mr Justice Darling said, 'You are in the Police Force, and so is Brogden and so are the others. Had that fact anything to do with your not mentioning it at the police station, but writing to Mr Abinger?' Greaves replied, 'No' – but it did not sound convincing.

For a uniformed police constable to be transferred 'four or five times' with under eight years' service did suggest that Greaves was an officer who courted trouble, and his association with ex-Inspector Syme attracted further hostile cross-examination, interventions from Abinger and firm rulings from the judge. Here was a constable who had previously made accusations against a sergeant and had said three other constables could substantiate his claims, only for them to deny that this was the case. He denied that Wensley had reprimanded him for interfering with plugs on the telephone board whilst Wensley had been making a call to Sir Melville Macnaughten. And there was one other very pertinent matter. It was suggested to him that after Morrison had told Wensley that he had accused him of murder, Wensley had called all of the officers, including Inspector McKenzie – and, most importantly, Greaves – into the charge room to ask them if anyone had mentioned the charge of murder to Morrison. Greaves denied this had ever happened.

Closing speeches ended with a great deal of hostility on both sides, and after the judge finished summing up the evidence the jury was sent out to consider their verdict at eight o'clock. They returned thirty-five minutes later, having unanimously found Morrison guilty of the murder of Leon Beron. Asked by the deputy clerk of the court if he had anything to say as to why the court should not pass the death sentence upon him, Morrison replied, 'I have a great deal to say. For one matter, the evidence against me as to the funds which had been seen on me on 1 January being the proceeds of the murder. I can prove that in November I had the sum of £300 and out of this £300, I have still got £220. If I can prove that, will that in any way alter the jury's verdict?'

Without going into detail to the jury, Morrison was referring to a fraud which he and three others had carried out on a bank on 30 November 1910 – about the time that Morrison said he had received the miraculous windfall from his mother in Russia – which netted the gang £300. Morrison's share would possibly have been in the region of £75, but incredibly, even in this last ditch attempt, he found it impossible, thanks to his overpowering ego, to admit that his share would have been less than £300. But it was all too late for Morrison. The judge donned the black cap, passed the death sentence and invited the Almighty to have mercy on Morrison's soul.

Characteristically, Morrison had one last piece of invective for the court. 'I decline such mercy!' he screamed. 'I do not believe there is a God in Heaven, either!'

But Morrison did not hang. He was scheduled for execution on 20 April 1911, but a petition to save him attracted 75,000 signatures, and on 13 April he was reprieved by Winston Churchill, who commuted his sentence to one of twenty years' penal servitude. Morrison attacked warders who conveyed him by train to Dartmoor; upon his arrival, he was placed in a straitjacket. Eleven days after his reprieve, and after some very quick work, a waxwork of Morrison appeared in Madame Tussaud's Chamber of Horrors. For years, the controversy about Morrison's guilt rumbled on, with various people from time to time emerging to confess to Beron's murder, admissions which were as inaccurate as they were odd. Morrison continued to be a troublesome prisoner, pleaded four times with the Home Secretary to be executed, then changed his mind and petitioned for his release on thirty occasions. He eventually went on hunger strike and died in Parkhurst Prison on 24 January 1921.

★ ★ ★

Wensley always believed that Morrison had had an accomplice in Beron's murder. One such prospective candidate had told Wensley that Morrison had approached him with details of the plot, but that he had refused to take part. Morrison was furious, pulled out his revolver and threatened to shoot him. It might, or might not have been true.

Ethel Clayton, a prostitute, told Ward that on the night of New Year's Eve, her pimp, Hugo Pool (she referred to him as 'her husband'), had left the house in company with Morrison and that when he returned three days later he was in possession of gold and silver, and his shirt, which he burnt, was covered in blood. If Pool was involved, it could be that he and Morrison travelled separately to Clapham Common, attacked Beron and then travelled back together from Kennington Church. Had Pool used the blunt object and Morrison the knife, it would account for Pool's shirt being covered in blood and Morrison's clothing having just a few spots – if, of course, that blood was Beron's. It was the first of several rambling and contradictory statements made over a period of years by Ethel Clayton, beginning in February 1911, prior to the trial. Pool was questioned but released through lack of evidence. During the trial, Morrison denied knowing either Clayton or Pool. They were brought into court, whereupon he was obliged to admit that he did know them. In fact, Morrison had known Pool, a violent and convicted thief, since he had arrived in England, and Pool was almost certainly one of the three others involved in the bank fraud with Morrison. However, he denied being in Pool's company on the night of the murder. Neither Clayton nor Pool was called at the trial. Two months after Morrison was reprieved, Hugo Pool made an honest woman of Ethel Clayton; this meant that as his lawfully wedded wife she was neither competent nor compellable to give evidence against him.

Wensley said he heard that Pool had left for America shortly afterwards, where he was executed for robbery and murder; in fact, Pool was sentenced to four years and eight months in New York State for receiving stolen property in 1914.

There was a public enquiry which commenced on 30 March 1911, under the auspices of George Cave KC, MP, in which the police were exonerated of any impropriety, although with regard to Greaves, who was regarded as 'eccentric' by his contemporaries, Cave noted, 'I am disposed to think that this epithet was not undeserved.' Greaves was transferred to Ruislip, probably as far as it was possible to send him from his address at 65 New Road, Whitechapel. He later resigned, and it is thought that he emigrated to America.

So did Wensley tell Morrison in the restaurant that he was wanted for murder? Almost certainly not, and for this reason: when Wensley made an arrest, he would invariably address the suspect by name, followed by the words, 'I want you', just as he did at the time of Morrison's arrest. This is documented by extracts from the transcripts of trials at the Old Bailey, prior to Morrison's arrest, when he used those exact words.

At the conclusion of the case Wensley was exhausted. For three months he had been working night and day on the Houndsditch murders and the Morrison case, neither of which, in all fairness, was his own investigation. He had been thwarted left, right and centre by lying witnesses, shot at, subjected to a near-hysterical series of denunciations by Abinger and made the subject of a damaging attack by a fellow police officer; he must have felt he was at his wit's end. Sir Melville Macnaughten endorsed his application for leave with the words:

> Divisional Detective Inspector Wensley has been hopelessly overworked for the last three months and is perilously near to a breakdown. I cannot speak in sufficiently high terms of the work he has done and I strongly recommend that he be granted special leave for fourteen days.

Sir Edward Henry was one of the great commissioners and a humane one; when a gunman shot him three times, a year later, Sir Edward intervened on his behalf and had his life sentence reduced to one of fifteen years' penal servitude. Sir Edward was also the son of a doctor and he fully supported Sir Melville's endorsement:

> I entirely concur. I will sanction as much special leave in excess of fourteen days as may be required, so that Mr Wensley may have a real good rest.

In addition to a much-needed rest came promotion to divisional detective inspector on 16 March 1911 – this rank had replaced that of 'local inspector' since January 1909 – and the commendations came flooding in, from the commissioner, the trial judge, Sir Charles Matthews, the Director of Public Prosecutions, Messrs Wontner, the Metropolitan Police solicitors, and the prosecuting counsel, Sir Richard Muir.

Only Edward Abinger seemed reluctant to offer his congratulations.

# CHAPTER 17

# Harding v Wensley: Round Two

It is now time to return to Wensley's nemesis, Arthur Harding. Having had a brush with Wensley during the 1908 Royal Commission, it would have made good sound sense for Harding to have given Whitechapel a very wide berth indeed. For one small segment of his chequered career, he did – by touring the country distributing counterfeit currency. But not for long. He continued his career as the leader of a gang of pickpockets as well as running protection rackets; as an offshoot, he raided Jewish gaming clubs and relieved them of their winnings. His demands were reinforced by Harding's gang brandishing firearms, and Harding himself had obtained a Royal Irish Constabulary Webley revolver. Very few of his victims wished to testify against Harding, who with his overpowering arrogance was becoming more and more dangerous.

'A detective is the servant of the law,' Wensley wrote. 'His responsibility ends when he has brought a suspect before a court and stated fairly such facts as he knows … he has no right to let his personal views influence his duty.' Very laudable opinions, too. However, in Harding's case Wensley was prepared to make an exception.

★ ★ ★

Issac Bogard was known as 'Darky the Coon'; in fact he was Jewish, but his swarthy complexion and dark, curly hair provided him with his nickname, and his followers – many of them ex-boxers – were known as 'the Coons'. Bogard was born in 1888 in Spitalfields and was a pimp and a hard man. An enormously flamboyant character, he wore cowboy outfits – these included leather chaps and a Stetson – and affected an American accent.

'I am not a particularly violent man,' he told a court, but the authorities would have begged to differ. He had been convicted of punching a police officer in the face; following this attack, he escaped to the rooftops and pelted the pursuing officers with tiles. He had also been sentenced to fifteen months' hard labour in 1906 (in the name of 'Ike Bogard') for robbery with violence. In 1908 he was convicted and flogged for living off immoral earnings, the following year he was convicted of assault and in 1910 he was sentenced to nine months' hard labour for maliciously wounding a woman.

Bogard and Harding were at daggers drawn. In 1907, George King, a renowned burglar, who had served a sentence of five years' penal servitude and who had been a member of Harding's gang, sided with Bogard and another gangster, Philip Shonck, to murder Harding; but before this plan could come to fruition, Shonck was shot by Tommy Taylor, one of Harding's men. To add insult to injury, Taylor tried to recruit one of Bogard's prostitutes, which led to Bogard beating up Taylor, although Bogard later said that it was because he had used foul language to his wife. Perhaps the two incidents were somehow intermingled. Although Taylor was deeply involved with Harding's gang, especially their practice of robbing Jewish gamblers, he also lived off prostitutes' immoral earnings and had just the one conviction in 1906, for gambling with dice, although according to the police, 'He was never known to have done any work'.

Matters came to a head on 10 September 1911. At 9.00 pm, Bogard – he had been warned by his wife to stay away from his usual haunts – and a friend, Philip Lipmann, entered the Bluecoat Boy public house. An hour previously, Jack Burman had been outside the Phoenix public house, a short distance away. Burman, who had been twice convicted of assault (one of them a stabbing), was approached by Harding and some of his gang, whom he knew. 'Where is Isaac Bogard, commonly known as Darkie the Coon?' he was asked in a rather formal manner, and he replied truthfully that he did not know. He was then told, 'There won't be no Bogard after tonight.' He later gave evidence to that effect, mid-way through a sentence of three months' imprisonment for being a suspected person, although his account was disputed by Harding, saying it was 'a wicked, deliberate lie.'

But whether Burman's account was truthful or not, Harding's intelligence was good; within five minutes of Bogard entering the bar, Harding and companions arrived, including twenty-nine-year-old William Spencer – known as 'Emms' – the proud possessor of twelve convictions since 1899, three being for assault. He was currently a convict on licence. Stephen Cooper, aged thirty, was one of the more dangerous of an already dangerous bunch; since 1898 he had acquired sixteen convictions, of which five were for assault, and on three occasions he had been found in possession of firearms. William Newman, aged twenty-seven, who since 1898 had collected eleven convictions (five of which were for indictable offences) was also present, as was twenty-three-year-old Thomas

Taylor, who certainly had a score to settle. All of them – Taylor especially – were described as 'looking excited'.

Bogard knew immediately he was in for a rough time; sensibly, he tried to defuse the situation. 'Hullo!' he called out to Harding. 'Going to have drink?'

Harding initially ignored him, but later returned and said, 'I thought you were going to pay for drinks?'

Bogard duly ordered drinks and paid for them, and then Harding said to him, 'Do you know what we are going to do to you?'

Although it is highly likely that Bogard did know, he simply replied, 'I'm surprised at you.'

Bogard then received a tap on the shoulder and, as he turned, Taylor cut his throat with a knife, and Newman, Harding and Spencer all smashed their tumblers and rammed them into Bogard's face and hands. Lipmann, who had emerged from the urinal, rushed to Bogard's assistance and was cut on the hand. As they ran out, Newman shouted, 'That's for Taylor, you fucking bastard.'

The manager of the Bluecoat Boy was Harry Samuels; he witnessed the incident, jumped over the counter and blew a blast on his police whistle. Thereafter, his courage failed him, he beat a hasty retreat for Southend and was unavailable for the trial. His mother Kate, however, was made of sterner stuff; she had been splattered with blood from Bogard's injuries but she testified that Harding was responsible for the attack.

In Shoreditch, about fifteen minutes later, Bogard saw Spencer, who said to him, 'Look at how you're bleeding, Coon', and offered him his handkerchief.

'Do you mean to give me a handkerchief after you've struck me with a glass?' asked Bogard, adding ironically, 'You are a good fellow!'

'It wasn't me who done that,' untruthfully retorted Spencer, who then saw a police officer approaching and made himself scarce.

Dr William Cliff Hodges, the Relieving Room Officer at the London Hospital, saw Bogard at one o'clock the following morning; had he been asked, he would have undoubtedly agreed with Harding's later gloating assertion that 'the Coon had a face like the map of England'. He inserted stitches in a number of deep cuts in and around Bogard's mouth and lips which were consistent with the use of broken glasses. The deep cuts on his throat 'would have been dangerous if they had been any deeper'.

The following Sunday, Bogard and George King were attacked once more, near the Horns public house, by Harding and his gang. Harding, referring to the bandage around Bogard's throat and the sticking plaster on his chin, said, 'That's only half of what you've got; the rest will come.'

Newman kicked Bogard and said, 'All right, you black bastard – come on, we'll do it, now.'

Fighting broke out, and Police Constable 23 'H' Harry Gibson arrived, to see Stephen Cooper fire a revolver at an unknown man[15] who was fighting with Robert Wheeler. PC Gibson caught hold of Cooper's gun arm and the two men fell to the ground, with Cooper on top. Then another of the gang called out, 'Give it here, Steve', snatched the revolver from Cooper's hand and ran off; Tommy Taylor then tried to rescue Cooper. PC Gibson was assisted by Police Constable 51 'H' Harry Gurney; Cooper stated, 'I've done nothing, guv'nor', and Taylor, who had run away, was caught by Police Constable 522 'H' William Robins, who, upon searching him, found a five-chambered revolver, fully loaded, in his pocket.

Amongst those detained by police were, oddly, Bogard and King, who were arrested for disorderly behaviour.

On the following morning the two men appeared at Old Street Police Court, and although the account given was 'confusing' to the magistrate, Sir Charles Biron, he decided to bind over both Bogard and King, who asked Sir Charles for police protection. Having heard that Harding and an armed gang were waiting for them, he ordered the two men detained whilst the police were contacted. It seemed not a moment too soon; Old Street Court was literally being besieged by Harding and his gang.

Wensley and eight of his men arrived in a covered van and were able to see exactly what was going on. Harding's behaviour, born out of arrogance, was nothing short of incredible, brandishing a revolver in the presence of large numbers of police. As Bogard and King were released from court, the gang rushed them; William Andrews hit Bogard and was arrested, as was Harding. Several other members of the gang who escaped were identified and warrants obtained for their arrest; amongst their number was Charles Callaghan, PC Carr's former prisoner. Aged thirty-one, Callaghan had acquired eight convictions since 1902, one of which was for assault and another for shooting with intent. He described himself as 'a labourer', but the only employment he had carried out had been at Harding's behest; the police had 'never known him to have done any work'.

---

15 In fact, the 'unknown man' was William Spencer; Cooper had shot at him because Spencer had previously punched him in a pub.

The prisoners were kept on remand for fourteen weeks, an astonishing length of time by any standards, and Wensley had his work cut out keeping hold of the independent witnesses for the prosecution. One of the most problematical witnesses was Bogard; he was served with a subpoena after his appearance at court to give evidence on 26 September but did not attend. It was only on 3 October that he finally appeared, as the result of receiving a witness summons. In the witness box at the committal proceedings, Wensley's life and that of his wife and children were threatened, but eventually Harding and seven of his gang were committed for trial at the Old Bailey on a variety of charges, including shooting with intent to murder and also to cause grievous bodily harm, feloniously wounding Bogard and, together with other persons to the number of twenty and more, assembling to commit riot and committing riot.

The trial judge was Mr Justice Avory, and Richard Muir once more led for the prosecution; the defendants were represented by a multiplicity of legal talent.

Bogard, who described his occupation as 'comedian', of 1 Hamlyn Place, St George's-in-the-East, gave impressive evidence. His wife, who had forewarned him by telegram of impending danger from Taylor, who, she said, was in possession of a knife, was not called as a witness; at the time of the trial, Wensley told the court, she was serving a sentence for disorderly conduct. It was alleged that Bogard had been in possession of a knife, had been drunk and had thrown a water jug at Harding – all of which was denied by Bogard and other independent witnesses.

When Harding gave evidence, he was quick to put the blame on Taylor, who, he said, had followed him in the pub and had punched Bogard. The latter told Harding, 'You was with him', which Harding denied. He told the court that Bogard had started to open a penknife and therefore, in self-defence, he had hit him in the face with his unbroken glass and then left the pub.

The following day, Harding said that he saw Bogard again, who asked him why he had been attacked. Harding's alleged reply was, 'Look here, Coon, I know you would have given me one last night; it was only tit-for-tat.'

Bogard's reply was, 'I know, it was a mistake. I was half drunk, but when Taylor done it on me I thought you was with him.'

Pointing to the bandage around Bogard's throat, Harding innocently said, 'Surely I did not do that?'

Bogard replied, 'No, Taylor done that', whereupon the two men had a drink and parted on friendly terms.

It sounded unbelievable, and it was.

Far from having 'done that', Taylor entered the witness box to say that he was not in possession of a knife but that he had been confronted in the Bluecoat Boy by Bogard, who had punched him, and that he had punched him back. Although he had not noticed any blood on Bogard's neck, it was possible, he told the court, that if there was blood, it could have come from his nose, which was bleeding.

William Spencer and William Newman both gave evidence, and their testimony was as fanciful as that of their associates. They were all speedily found guilty, as was Cooper for feloniously shooting at a person unknown; and Harding, Callaghan, Spencer, Taylor and Wheeler changed their pleas of not guilty to guilty of riot. William Andrews pleaded guilty to assaulting George King and Harding to assaulting Bogard on 18 September.

On 19 December, before passing sentence, Mr Justice Avory said:

Such of you as have pleaded guilty to this riot must know perfectly well that it was one of the most serious riots which could be dealt with by the law; for it was a riot in which some of you at all events were armed with loaded revolvers, a riot which took place in the very precincts of a court of justice, a riot the purpose of which was either to intimidate or punish in your own way persons who were attending that court of justice, and a riot the purpose of which was, in fact, carried out by the assaults which were committed upon the men upon whom you meant to have your revenge. I wish to say that for any portion of London to be infested by a number of criminal ruffians armed with loaded revolvers is a state of things which ought not to be further tolerated, and if the existing law is not enough to put a stop to it, some remedial legislation must be effected.

Newman, for wounding Bogard, was sentenced to fifteen months' hard labour. He later enlisted in the army and after demobilization commenced trading as a bookmaker. Callaghan was sentenced to two years' hard labour for the riot and later worked with Newman in his bookmaker's business.

Spencer was sentenced to eighteen months' hard labour for riot and three years' penal servitude for wounding Bogard, the sentences to run consecutively. Following his release, he joined the army and served with the Royal Army Service Corps.

For assaulting George King, Andrews was sentenced to twelve months' hard labour; thereafter, he, too, joined the army and was killed in action.

Cooper was sentenced to three years' penal servitude for shooting at a person unknown; always rather unstable, he cut his throat whilst he was serving his sentence in Wandsworth prison and was transferred to Broadmoor, where he died.

Wheeler was sentenced to fifteen months' hard labour for riot; after his discharge he worked as a look-out man for a firm of bookmakers.

For both riot and wounding Bogard, Taylor (whose character was described in court as being 'a record of acquittal') was sentenced to two years' hard labour on each count, the sentences to run concurrently. Upon his release, Taylor was convicted of making counterfeit coins and received a four-year sentence; he died of venereal disease in 1915.

But when it came to Harding, it was certainly 'pay-back' time for Wensley, who told the court:

> At the age of seventeen, he [Harding] became a terror to Bethnal Green, and captained a band of desperadoes. In all, he has been convicted fourteen times, yet he was one of the complaining witnesses before the Police Commission. He has developed into a cunning and plausible criminal of a dangerous type. I have never known him do any work.

Harding received the stiffest sentence of all: for riot twenty-one months' hard labour, and for wounding Bogard three years' penal servitude, the sentences to run consecutively.

Four days after sentence, the *Illustrated Police News* reported, 'East End Vendetta. Gang of ruffians broken up at last'. Harding's gang had acquired an identity of their own: the Vendettas. It is doubtful if any of them were able to spell it, let alone knew what it meant.

★ ★ ★

Bogard enlisted in the army following the outbreak of war. As Private 263049 I. Bogard of the South Wales Borderers, his award of the Military Medal for bravery was gazetted on 22 February 1918. And following Detective Chief Inspector Fred 'Nutty' Sharpe's retirement as head of the Flying Squad in July 1937, he set up a bookmaker's business in Wandsworth; fifty-one-year-old Isaac Bogard was one of the first men he employed. 'They're a colourful, rascally lot, these wide 'uns,' said Sharpe.

Harding received a number of other prison sentences. He still mixed with the criminal classes, even after marrying and raising a family. He had his spectacularly biased and inaccurate memoirs published and, astonishingly, stated that he worked as an informant for the post-war Ghost Squad, which operated from 1946 to 1949. He said that his estimation of the police fell a tremendous amount and that he claimed the Ghost Squad was crooked from top to bottom.

In fact, Harding never held the police in any kind of estimation; it was his way of firing a parting shot at the Metropolitan Police, which he hated in general, and at Wensley, in particular.

# CHAPTER 18

# Chief Detective Inspector

Wensley's rest cure – such as it was – following the Sidney Street, Morrison and Harding cases was over. Five days after the conclusion of the Harding case he had a double murder to deal with.

Although Myer Abramovitch was known as 'Myer the Insane' (and told a friend, 'I don't know what's the matter with my head'), everybody agreed that he was a quiet, inoffensive and respectable fruit seller, who sold his wares at a restaurant at 62 Hanbury Street, Spitalfields. He was friendly with the proprietor, Solomon Milstein, and his wife Annie, in whose basement illicit games of faro were played, in which Abramovitch sometimes participated.

On Sunday, 24 December 1911 a customer named Abraham Rockman had lost all of his money gambling, so he handed his watch and chain with a Kruger sovereign to Joseph Goldstein, a pugilist hired to keep order, and asked if he could be advanced a sovereign. Milstein agreed and was seen by Abramovitch to hand over the money from a purse. The previous day, a gambler named Hermann Lasserson had done exactly the same with his watch and chain and had received £2 10s 0d for it. On the evening of Boxing Day, when the gambling finished, the house winnings were put into a small cash box in the Milsteins' bedroom.

A few hours later, Marks Vekbloot, who occupied a flat above the Milsteins' bedroom, was woken by the sounds of groaning but then went back to sleep. At 3.00 am he smelled smoke coming up from the floor below and blew a police whistle, which was heard by Police Constable 457 'H' Roderick Stewart, who arrived and helped put out the fire, which came from some bedding. There, on the floor, lay Solomon Milstein; under the bed was the body of his wife and under the bed's pillow was a bloodstained knife, together with a bloodstained blue handkerchief which smelled strongly of paraffin.

It was clear there had been a severe struggle; there were abrasions on Solomon's face and chest and cuts on his arms, but death had been caused by a knife plunged into his lung to a depth of five inches. There were cuts and abrasions on Annie's face, head and hands, possibly caused by a fire-iron found in the room, and a five-inch long wound on her chest and stomach, an inch deep, which had caused her death. Dr Percy Tranter Goodman, who examined the bodies, stated that, 'It was a very brutal outrage,' adding, 'Not the slightest mercy was shown.'

Everyone who had been in the restaurant prior to the murder went to the police station to assist in the investigation – save one. Hours later, Myer Abramovitch was brought in to Leman Street police station, where he was seen by Wensley. Before Wensley could open the door of his office, Abramovitch said, 'I know what you want. You'll find it in this pocket', and indicated the left-hand inside pocket of his overcoat. There were both Rockman's and Lasserson's watch and chain. Then Wensley was handed a leather purse, with the words, 'This is his; you'll find all the money there.' Contained in Mr Milstein's purse was £2 10s 0d in gold and, in various pockets, 5s 11¼d. Abramovitch was wearing two suits; the inner suit had a large quantity of blood on it, as had his singlet, pants and shirt. A pocket in the overcoat was saturated with blood, and Abramovitch admitted that the overcoat and the outer suit belonged to Milstein. Pointing to the paraffin-soaked handkerchief on Wensley's table – it had been identified by several witnesses as belonging to Abramovitch – he said, 'That's mine. I done it because I lost all my money at gambling.'

At the Old Bailey trial the Divisional Surgeon, Dr Percy John Clarke, admitted that he was no expert regarding insanity but thought that the killings had been committed by a sane man. This was at variance with the case for the defence, who were doing their best to convince the jury that Abramovitch was clearly unbalanced and cited the fact that at the time of his arrest the prisoner was wearing two suits. 'He was not an extraordinary object in Whitechapel to walk about with two suits on,' replied the doctor. 'They sometimes wear three suits in Whitechapel and they are not insane; it is a foreign habit.'

The prosecution decided to resolve the issue by calling a doctor to see if there was any foundation to the matter of insanity, and the trial judge, Mr Justice Ridley, agreed. Sidney Reginald Dyer, the medical officer at Brixton prison (who told the court he had seen prisoners who wore as many as *six* suits), had examined Abramovitch and come to the conclusion that he was not insane. The prisoner was therefore sentenced to death.

While Wensley was waiting for the Abramovitch case to be committed to the Old Bailey, he dealt with a *ménage à trois* at the insalubrious surroundings of 22 Newman's Buildings, 3 Pelham Street.

John Chesnovski had first met Vincent Gonzewski and his wife Victoria in 1907, and in Mr Gonzewski's absence Chesnovski and Victoria commenced an amorous affair. Their dalliance was discovered, there was a quarrel, the Gonzewskis separated and Victoria and Chesnovski began to live together as man and wife.

But it was clear that Gonzewski had not forgotten or forgiven the adulterous lovers, because on 15 January 1912 he burst into their room, blazed away with a revolver and shot Chesnovski in his hand and his elbow. Victoria sustained several bullet wounds: two to her left upper arm, another to the left side of her chest – although this may have resulted from one of the bullets going through her arm – and one when a bullet entered close to the right side of her spine and exited from the left side of her chest. Aubrey Barker, the chief surgeon at the London Hospital, would later tell an Old Bailey jury that her legs were paralysed for fourteen hours thereafter; indeed, he thought it possible that complications might ensue which would prevent her from leaving hospital at all.

Chesnovski wrestled the revolver away from the betrayed husband and cracked him over the head with it. Rosie Gotthelf, who lived in the flat next door, was alerted by the sound of shots and Victoria's screams, ran to her window and shrieked, 'Police!' When Wensley arrived and was handed the revolver, he found that it contained five spent and one live round, so it was clear that Gonzewski had reloaded. He certainly had the capability to do so: when he was searched, he had seventeen live cartridges in one pocket and thirteen in another, and on the landing there were two spent and one live cartridge; there were also two further bullet holes in the room.

Gonzewski was found guilty of wounding with intent to murder his errant wife and was sentenced to three years in a Borstal institution. The Borstal system had been in use since 1902 and had been devised for recalcitrant offenders between the ages of fifteen and twenty-one. This sentence thus appeared quite irrational, since Gonzewski was twenty-six at the time.

★ ★ ★

Wensley was more active than ever; he was commended by a coroner for his presentation of a murder case and then, six days later, commended by the jury at an inquest for his preparation and presentation of the evidence in another murder. Two weeks later, he was commended twice in one day: first, by a judge at the Old Bailey for skill in a case of larceny, and then by the judge and petty jury at the County of London Sessions for the apprehension of two persons in a case of burglary and for recovering the stolen property.

Therefore, it was perhaps not too surprising that after just eleven months in the rank of divisional detective inspector, Wensley was promoted to the rank then known as chief detective inspector. Freemasonry probably helped: Wensley had been an active mason for years and in 1916 he would be invited to join Temple Lodge 101.

Wensley was still two weeks away from his forty-sixth birthday, and with twenty-four years' service he had done tremendously well to have attained this rank. He had replaced John Kane ('whose experience', stated the *Daily Mail* on 10 May 1906, 'is very wide'), who was one of four chief inspectors. Originally, the others had been Fred Fox, Walter Dew (who had arrested Dr Crippen) and Charles Arrow; in 1907 they had been gathered to assist other divisions and constabularies with their considerable expertise in major investigations.

It was usual for these chief inspectors to be transferred to the Yard – this was the case with Tom Divall, who had similarly been promoted to chief inspector – but Wensley dug his heels in and stayed on 'H' Division. He would gladly assist neighbouring divisions with their investigations, but leave Whitechapel he would *not*. In this he was undoubtedly assisted by his friend, Sir Melville McNaughton, Wensley's staunchest ally amongst Scotland Yard's senior officers; but if this was the case, it would be the last favour Sir Melville could bestow upon his protégé. In the same year as Wensley was promoted Sir Melville was appointed Companion of the Bath, but he was already in poor health and the following year he was awarded the King's Police Medal and retired, having served ten years as Assistant Commissioner (Crime). He was widely admired; appointed Knight Commander of the White Military Order of Spain and also Commander of the Order of the Dannebrog, he died, following an all too short retirement, in 1921.

Wensley could have now sat back and issued avuncular advice to his subordinates, but he was determined not to become a desk-bound warrior, any more than when he had been promoted to divisional detective inspector. He continued to tear through the underworld, and within two months of his appointment he was commended at Mansion House police court for the manner of his evidence in the case of six receivers, followed two months later by a coroner's commendation for his presentation of a case of a suspicious death. One month later, he was complimented at Tower Bridge police court regarding his actions in a case of larceny, and two weeks after that a further commendation came his way at the County of London Sessions, for perseverance in a case of larceny.

His next murder case was as sordid as could possibly be. Lilian Rose Caroline Pease was thirty-eight years of age and had been separated from her husband for some considerable time; she was a prostitute and was known as 'Darky' or 'Little Darky'. On the evening of 16 November 1912 she met up with Isaac Parkes, a forty-two-year-old labourer, and, purporting to be man and wife, they went together to 8 White's Row, Spitalfields, a common lodging house. Later, accusing her of stealing his money, Parkes demanded that she return it and promised to strangle her if she did not. Following her refusal, he later admitted, 'I did.'

Taking the deceased's fur stole with him, Parkes went to another lodging house at 30 Duvall Street, where he unsuccessfully tried to sell the fur; he then went to 35 Duvall Street and asked Annie Mahoney, an attendant at the common lodging house, 'Who wants to buy a fur for fourpence?'

He received the crushing (and quite accurate) reply, 'I dare say you've taken that off some poor creature', and was again turned away.

Parkes next met Ada Paul (an 'unfortunate') and, posing as a married couple, they rented room no. 7 at 30 Duvall Street. Many of these common lodging houses were little more than brothels; the proprietors knew perfectly well that many of the couples who used them were not man and wife, and in this case they certainly knew Ada Paul's real identity, as well as her profession. But when Miss Paul demanded money for her services, Parkes told her he had been robbed, and he departed shortly thereafter, leaving behind the late Mrs Pease's fur and also a bag with two spoons in it. Rather shamelessly, Miss Paul admitted, 'I put the fur on ... I sold the spoons for a penny. I wore the fur for a day or two.'

When Lilian Pease's body was discovered, Wensley immediately arrested a costermonger named Patsy O'Shea, who had been in Mrs Pease's company earlier that evening; but the following day, Katie Webb, the sister of Inspector Webb, saw a man leave a piece of paper on the steps of Commercial Street police station before hurrying away. It read:

The super. of Commercial police station. Sunday. Dear Sir. I want you to send one of your officers to White's Row and there up in the top room you will find the body of a woman. I strangled her in the early part of this morning. This is the second woman I have done in. After this I will tell you more about it when you catch me. Yours truly, I.P.O.W. I am started on the road now for W.W.

It appeared that W.W. stood for West Ham Workhouse, and it was there that Parkes confessed to William Chandler, the superintendent of the casual ward. The police were called, and when Wensley saw Parkes at Leytonstone police station he took a written statement from him and charged him, to which Parkes replied, 'That is quite right.'

Wensley then ensured that the charge against Patsy O'Shea was dismissed. He later told an Old Bailey jury, 'I have for years been accustomed to compare handwriting', and, referring to the note left at Commercial Street police station and the signature on the statement, was quite emphatic in declaring, 'I should say it's in the prisoner's writing.'

The jury's verdict was, 'Guilty of causing the death of the woman but without unlawful intention', at which Mr Justice Darling grumpily declared, 'This is no verdict', and refused to accept it. He put the case over to the next sessions, when, perhaps rather high-handedly, he directed that the verdict should be recorded as one of guilty of manslaughter and sentenced Parkes to fourteen years' penal servitude.

As 1912 came to a close, Wensley was commended twice more, at the County of London Sessions for his actions in a case of housebreaking, and by a coroner for his presentation in a murder case.

★ ★ ★

The number of Metropolitan Police officers increased to 22,048 in 1913 and, what was more, they were now permitted one day off per week. And now the Wensley family was on the move; the house at 98 Dempsey Street was vacated, and in April they moved into a new suburban development, 'Lucholm' at 76 Powys Lane, Palmers Green, North London. Wensley's mother accompanied them; she had lived with the family since her husband's death and would continue to do so until her own death, aged ninety, in 1927.

With the move into the new house, Lollie was in her element; unlike Dempsey Street, it had a large garden, and she kept the house immaculate. Never easily upset, she loved Wensley deeply, although he could be forceful, impatient and sometimes tempestuous; he did not suffer fools gladly. Nevertheless, he loved Lollie in return, as he did his children, although he was a firm disciplinarian.

So it was a longer journey to work, certainly; but it was an infinitely more salubrious neighbourhood than the one Wensley had just left, particularly with regard to the close proximity of

Dempsey Street to 254 Commercial Road, a tobacconist's owned by fifty-year-old Morris Loufer.

To say Loufer was in a parlous financial state was an understatement; his cheques were dishonoured, his accounts were in arrears, the gas company sent a demand note and the bailiffs were called in. During the early hours of 24 January 1913 there was a fire at 254 Commercial Road; sixteen people, including the Loufer family, were there. Police Constable 166 'H' Noah Jones acted with great bravery, entering the house on three occasions and rescuing seven of the occupants (including Loufer's wife and two small children) before being overcome by smoke. He had also noticed Morris Loufer there and, although it was 3.00 am, seen that Loufer was fully dressed. Two of the occupants, Morris Kovalsky and Cornelius King, died in the fire.

When Wensley commenced his investigations, he discovered that three months previously Loufer had insured the contents of the premises for £400, and the premium had cost him every penny he possessed. He had told several people that he was in a great deal of trouble and that 'there must be a fire', and four days before the fire, Loufer's son Samuel had brought six gross of matches and a dozen wax tapers into the shop.

Father and son were charged with murder. Samuel was acquitted, but after Morris Loufer had told the Old Bailey that every witness was a liar, including the plucky PC Jones, since Loufer claimed he had been wearing only his underpants when he answered the door to the officer, he was convicted of manslaughter, sentenced to ten years' penal servitude and recommended for deportation.

Wensley ensured that PC Jones was awarded the King's Police Medal for his bravery and was himself commended by the coroner, as well as receiving another award. On 18 July 1913 he escorted the Maharaja of Mysore around London's East End, and so impressed was the potentate with Wensley that he presented him with a silver tray. But that was a brief interlude; as 1913 ended and 1914 commenced, war clouds were beginning to gather over Europe.

\* \* \*

With the outbreak of war in August 1914, 24,000 special constables were sworn in – by the end of the year, they would total 31,000 – and the order regarding the day off, which had been granted the previous year, was rescinded, as was all annual leave, for the first year of the war. Crime was flourishing and Wensley continued to be commended by coroners, once for his presentation in a case of murder and once in a case which turned out to be an accidental death.

But on 5 August 1915 tragedy struck the Wensley family; their eldest son, Frederick Martin, a second lieutenant serving with the Lincolnshire Regiment in France, was about to participate in a bombing raid when he was struck by a shell and died immediately.

Despite his grief – or perhaps to subjugate it – Wensley immersed himself in his work; he gave evidence in the case of Aaron Lechtenstein and Reuben Michaels, who had attempted to bribe a superintendent, was commended by a coroner for his 'smart apprehension' of a woman for murder, privately rewarded in another case, was commended at the County of London Sessions in a case of larceny and a month later further commended, together with a £1 reward, in a case of larceny and receiving.

Then on the night of 23/24 September 1916 there was an air raid over London by German Zeppelins. With a top speed of 63 mph, these giant cigar-shaped airships, 536 feet long, had been carrying out bombing raids on London since 31 May 1915; by the end of the war 52 raids would result in over 500 fatalities. Now, on this night, the four Zeppelins – L31, L32, L33 & L34 – were intercepted by the Royal Flying Corps and three were destroyed, but not before dropping bombs which resulted in 38 casualties, one of whom was Chief Detective Inspector Alfred Ward. He died in a London hospital the following day.

Wensley was enormously saddened to hear of his old friend's death, and the news was flashed around the world, because Ward had been a hugely successful investigator both at home and abroad. One who did not express grief at Ward's death was Stinie Morrison, who in his cell at Parkhurst prison was said to have wept tears of joy at the news, declaring that now he really did believe that there was a God in heaven.

But it also left a vacancy at the Yard, and now there was no Macnaughten to champion Wensley's cause; since 1913 the Assistant Commissioner (Crime) had been Basil Thomson. From the beginning of the war, the CID had become the striking arm of the security services, who had no powers of arrest. In 1916 Thomson was involved in the trial of Sir Roger Casement and had interviewed the exotic Dutch dancer and spy, 'Mata Hari'; both of these were executed for treason. He had just been appointed Companion of the Bath, he wanted the best detectives around him and he got them; on 6 October 1916, less than two weeks after Ward's death, and after twenty-five years' service in Whitechapel, Wensley was transferred to the Yard.

\* \* \*

The Yard had changed considerably from the building where Wensley had been sworn in as a constable in 1888; now Wensley occupied one of the offices in the Norman Shaw building, next to Cannon Row police station on the Embankment. In 1913 the Criminal Records Office had been formed at the Yard, by the merging of the Habitual Criminals' Registry, the Convicts' Supervision Office and the Fingerprint Office – this last would have its own department in 1919. Superintendent John McCarthy was in charge of the five chief inspectors: Fowler, Gough, Hawkins, Carlin and now Wensley, as senior chief inspector.

There was a multiplicity of work to deal with: murders, of course, but also governmental enquiries which required great circumspection, confidential enquiries on behalf of the Director of Public Prosecutions and matters concerning the war, including prosecutions under the Defence of the Realm Act and offences against the Food Control Orders and the Military Service Acts.

It was not long after his arrival that Wensley was asked by Thomson if he could devise a system for making the CID a more fluid organization, since until then the divisional detectives had worked under the direction of their inspectors to deal with crimes committed on their own divisions. Because if the CID did not adapt, criminals would; with the advent of the motor car, for example, criminals were moving faster and no longer confining their exploits to the areas in which they lived.

Wensley explained how this situation could be turned around; he envisaged senior officers being given the responsibility of co-ordinating the work of several divisions, and specially selected detectives being given a roving commission to go where they were needed – or where their informants directed them – to effect arrests. To prove the point, he had already achieved considerable results with these methods, using disguises, running informants and borrowing horse-drawn wagons to trail suspects, notably in the jewel robbery of Mr Cox and the Weiner gang, as well as tracking a miscellany of other criminals who had crossed divisional boundaries. However, there were also the failures to learn from.

As early as May 1875, three detectives had been struck off general duties and provided with the sum of £20 to purchase information to detect a gang of notorious jewel thieves, one of whom was known as 'Soldier Billy' and another as 'Billy the Greek'. But none of the gang were arrested, and there was no accounting for the £20 advance; perhaps it disappeared into the deep pockets of one of these officers, the corrupt Detective Sergeant John Meiklejohn, who two years later was one of three detectives sentenced in the infamous 'Trial of the Detectives'.

And in 1906, Fred Fox, one of the original chief inspectors at the Yard, had been permitted to form a squad of officers to detect 'coiners'; they were given carte blanche to go anywhere in their quest. The scheme collapsed after the young, inexperienced officers on the unit were sent out without proper guidance or supervision. So these previous schemes had failed; Wensley was determined that his would not.

But it was not to be, in 1916. There was a war on, and Thomson politely thanked Wensley for his input, concentrated his energies on catching spies, and there the matter rested. In fact, as far as Thomson was concerned, Wensley's concept was stillborn, because by the end of the war he was knighted, became director of intelligence in Special Branch and retired in 1921. Wensley, however, did not forget; but it was not something which could immediately be implemented. The following year, 1917, the numbers of Metropolitan Police officers were depleted, with 2,300 of them serving in the armed forces.

# CHAPTER 19

# 'Blodie Belgiam'

Whenever it was possible for Wensley to roll his sleeves up and get out of the Yard, he did so. The murder of Madame Émilienne Gerard provided just such an opportunity.

On 2 November 1917 Thomas George Henry, a packer, discovered a parcel in the interior of the gardens of Regent Square, Bloomsbury. Inside the parcel were the trunk and arms of a woman; her head, legs and hands had been removed. The trunk was wrapped in a bloodstained sheet bearing a laundry mark 'II H' and also in sacking marked 'Argentina La Plata Cold Storage'. In addition, there was a piece of brown paper upon which the words 'Blodie Belgiam' were scrawled. A search inside Regent Square revealed a brown-paper parcel, in which were found the woman's legs.

Superintendent McCarthy directed Wensley to attend Bow Street police station to supervise Divisional Detective Inspector John Ashley on the case. It required the Yard's involvement because no one had any idea as to the woman's identity or where she had been killed.

Within twenty-four hours the laundry mark on the sheet was identified as belonging to thirty-two-year-old Mme Émilienne Gerard, who lived at 50 Munster Square and whose husband was serving in the French Army. She had not been seen since 31 October, when there had been a particularly heavy air raid over London: 22 Gotha biplanes had dropped 83 two-kilogram incendiary bombs, killing ten civilians. She had left the house to take shelter, and her absence simply had not been the subject of comment; she could, of course have been one of the bombing casualties or she could have gone to France, which she quite often did – on mysterious missions for the Government, some said, although it was far more likely that she went to visit her husband. But whatever the reason, nobody really cared.

The police surgeon who examined the remains came to the conclusion that the body's dissection had been carried out by someone with a knowledge of anatomy – possibly a butcher. And when Wensley examined Mme Gerard's rooms and discovered bloodstains, a photograph of a man and an IOU for £50 in the name of Louis Voisin, his further enquiries revealed that the man in the photograph was Louis Voisin, who lived at 101 Charlotte

Street, a quarter of a mile from Regent Square, and that by trade he was a butcher.

When Wensley arrived at the basement flat in Charlotte Street, there was forty-two-year-old Voisin, together with a woman named Berthe Roche; both were French, and although Voisin, a short, powerfully-built man, spoke only broken English and Roche even less, Wensley had the assistance of Detective Sergeant Read, who spoke fluent French. After he had discovered that, the night before the body was found, neighbours had heard the voices of more than one woman coming from the basement, Wensley decided to bring them both in.

Voisin stated that he had known Mme Gerard for eighteen months; at one stage she had been his housekeeper, but he had been to her rooms only once, on 31 October, after Mme Gerard had asked him to feed her cat, since she was going to France with a friend named Marguerite. He neglected to say that they had been lovers and that he paid the rent for her rooms at Munster Square. Wensley carried out house-to-house enquiries and discovered that a man named Evrart had dined with Mme Gerard at an Italian restaurant near Soho Square on the evening of 31 October, at which time she had said nothing about going to France.

The following day, Wensley interviewed Voisin again; this time, he asked him through the interpreter if he had any objection to writing the words, 'Bloody Belgium'. 'None at all,' replied Voisin, who wrote, 'Blodie Belgiam' five times.

In Voisin's possession was a key which fitted the door of the cellar next to his basement flat; in the cellar was a cask and in amongst the sawdust were the murdered woman's head and hands. Sir Bernard Spilsbury was called in. His examination revealed that the head had been reduced to a pulp after receiving at least eight savage blows, but these had not killed her. She had been strangled, and a towel had been used since one of her earrings was found attached to it. Although human bloodstains were found in Munster Square, Spilsbury believed that they were so slight that the murder had not been committed there. No, it was at Charlotte Street that Mme Gerard had been butchered; and Spilsbury's findings painted a grim picture. The attack took place by the back door, through which the unfortunate victim had been trying to escape; there was a spot of blood on the wall of the yard outside. But in the back room there was blood everywhere, human and animal blood mixed, on the door leading to the yard, the floor, the wall, even the ceiling. There was more blood on the sink and draining board, and in the cellar were a man's shirt and jacket, a towel and three pieces of cloth – all soaked through with blood. A similarly bloodstained butcher's overall was found in the back yard, and in the kitchen were found a chopping block and a butcher's knife. In the yard was a stable used by Voisin for his horse and trap; there, saturated with blood, was found a hearthrug, together with human hairs resembling those of Mme Gerard.

Surrounded by such damning evidence, Voisin made a written statement in which he stated that on the day of the murder he had gone to Munster Square, where he found the floor and carpets to be blood-soaked and where he also found Mme Gerard's head and hands on the kitchen table; none of the other body parts were there. Astonished, he thought a trap had been laid for him and, not knowing what to do, he cleaned up the blood – that was how his clothing became soaked with it – went home, had lunch, returned to Munster Square, collected the head and hands and went back to Charlotte Street. He denied killing her, said neither of them owed anything to the other (conveniently forgetting the £50 IOU) and completely exonerated Mme Roche from any involvement in the case.

When both Voisin and Mme Roche were charged with murder, Mme Roche immediately jumped to the conclusion that Voisin had incriminated her and shrieked profanities at him; he responded with a Gallic shrug of his shoulders and the comment, 'It's unfortunate.'

As was fully expected, Wensley's masterly evidence was hotly contested by the defence, who stated that the writing of the words 'Blodie Belgiam' was inadmissible; but the trial judge, Mr Justice Darling, held that 'there was no reason for thinking that the statement was involuntary', and this was later backed up by Mr Justice Lawrence in the Court of Appeal.

On the second day of the trial, the case against Berthe Roche – which had never been very strong regarding the murder – was thrown out. Voisin was found guilty, Mr Justice Darling helpfully pronounced the death sentence in French and on 1 March 1918 Mme Roche was indicted on a charge of being an accessory after the fact. She appeared before Mr Justice Avory, a judge with a droll sense of humour (once, at Winchester railway station, he tipped a porter sixpence. 'Is that all?' asked the porter and received the sardonic reply, 'You're lucky; the last time I was here, I gave a man seven years!').

And so it was in this case; Berthe Roche was sentenced to seven years' penal servitude. She went mad in prison, was transferred to an Insane Asylum and died there on 22 March 1919.

The day after her sentence, Voisin was hanged at Pentonville Prison, and the true circumstances of the murder died with both parties. So what really had brought about Mme Gerard's murder?

It is, of course, conjecture, but the pooled opinions of all of the interested participants for the prosecution were as follows.

On the night of the air raid, Mme Gerard had left her flat, initially seeking shelter but then deciding to seek comfort in the arms of her lover, Voisin. But upon her arrival at Charlotte Street, she discovered Voisin with Mme Roche, perhaps in bed, and the combination of the terror of the air raid and the shock of finding a rival who, quite possibly, had a temperament as excitable as her own, resulted in a furious row. It is more than probable that Mme Roche struck the blows to Mme Gerard's head, possibly with a poker; had Voisin, with his enormous strength, hit her, it is highly likely that her skull would have been shattered by the first blow. So it is likely that Voisin then throttled her with the towel to drown out her screams – the sound of the air raid and the anti-aircraft guns assisting – whilst Roche continued to frenziedly batter her rival. Now came the problem of how to dispose of the body, but Voisin relied on his trade as a butcher and dismembered it. Berthe Roche drew water from the communal tap in the yard to clean up the blood and informed a neighbour that Voisin had slaughtered a calf, in order to explain the bloodstains on his clothing. Now it was necessary to show – when the body was discovered – that the murder had taken place at Munster Square. Voisin went there the following morning and, possibly taking the head and/or hands with him, deposited drops of blood in the rooms. But then there was a change of plan; he took a sheet from the bed, returned home and, that night, wrapping the sheet around the unfortunate Mme Gerard's trunk, took that parcel and the parcel containing the legs in his horse and trap to the area of Regent Square, where he deposited them.

So why did he write those illiterate words, 'Blodie Belgiam'? Whatever the reason, the murder provided another gripping story for Wensley's casebook; and it also ensured Voisin's very brief meeting with a man named John Ellis.

He was the hangman at Pentonville.

* * *

On 29 August 1918 the police went on strike, demanding better pay and conditions plus union recognition. Two years previously, the Commissioner, Sir Edward Henry, had signed a Police Order threatening with dismissal any police officer who joined a union. Out of a force of 18,000, one third struck; Sir Edward, who had thought this to be a particularly suitable time to go on holiday, resigned. The strike leader, Police Constable Tommy Thiel, who had been sacked, was immediately reinstated on the directions of the rascally little Prime Minister, Lloyd George, who informed the aggrieved officers that immediate and substantial pay and pension improvements would be forthcoming.

For once, Lloyd George was as good as his word; no fool, he could sense the possibility of disorder and political disaster should just 12,000 police officers be available to police the capital. A constable's pay was immediately increased by 13s 0d per week. There was a war bonus of 12s 0d, a child allowance of 2s 6d for every child of school age, widows were given a weekly pension of 10s 0d and after twenty-six years' service a constable's pension of £1 15s 6d per week was granted. In addition, an organization to represent the officers' interests was set up. Unsurprisingly, the strike ended there and then.

And then, ten weeks later, the war came to an end. The general jubilation was marred by the news that Wensley's younger son, Harold William, who had passed through Sandhurst with flying colours, had been gazetted, like his brother, to the Lincolnshire Regiment and had been sent to the front, had contracted influenza on Armistice Day. Four days later, he was dead.

'These were the boys whom I showed how to live,' Wensley wrote in his memoirs, 'and who showed me how to die.'

# CHAPTER 20

# The Flying Squad

Harold Wensley was not the only person to fatally succumb to influenza; since March 1918 a particularly virulent form of the disease, known as Spanish 'flu, swept the world, and before it was contained, two years later, it claimed the lives of 100 million people, over six times the number of people who had perished in the war, which lasted twice as long as the pandemic.

So Wensley grieved for his sons and administered Harold's will, which left the sum of £334 9s 5d to his beneficiaries, then once more plunged into his work. This included two provincial murder investigations; and the fact that nobody was convicted was hardly Wensley's fault.

The first was the murder of Mrs Elizabeth Ridgley, a fifty-four-year-old shopkeeper, whose body was found on Monday, 27 January 1919 in her shop's kitchen in Hitchin, Hertfordshire; she had last been seen on the previous Saturday evening, and although moaning had been heard a few hours later, nobody had done anything about it. There were lacerated wounds on the back of her head and face and bruises on her back and arms. A bloodstained 4lb weight was found by her body, and her Irish Terrier had also been killed by a blow to the head.

The gormless local police came to the conclusion that death had occurred 'due to an accidental fall', and Wensley and Spilsbury were not called in until February, a fortnight later. The police's theory, said Wensley, 'was unaccountable to me', and although a local labourer named John Healy had been arrested, the judge at Hertfordshire Assizes, Mr Justice Darling, castigated the local police's assertion as 'absurd', adding, 'Every precaution seems to have been taken to ensure that no one should be detected.' Healy, who was said to have been 'lurking' near the shop, was acquitted within a few minutes of the jury retiring.

The second case was equally frustrating. Nellie Florence Ruby Rault was a nineteen-year-old member of Queen Mary's Army Auxiliary Corps who had been posted to the Haynes Park Royal Engineers Signals Service camp in Bedfordshire. She was last seen on Friday, 9 May 1919, but when she was missed at roll call the following morning a search was organized, and on Monday, 12 May her body was found in woodland 150 yards from the camp's gates. She had bruises on her face and had been stabbed five times, including twice in the breast and once in the heart. A long, sharp table knife was found by her body; it had been wiped clean of fingerprints.

Company Sergeant Major Montague Cecil Keith Hepburn of the Royal Engineers had been arrested and charged with her murder the day following the discovery of the body; he replied, 'I can say, sir that I am innocent; quite innocent, sir. A mistake has been made.'

The day after Hepburn's arrest, Nellie Rault was buried, and a week later, an inquest was opened. Hepburn refused to give evidence, but the coroner told the jury that he did not want them to be influenced by the fact that he had been arrested and stressed Hepburn's impressive army career: he had been Mentioned in Dispatches and awarded the Military Medal and the Belgian *Decoration Militaire avec Croix de Guerre.*

The verdict was that Nellie had been murdered by some 'person or persons unknown', and after two remands at the Bedford Divisional Court, in which the evidence was confused and contradictory, the charge against Hepburn was dismissed.

So with the body buried, the inquest concluded and the prime suspect discharged, someone suddenly had the bright idea of calling in Scotland Yard. It was not until 7 June that Wensley arrived; he carried out a proper investigation, his enquiries totally discredited Hepburn's alibis and a report was submitted to the Director of Public Prosecutions. Although no further action was taken, the Director concluded, 'I entertain a strong personal opinion as to the identity of the person who committed this offence.'

Whilst Wensley was carrying out this thankless task, the police went on strike once more. Out of the 18,200 Metropolitan Police officers, 1,056 struck – they were immediately dismissed, which brought about the end of the strike.

One of Wensley's other missions was to be sent to Ireland, to carry out investigations into the upsurge of violence by the Irish Volunteers (later known as the IRA) against members of the Royal Irish Constabulary and British troops. Over 300 people died in this campaign, and Wensley, certainly no coward, believed he would not return alive. Prior to his departure, he handed a parcel to Detective Inspector George Wright, asking him to retain it and, if he could not return it to him, to give it to Lollie. Like many mainland officers who have been sent to investigate terrorist activities in that troubled island, he never referred to it afterwards.

On 20 October 1919, Wensley's suggestions – previously made to Sir Basil Thomson, three years earlier – regarding the formation of what would become the Flying Squad, were eventually heeded; the new Commissioner, General the Right Honourable Sir Cecil Frederick Nevil Macready Bt, GCMG, KCB, split the Metropolitan Police District into four areas (they had previously been referred to as 'districts'), and Wensley was promoted to superintendent, as was Albert Hawkins; Arthur Neil and Francis Carlin were promoted to acting superintendents. This appointment for 'Special Duty' meant that Wensley now had control of all of East and some of North London.

Hawkins – he was known as 'Bouncing Albert' – was a stout, hearty, humorous man who never forgot a criminal's face or his voice; he once heard someone speaking in a West End office, recognized the voice as being that of a wanted man and arrested him. Hawkins was given control of most of South London.

Carlin was short and immaculately dressed. Much of his career had been spent in the West End; he had solved the Berkeley Hotel robbery in 1913, and when he dealt with a cheque forged in the name of Lord Lonsdale and told Luigi, the Berkeley's maître d'hôtel, that he knew who was responsible, Luigi bet him he was wrong. Luigi lost, and within a week the culprit was arrested, following a chase from a barber's shop. Carlin was to administer Central and West London.

Arthur Neil was known as 'Drooper Neil' because he had a most lugubrious expression. Years after the Jack the Ripper murders, he was convinced that the Ripper and Severin Klosowski, alias George Chapman, whom he sent to the gallows for three murders, were one and the same. He was given the task of supervising some of Central and the rest of North London.

Fred Thomas, the Superintendent Central (CID) remained in post as the chief executive officer for the Criminal Investigation Department, and Sir Trevor Bingham was appointed Assistant Commissioner (Crime).

The *Daily Mail* told its readers, 'It will be the business of "The Big Four" and their expert staff to apply up-to-date means to catch clever up-to-date criminals', adding optimistically, 'There is little doubt the police will win'.

They were all set to take the war against crime into the enemy's camp.

★  ★  ★

The end of the Great War was not the only cause of an upsurge in crime; the trend was also fuelled by ever-increasing unemployment and austerity. Soldiers who had fought bravely in France and

Belgium returned home to find not 'a fit country for heroes to live in' but a place where housing was poor, poverty was staring them in the face and world trade had all but collapsed. Now many of these men turned to crime. Younger men, too, who had known little parental guidance during the war, joined their ranks, as did large numbers of the lawless members of the immigrant communities.

Cars were stolen to be used in crime, especially of the 'smash and grab' variety – shop owners were forced to spend more money in putting up grilles on their windows. Guns were finding their way into the country and they were used to great effect in bank robberies, masked burglaries and gang rivalry. Pickpockets infested the streets, music halls and race tracks, and gang warfare, which had largely been confined to race meetings, now flooded out into the streets, where pitched battles were fought. Cashiers were being knocked down and robbed. Matters had gone quite far enough.

Within days of his new appointment, Wensley welcomed a number of detectives, including Detective Inspector Walter Hambrook, into his office.[16] These men had been specially selected for their skill at thief-taking and running informants and for their physical toughness, and Wensley outlined the plan of the new unit to them. The boundaries which had existed in the past were to be forgotten; they would work anywhere in London where they were needed, he told them. The gangs responsible for the current crime wave were to be smashed, broken up and convicted. 'The success or not of this mobile patrol scheme will depend on you,' he told them. 'But in twelve months' time, the commissioner must report to the Home Secretary. He will decide whether this experiment should either continue or be disbanded.'

The 'mobile' element that Wensley referred to consisted of two horse-drawn covered wagons, leased from the Great Western Railway. And as they trundled out into Whitehall, the only difference between these wagons and the thousands of others in the capital was that the boards showing the names and addresses of the businesses they purported to represent were fixed into slots. They were interchangeable, to suit any area of London where they were patrolling. That, and their cargo: half a dozen detectives in the back, peering out of spy-holes cut in the canvas covering.

The whole concept was simple and it was cheap: a dozen detectives, 'on loan' from their parent stations, being conveyed to

---

16 For a full account of the formation of the Flying Squad, see the author's *The Sweeney – The First Sixty Years of Scotland Yard's Crimebusting Flying Squad 1919–1978* (Wharncliffe Books, 2011).

their destinations to carry out observations, both static and mobile, able to be dropped off, to follow suspects on foot, on a bus, a tram or the Underground or to jump out and pluck the criminals, literally, out of thin air as they were in the act of stealing a car, picking a pocket or about to carry out a smash and grab raid.

The intended twelve months' trial was an unqualified success; so much so that by July 1920 two 26hp Crossley Tenders, formerly the property of the Royal Flying Corps, were purchased. Heavy, ungainly vehicles with thin tyres and no front brakes, only when they were specially modified were they able to reach a maximum speed of 40 mph. But they were considered to be mechanically sound, and beneath their khaki hoods they could conceal a dozen officers; on the roof, aerials manipulated by wires were used to receive radio signals. Unsurprisingly, due to the combination of wires and metal bars on the roof, the odd-looking Crossleys were nicknamed 'Bedsteads'.

On the evening of 15 September 1920 these two tenders set off on their first patrol, with Hambrook in charge. Their quest was to detect a gang who worked areas both north and south of the Thames; they had been carrying out smash and grab raids, terrorizing shopkeepers, and, two nights prior to the patrol, three of the gang had attacked an off-duty police constable named Nealon, who had attempted to intervene during one of their raids. He had been struck with a heavy, eight-sided iron bar and left for dead.

On the second night, Hambrook's men spotted the gang in a half-ton covered van and followed them all over South London, watching them reconnoitring various shops before returning to the Elephant & Castle, where they garaged their van before drifting away.

Now Hambrook had a focal point to which the gang must return before carrying out any further raids. He contacted the other tender, and the two teams of detectives kept observation on the garage in relays. After thirty-one hours of observations, at 4.00 am on 18 September, the gang returned. Their van was followed to Pimlico Road, where they fled after being disturbed attempting to break into a clothier's shop. After a pursuit by the detectives there was a tremendous fight, during which severe injuries were inflicted on both sides; and following the gang's arrest, a search of their van revealed a complete burglar's kit – plus the eight-sided iron bar used to batter PC Nealon a few days earlier.

Hambrook and his officers were warmly congratulated, both at Westminster police court and the Old Bailey, where the gang were sentenced to hard labour and penal servitude. In addition, the commissioner highly commended PC Nealon, to whom he awarded the sum of £5 – well worth having, when a constable's weekly wage was £3 5s 0d. Hambrook (by now a divisional detective inspector) was also commended, as were eleven of the Squad officers, who were each awarded £1 5s 0d.

There was now further publicity for the Squad's work: four days after the arrest of the gang, Mr G.T. Crook, the aptly named crime correspondent of the *Daily Mail*, published an article in which he referred to the work of the new unit, using the words 'flying squads of picked detectives' and referring to the criminals they arrested as having been 'picked up by the flying squads at all hours of the day and night ...'

The description stuck; the official name 'Mobile Patrol Experiment' was out, and the 'Flying Squad' was in.

Over the years, the vehicles were greatly improved, the personnel increased and the Squad has gone from strength to strength; and although it has sometimes proved as controversial as its creator, it has remained the premier crime-busting arm of the Metropolitan Police.

★ ★ ★

With promotion came a change. Wensley's waxed moustache came off, although his driver, Police Constable Webber, failed to notice until two weeks after its removal. Clean-shaven Wensley busied himself with all aspects of police work. In order to minimize the risk of being seen, a sophisticated gang rented a house close to a warehouse which they broke into, stealing furs and cloth to the value of £3,600. At the Old Bailey, nine of the gang received sentences varying from five years' penal servitude to nine months' hard labour. And when Harry Alfred Hawkins and William Dries stole 51,143 yards of khaki flannel, valued at £11,880 5s 4d, from the United States Army, Wensley was on hand to recover it.

Peter Beveridge, later to become head of the wartime Flying Squad and, later still, one of the 'Big Five' himself, recalled Wensley arriving in 1919 at the 'Eagle Hut', the recruits' training school in the Strand, there to instruct the embryo officers in the art of identifying criminals and how to register their features: 'Go from the top; hair, eyes, nose, mouth, age and build.'

Wensley's own description was provided by William Rawlings OBE, MC, then a new detective constable at Central Office (and later to become deputy commander of the CID): 'Thin, angular, very Jewish in appearance, with bright, piercing eyes that bored into you, slow and hesitant in his speech'. Although he spoke very slowly when questioning a suspect – so that the prisoner would be in no doubt what had been said – and his speech became almost like a stammer, there was nothing hesitant about Wensley's approach to picking the right officers for his brainchild. In 1922 Wensley sent for Fred Sharpe – then a detective sergeant (second class) – and told him, 'We're putting you in the Flying Squad'. Sharpe was still attached to 'J' Division, so he was merely 'on loan' to the Squad, as were many others, but he remained there for nine years; he would eventually complete his career by becoming the head of the Squad.

Wensley never believed in putting his subordinates 'on the report' for minor disciplinary matters, which he referred to as 'official naggings'. He thought that instituting disciplinary proceedings for a minor breach of the regulations was likely to break a man's spirit, when a firm word was all that was needed to rectify matters.

It is highly likely that he recalled the times when he himself had been unfairly treated, firstly when he was initially refused admission to the CID and secondly when obstacles were put in the way of promotion. Nevertheless, Wensley was a strict disciplinarian; although he had no objection to his Flying Squad officers discarding their jackets on a hot day, he insisted that they must also remove their braces as well. 'I expect you all to behave like gentlemen,' he said, 'and you never see gentlemen in their motor cars in their braces!'

Then there was Ted Greeno, the two-fisted terror of the racetrack gangs; of Wensley he said, 'He spoke slowly in a way that made criminals think he was soft. It was a mistake they made only once.' Greeno regarded Wensley as 'the greatest policeman of my time, or anybody else's', so on 15 September 1923 he was delighted when Wensley told him, 'We have been watching your career and we think it is a career worthy of the Criminal Investigation Department.' Greeno was a member of the Flying Squad for seventeen years and bowed out of the Metropolitan Police after over thirty-eight years' service. He was one of the 'Big Five', had been commended by the commissioner on eighty-six occasions and was appointed MBE.

Wensley, too, had been appointed MBE in April 1920, and still the congratulations were flooding in: by a judge at the Old Bailey and the Director of Public Prosecutions, firstly for 'brilliant work in respect of the arrest of seven persons dealing in gold coins' (the prisoners included a barrister and diamond merchants) and then, six weeks later, for 'valuable assistance in a case of manslaughter'. Six weeks after that, there was another commendation from a judge at the County of London Sessions for his action in a case of officebreaking, before Wensley involved himself in another murder investigation. It was considered so sensitive that in December

1921 he was summoned by the Director of Public Prosecutions to discuss the case.

Suspicion had fallen upon a solicitor, Major Herbert Rowse Armstrong TD, MA, who lived in Hay, in Brecon. It was believed that he had been endeavouring to murder a rival lawyer, Oswald Martin, by means of arsenical poisoning. On 26 October 1921 Mr Martin had been invited to tea by Major Armstrong; and after pouring him a cup of tea, Armstrong, with incredible uncouthness, handed Martin a buttered scone with the words, 'Excuse my fingers'. Martin ate it. That evening, after dinner, Martin was violently sick, and his illness continued for five days. The family doctor, Dr Tom Hincks, was called; initially, he believed that this was a severe bilious attack but he was puzzled by Martin's high pulse rate. But when Martin's father-in-law, who was the town's chief chemist, remarked that Armstrong regularly purchased large quantities of arsenic from his shop, Dr Hincks recalled that Martin's sister-in-law had displayed similar symptoms after eating a chocolate from a box which had been anonymously delivered to Oswald Martin's house. He also remembered the death of Major Armstrong's wife that February; at the time he had thought the reasons for her demise confusing, but had believed the cause was heart disease, arising from nephritis and gastritis.

Something was badly wrong; Dr Hincks sent the remaining chocolates, plus a sample of Martin's urine, to the Clinical Research Association in London, and at the same time he wrote to the Home Office, outlining his suspicions. They were well founded; two of the remaining chocolates had been tampered with and one was found to contain 2.12 grains of arsenic. Martin's urine sample was found to contain one thirty-third of a grain of arsenic, and the Association's report duly met up with Dr Hincks' letter on the desk of the Director of Public Prosecutions.

Martin had received at least twenty further invitations to tea, so it came as a relief when Armstrong was arrested in his office on 28 December. In his pocket was one-twentieth part of an ounce of arsenic – used, he said, to eradicate dandelions – and there were another two ounces in his desk. Within days, his wife's body was exhumed from the graveyard at Cusop churchyard. Three and a half grains of arsenic were all that was left of the massive dose used to murder her; it was, said the analyst, 'the largest amount of arsenic I have found in any case of arsenical poisoning'. At six inches shorter than his neurotic, domineering wife, Armstrong had been badly hen-pecked, but after forging her will to make himself the sole beneficiary, his wife died, whereupon he started smoking, drinking and going on European holidays; he also became infected with syphilis and proposed to a rich widow. Not altogether unsurprisingly, he was charged with his wife's murder.

As a lawyer, Armstrong was used to court procedure; but at his trial, which commenced at Hereford Assizes on 3 April 1922, his scathing questioning by Mr Justice Darling resulted in him being found guilty. It was not lost on the jury that the time of his arrest, just before New Year, was hardly the season for poisoning dandelions; and within a month, he was hanged at Gloucester prison.

★ ★ ★

In May and also September 1921 Wensley was granted periods of leave; they were undoubtedly needed to recharge his batteries, because on 30 November 1921 Superintendent Thomas retired and Wensley assumed responsibility for CID Central, as well as Central and East London. Hawkins remained in post, and Carlin and Neil received promotion to substantive superintendent.

Ronald True was as mad as a March hare; he hit Olive Young (an 'unfortunate') on the head with a rolling pin, then stuffed a towel down her throat and throttled her with her dressing gown cord, before stealing her jewellery; and when he was arrested by Superintendent Hawkins, he was in possession of a loaded revolver. Whilst on remand, he struck up a friendship with Henry Jacoby, who, while working as a pageboy at the Spencer Hotel, Portland Place, had battered the elderly Lady White to death. There was a great deal of public controversy after both men were convicted and sentenced to death, since Jacoby, who was nineteen, was hanged on 7 June 1922 but True was reprieved. He was sent to Broadmoor, where he was regarded as a popular inmate; he died there in 1951, aged sixty.

Wensley had supervised the investigations of those two cases, but his next case was one where he rolled his sleeves up and got actively involved in the enquiry. The victim was George Stanley Grimshaw, a married family man who was aged fifty-four and had been found battered to death in Highams Park, Chingford on 17 May 1922. It was an area frequented by courting couples, and it was initially thought that Grimshaw was a voyeur who had been attacked as a result of his activities; in fact, this theory was given some credibility by the fact that a young man and woman had been seen leaving the area of the killing. But it was nothing of the kind; it had been a carefully thought out, premeditated murder, devised by the young couple themselves.

They were twenty-three-year-old William James and Elsie Yeldham, a year younger – they had married three days after the murder, so that she could not be compelled to give evidence against her husband. Grimshaw, said to be infatuated by Elsie, allowed himself to be enticed by her into the woods, where he was attacked by Yeldham, wielding a heavy spanner. The pair then rifled his pockets and found themselves £15 the richer. It was a painstaking investigation, and both were convicted of murder and sentenced to death. Only Yeldham was hanged, on 5 September 1922 at Pentonville Prison, courtesy of hangman John Ellis; Elsie was spared a meeting with him because her sentence was commuted to one of life imprisonment.

So that was a case involving two lovers bringing about the death of a third party; very much like Wensley's next case, which would become the most controversial of his career. Almost a century later, it still arouses fierce polemics.

# CHAPTER 21

# The Star-Crossed Lovers

From time to time during his career, Wensley – through no fault of his own – became embroiled in cases which should have been nothing to do with him. It happened with the Houndsditch murders, which was a City Police case; it happened with Stinie Morrison, and that was a 'W' Division case.

So when Detective Superintendent Arthur Neil – who now had charge of 'K' Division – went on leave in 1922, it fell to Wensley to take over his area in his absence; this would involve him in one of the most controversial cases of the twentieth century.

★ ★ ★

Edith Jessie Graydon and Percy Thompson were married in January 1915; she was twenty-two and he was twenty-six. Thompson had enlisted in the London Scottish Regiment in 1916, but was discharged as unfit, suffering from an enlarged heart which would continue to give him problems. He was a shipping clerk in the City, his wife was the manageress of a wholesale milliner's business and both of them were earning good money: a total of £12 per week. There were no children of the marriage, and they lived at 41 Kensington Gardens, Ilford. It was a respectable area, and it appeared the Thompsons were a contented couple. However, Edith Thompson thought – perhaps with some justification – that her husband was as dull as ditchwater, and opinion would become divided on whether she was, at best, an adulterous romantic dreamer or, at worst, a scheming murderess.

During the evening of 3 October 1922 the Thompsons had been to the Criterion Theatre to see a play, *The Dipper*, with friends and, having caught the 11.30 pm train from Liverpool Street, they arrived at Ilford and began the walk home along Belgrave Road, which was a poorly lit thoroughfare. Just before midnight, they had reached the junction with Kensington Gardens when a man suddenly overtook them, pushed Mrs Thompson aside and attacked Percy Thompson with a knife. He suffered four slight cuts below the ribs, two more on the right of the jaw and a longer cut on the inside of the right arm, all of which would have caused him some discomfort. But there were also two cuts, both two inches deep, in his neck ('which required considerable force', said Dr Percy James Drought later), one of which severed his carotid artery. These were the cuts which resulted in Percy Thompson's almost immediate death.

But there were witnesses at the scene almost instantly, to whom Edith Thompson made no mention of her husband being stabbed. 'Oh my God,' she cried to Dora Finch Pittard, who was walking along Belgrave Road. 'Will you help me? My husband is ill; he is bleeding.'

And John Webber, who lived nearby at 59 De Vere Gardens, heard Edith Thompson cry, 'Oh, don't, oh, don't!' which, Mr Webber added, 'was in a most piteous manner'.

When Edith Thompson was visited by Police Sergeants Walter Grimes and Walter Mew, three hours later, and asked what had happened, she replied, 'I don't know; I can't say – I only know my husband suddenly dropped down and screamed out, "Oh!" ' She added that she and her husband had not spoken to anybody in Belgrave Road.

Later that morning, Wensley received a telephone call from Divisional Detective Inspector Francis Hall, the head of 'K' Division's CID, and consequently made his way to Ilford police station. There he saw Edith Thompson, still in her evening gown and quite obviously distressed; she had been asked by Detective Inspector Richard Sellars to accompany him to the station. There appeared to be no rhyme or reason for the attack. Could the person responsible have been some shell-shocked veteran of the Great War? Nobody knew.

Wensley spent some time talking to Edith Thompson to determine why her husband had been murdered, without success, and she later returned home. He then spoke to Richard Halliday Thompson, the dead man's brother, and discovered that the Thompsons had had a lodger, Frederick Edward Francis Bywaters, aged twenty, and that it appeared a romantic relationship existed between him and Edith Thompson.

It was quickly discovered that Bywaters was a ship's writer and that he might well be away on a voyage; but if he was not, it was important to find him, even if only to eliminate him from the enquiry. It was discovered that Bywaters had visited the parents and sister of Edith Thompson at their home at 231 Shakespeare Crescent, Manor Park, a short distance away from the Thompsons' address, on the night of the murder; he had known the family for some time, because he had gone to school with the sons of the household. The daughter, Avis Graydon, mentioned to Bywaters that her sister and brother-in-law had gone to the theatre that evening, and Bywaters had left the house at approximately 11.00 pm.

Wensley discovered that Bywaters' widowed mother lived at 11 Westow Street, Upper Norwood, and now he made use of his creation, the Flying Squad, to race across London and see if he was there. Late that evening, Detective Inspector Frank Page interviewed Mrs Bywaters – her son was absent – and took possession of a number of letters and a telegram from Mrs Thompson.

The same evening, Bywaters went to Shakespeare Crescent in possession of a copy of the *Evening News* which carried a report of the murder and told Edith Thompson's father, 'This is a terrible thing if it is true.' Detective Ernest Foster arrested him there for murder, and he was taken to Ilford police station, where he was seen by Inspector Sellars, who took possession of his overcoat. This was examined by Dr Drought, since there appeared to be blood spots on the sleeves. Told he would be detained, Bywaters truculently exclaimed, 'Why? I know nothing about it.'

In the presence of Sellars and Wensley, Bywaters made a voluntary statement. He said that he had been a paying guest at the Thompsons' address between 18 June and 1 August 1921, had been 'exceedingly good friends' with Edith Thompson, and had left after he had interfered in an altercation between the Thompsons. He added that he had written a few letters to her, as she had to him. On the night of the murder, he said, having left the Graydons' house he had caught a train at 11.30 pm to Victoria and gone from there to his mother's house in Upper Norwood. He made no admission to the murder, signed the statement as correct and was detained.

The following day, 5 October, Sellars asked Edith Thompson if she could give any further information as to her husband's attacker, and she agreed to make a voluntary statement, saying, 'I will tell you if I possibly can.'

In a typewritten statement she stated that she knew Bywaters and that they had corresponded, saying that 'his letters to me and mine to him were couched in affectionate terms'. At the time of the murder, she said, her husband had gone into the roadway, he staggered and was bleeding, and 'I cannot remember whether I saw anyone else there or not'.

She signed that statement as being correct; and then an anomaly occurred which has never been satisfactorily cleared up.

Sellars gave evidence that, following her making of the statement, he escorted Edith Thompson to the matron's room and that as he did so they passed the library, where Bywaters had been detained. Upon seeing him, she cried, 'Oh, God, oh, God, what can I do?

Why did he do it? I did not want him to do it!' She then added, 'I must tell the truth' and volunteered a further statement, which read as follows:

> When I got near Endsleigh Gardens, a man rushed out from the Gardens and knocked me away and pushed me away from my husband. I was dazed for a moment. When I recovered I saw my husband scuffling with a man. The man whom I know as Freddie Bywaters was running away. He was wearing a blue overcoat and a grey hat. I knew it was him although I did not see his face.

All well and good. However ... in her memoirs, *A Woman at Scotland Yard*, Detective Inspector (Second Class) Lilian Wyles BEM spoke of being told by Wensley to go immediately to Ilford police station. There, Wensley instructed her to go to the room where Edith Thompson was detained, to listen to what she said and to keep her own answers noncommittal. Later, Miss Wyles said, Edith Thompson got a glimpse of Bywaters. 'Her hand flew to her mouth, there was a slight scream and Mrs Thompson moaned, "Not that, not that! No! No! Why did he do it? Oh, God!" '

This was rather at variance with the circumstances of the identification and the blurted-out admission as recorded by Sellars. Moreover, Wensley did not mention Miss Wyles' contribution in his memoirs, nor did Sellars admit, when he gave evidence at the Old Bailey, that she was present. To confuse matters even further, Thompson would later tell the jury at the Old Bailey, 'He [Bywaters] was brought into the CID room, where I was', and Bywaters agreed with that account. What was more, Miss Wyles did not give evidence at the trial. Perhaps Sellars' recollection was the better of the two; after all, Miss Wyles believed that this had happened in 1923, a year after the actual event.

But whatever the circumstances, it was sufficient for Sellars to tell Bywaters, 'I am going to charge you and Mrs Thompson with the wilful murder of Percy Thompson.'

'Why her?' replied Bywaters. 'Mrs Thompson was not aware of my movements.'

He then made a further statement, in which he said that he had waited for the Thompsons on the night of the murder:

> When near Endsleigh Gardens I pushed her to one side, also pushing him further up the street. I said to him, 'You have got to separate from your wife.' He said, 'No'. I said, 'You will have to.' We struggled. I took the knife from my pocket and

we fought and he got the worst of it. Mrs Thompson must have been spellbound for I saw nothing of her during the fight ... The reason I fought with Thompson was because he never acted like a man with his wife. He always seemed several degrees lower than a snake. I loved her and could not go on seeing her leading that life. I did not intend to kill him. I only meant to injure him. I gave him an opportunity of standing up to me as a man but he wouldn't. I have had the knife for some time; it was a sheath knife. I threw it down a drain when I was running through Endsleigh Gardens.

He and Edith Thompson were then charged; she made no reply, whilst Bywaters muttered, 'It is wrong; it is wrong.'

In the space of just one year, Thompson had sent Bywaters 62 letters, and during the course of the forthcoming trial, 32 letters, notes and telegrams were produced. It is possible that those that were withheld contained details of an abortion or miscarriage, which would have proved disastrous to Thompson, had the jury seen them. But all of the letters were of a highly passionate nature and many of them were accompanied by newspaper cuttings, fifty in all, some of which referred to cases of poisoning; in some letters she also made reference to putting something bitter in her husband's tea and using an electric light bulb, but 'he found a piece'. Later, she wrote, 'I was buoyed up with the hope of the "light bulb" and I used a lot – big pieces, too – not powdered – and it has no effect ... You tell me not to leave finger marks on the box.' In a further letter she mentioned the effects of digitalis and asked, 'Is it any use?' Many of these letters were found in a 'ditty box' belonging to Bywaters, a week later, on board the SS *Morea*.

The trial began at the Old Bailey on 6 December 1922. The judge was Mr Justice Shearman and the prosecution was led by the Solicitor General, Sir Thomas Inskip KC. Cecil Whiteley KC appeared for Bywaters and Sir Henry Curtis Bennett KC for Edith Thompson. Apart from being charged with Percy Thompson's murder, both were charged with conspiracy to murder; Edith Thompson was also charged with soliciting and inciting Bywaters to murder her husband, as well as causing Percy Thompson to be administered with poison and broken glass.

The witnesses duly gave their evidence, including Detective John Hancock, who had retrieved a sheath knife from a drain on the north side of Seymour Gardens, about 250 yards from Kensington Gardens, which was more or less where Bywaters had said it would be found.

Bywaters' testimony differed somewhat from the statement he had made to the police. Examined by his barrister, Cecil Whiteley, and referring to the confrontation with Thompson, he said, 'After I swung him round, I said to him, "Why don't you get a divorce or separation, you cad?" He said, "I know what it is you want, but I am not going to give it to you; it would make it too pleasant for both of you." I said, "You take a delight in making Edie's life a hell." Then he said, "I've got her, I'll keep her and I'll shoot you." As he said that, he punched me in the chest with his left fist, and I said, "Oh, will you?" and drew a knife and put it in his arm.'

So the defence now was that Bywaters, believing that Percy Thompson intended to shoot him, had acted in self-defence; what was more, he had no exact recollection of how Thompson had come to receive the stab wounds in the neck, but 'they had got there, somehow'.

In cross-examination Bywaters stated that he believed that the references made by Edith Thompson to the broken and powdered glass and the poisons were to do with her committing suicide; this did not sound particularly convincing.

The Home Office pathologist, Sir Bernard Spilsbury, performed a post mortem examination on Percy Thompson's exhumed body on 3 November. He was, of course, aware that glass had been mentioned in the case and possibly administered to Thompson, but could find no trace of glass or the scars it would inevitably have left on the walls of the gullet, stomach or intestines. In addition, there was no trace of poison being administered.

It was a triumph for Sir Henry Curtis Bennett, who appeared for Edith Thompson. 'Does it all come to this?' he asked. 'That there has been no trace whatever in the post mortem of any glass having been administered, either in large pieces or powdered?'

'That is so,' replied Sir Bernard.

'And as far as poisons are concerned, there is no trace whatever of any poison ever having been administered?' asked Sir Henry.

Once more, Sir Bernard concurred.

It appeared that the prosecution had shot itself in the foot; and possibly all would have been well for Edith Thompson had she heeded her counsel's advice and not given evidence. But she did.

One of the most telling pieces of evidence against her was a letter she wrote to Bywaters, the day before the murder, which included the words, 'Do something tomorrow night, will you?'

During her examination in chief, Edith Thompson denied having seen Bywaters during the attack, but when she was asked, 'Was it when you saw him [Bywaters] at the police station that you detailed the full story?' she replied, 'No. I made my second statement, which is the true statement after Inspector [*sic*] Wensley had said to me, "It is no use your saying he did not do it; he has already told us he has." The inspector then said to me, "Go back to the CID room and think about it, and I will come for you in half an hour." When at the end of that half-hour Inspector Hall came to me, I made my statement.'

But in cross-examination she performed poorly; there was a mass of letters to refer to and a lot of inferences to be drawn from them. In one letter to Bywaters she had written:

I'm going to try the glass again occasionally – when it is safe. I've got an electric light bulb this time.

During some blistering cross-examination by the Solicitor General she was asked, with reference to this letter, 'When was it likely to be safe?'

She replied, 'There was no question of it being safe; I was not going to try it.'

'Why did you tell Bywaters you were going to try it when it was safe?'

'Still to let him think that I was willing to do what he wanted.'

'You are representing that this young man was seriously suggesting to you that you should poison and kill your husband?' asked the prosecution.

By now, Edith Thompson was on the back foot, because she replied, 'I did not suggest it.'

'I thought that was the suggestion?' pursued the Solicitor General.

Again, Edith Thompson replied, 'I did not suggest that.'

'What was your suggestion?'

'He said he would give him something.'

And now the judge intervened: 'Give him something in his food; you answered my question a little while ago that it was to give him something to make him ill?'

This elicited the astonishing answer, 'That is what I surmised, that I should give him something so that when he had a heart attack, he would not be able to resist it.'

She was now putting the onus on Bywaters and claiming that she had had no intention of carrying out the plan.

The jury were present to try a case of murder, not adultery. But that was the slant put on the case, especially when in his summing-up the judge suggested that the two accused felt that the love that Percy Thompson had for his wife was 'something improper ... and that the love of a woman for her lover, illicit and clandestine, is something great and noble. I am certain that you, like any other right-minded person, will be filled with disgust at such a notion.'

It appears that the jury did feel that way; on 11 December 1922 they retired at 3.32 pm and two hours and eleven minutes later returned to find both Bywaters and Thompson guilty of murder.

'I say the verdict of the jury is wrong,' snapped Bywaters. 'Edith Thompson is not guilty. I am no murderer, I am not an assassin.'

When the death sentence was passed on Thompson, she cried, 'I am not guilty; oh God, I am not guilty!'

There were petitions and an appeal, which the appeal court judges described as 'squalid and rather indecent'; but nothing could save the star-crossed lovers. On 9 January 1923 they were both hanged, Thompson at Holloway prison and Bywaters at Pentonville.

With hindsight, it is easy to ask 'what if?' – but in a case such as this, the need to do so is irresistible. On the evidence available at the time of the arrest, Bywaters would have been charged with murder as would Edith Thompson; but if Bywaters had destroyed those incriminating letters and if Mrs Thompson had heeded her barrister's advice and kept well clear of the witness box, she would undoubtedly have been acquitted, and perhaps Bywaters too, on the grounds of self defence.

About Bywaters' guilt there seems little doubt, but Edith Thompson? Was she really a cold, calculating murderess, wanting to rid herself of an older, tiresome husband in favour of a dashing young lover who sailed the seven seas? Or was she a dreamer, someone in love with love who wrote long, passionate and perhaps rather silly letters to a very susceptible young man which led to tragedy?

Wensley – who, strangely, was never called to give evidence at the Old Bailey – had no doubt that it was a joint case of premeditated murder in which, he said, 'it was hard to see a redeeming feature'. Lilian Wyles, on the other hand, said, 'I never thought her wicked enough to plan Percy Thompson's murder. She had lived in a romantic fantasy, writing foolishly to an impressionable young man and not counting the consequences.' Spilsbury thought her guiltless of any attempt to poison her husband or to get rid of him in any other way.

Perhaps the last word on this very unhappy affair should be left to Edith Thompson's barrister, Sir Henry Curtis Bennett, who would later tell a friend:

I know – I am convinced – that Mrs Thompson would be alive today if she had taken my advice. She spoiled her chances by her evidence and demeanour. I had a perfect answer to everything, which I am sure would have won an acquittal if she had not been a witness. She was a vain woman and an obstinate one. She had an idea that she could carry the jury. Also she realized the enormous public interest and decided to play up to it by entering the witness box. Her imagination was highly developed but it failed to show her the mistake she was making. I could have saved her.

# Chapter 22

# Chief Constable of the CID

Sir Nevil Macready had been a good commissioner; he had a bluff and hearty manner, was able to communicate well with his men and had advanced great structural reforms. He was a resolute man, too, because when the Police Strike of 1919 was looming, he informed the Cabinet that he would resign if – as had happened previously – one single striker was reinstated.

His successor, Brigadier-General Sir William Thomas Francis Horwood GBE, KCB, DSO, was a disappointment. This was strange, since it appeared he had the right qualities for leadership: during a distinguished career in the First World War he had been Mentioned in Dispatches on seven occasions. He also had prior police experience: as head of the LNER Transport Police, a chief constable in the Metropolitan Police, then being advanced to Assistant Commissioner 'A' Department, then to Deputy Commissioner and finally, in 1920, to Commissioner. But he was not liked. He made no attempt to get to know his men by visiting them at their police stations or taking heed of their opinions. A clerk in his office described him thus:

> He was an unattractive man who mistook arrogance for leadership. I never saw him smile or return a courtesy and his attitude towards his job seemed to be one of distasteful necessity.

When a forty-two-year-old lunatic named Walter Tatam sent Sir William a box of chocolates on 9 November 1922, he ate them, thinking they were a present on his fifty-fourth birthday from his daughter Beryl. Unfortunately, the walnut whip chocolates had been laced with weedkiller, and within minutes he collapsed in agony. An unsympathetic Police Force immediately dubbed him 'The Chocolate Soldier', after Oscar Straus' successful 1908 operetta. It was also discovered that similarly poisoned chocolate éclairs had been sent to Assistant Commissioners Sir Trevor Bingham and Frank Elliott on the same day – but hearing the shrieks for assistance from Edith Ellen Drysdale, Sir William's secretary, may have prevented the two other senior officers from tucking into their unexpected treats.

Wensley assembled a small team to hunt down the would-be assassin, but it was not until 1 February 1923 that Tatam was traced. His flat was found to contain more poisoned chocolates, he rushed downstairs towards the arresting officers, babbling incoherently and brandishing a swordstick, and he was later sent to an asylum.

As far as the Metropolitan Police were concerned, the bad news was that Sir William survived for another twenty years; the good news for his secretary, Miss Drysdale, was that she married one of Tatam's other intended victims and became Lady Bingham.

★ ★ ★

A huge, fire-raising insurance swindle was so serious that Wensley took charge of it personally. Joseph Engelstein, James Bernard Stolerman and Julius Brust – all cabinetmakers – had for some considerable time been defrauding insurance companies out of vast sums of money. Engelstein demanded £100 to torch small premises and £1,000 for large ones, and had also defrauded a commission set up to award money to East End businessmen whose properties had suffered bomb damage during the war.

In two years Engelstein had set seven fires, which netted him and his associates £17,500; as a sideline, he also arranged bogus burglaries. However, fire-raising was his speciality, and Engelstein was good at it; he used wood-shavings doused in petrol which would be ignited at the bottom of staircases, and also a special petrol compound inside a zinc-lined box. 'The stuff I use will never be traced', he boasted. Not all of Engelstein's fire-raisings were initially successful; the damage in one of them was so slight that only a few pounds in compensation were awarded, but Engelstein soon put that right. Within ten days, there was another fire at the same premises which resulted in an £8,000 payout from the insurance company.

With Wensley's men– including the Flying Squad – working flat-out, two informants were forthcoming who pointed the finger in the right direction. But more concrete evidence was required, and it arrived in May 1923, when the three conspirators arranged to burn down a four-storey cabinetmaking factory in Columbia Road, Hackney – it belonged to Stolerman – which had been insured for £3,700. Stolerman had previously been paid out £5,349 for fire damage at one of his showrooms; now, his insurance company (whose suspicions were seriously aroused) declared that when his policy expired in June they would not renew it – hence the necessity for a fire prior to that date.

The zinc-lined box with its compound was found intact at the factory. A slow-burning fuse had been attached to permit the men to escape before the box exploded. But in order to make doubly sure of the fire, they had also sprinkled petrol all over the premises, and when the fuse was lit, the vapour from the petrol ignited. They were seen running from the building, Brust with his trousers alight. Engelstein and Stolerman both suffered burns, which Engelstein explained had been due to throwing paraffin on a furnace and Stolerman claimed were from an exploding geyser in his bathroom.

During the seven-day trial at the Old Bailey, the witnesses called by the conspirators to provide alibis for them were disbelieved, and the trio were sentenced to penal servitude, six years for Engelstein, five for Stolerman and four for Brust.

On 28 February 1924, during a Commons sitting, Mr Wardlaw-Milne MP thunderously demanded to know if the three accused were *foreigners*, and if so, would they be deported? He was soothed by the reply from the Undersecretary of State for the Home Department, who informed him that they were indeed foreigners and that they had been recommended for deportation at the conclusion of their sentences. But only Brust was actually deported; Engelstein died in prison and Stolerman, a White Russian, was not accepted by the Soviet government.

A few months after the fire-raisers had been sentenced, Wensley was out in the field again; this time it was to do with what at first glance appeared to be suicide, but turned out to be nothing of the kind.

A twenty-year-old girl named Florence Jones had become infatuated with a worthless individual named Robert Sheppard, aged twenty-three, who was clearly unbalanced. In March 1922 he had been charged with the murder of a woman near Reading; his confession was found to have been unreliable, and the case was dismissed. He had already tried to strangle Florence Jones but had later convinced her that he was now a reformed character. Not so; she was found dead in their flat at Tottenham, apparently the victim of gas poisoning.

Sheppard would later say that the pair had become depressed at their future prospects and that they had mutually agreed to commit suicide. Florence, he said, had turned on the gas tap in the kitchen, then asked him to wait in another room before returning. He did so, but then bitterly regretted what had happened and returned to the kitchen, but was too late. However, as well as having a gas tube near her mouth, Florence also had a belt tied tightly round her throat and could not have turned the gas on herself.

'I'm not having this,' said Wensley, and he didn't; although Sheppard was found guilty of murder at the Old Bailey, the jury added a recommendation for mercy. However, the judge, Sir Rigby Swift, sentenced him to death, telling the jury that their endorsement would be forwarded to the Home Office. Sheppard's barrister stated that an appeal would be lodged, but Sheppard refused it, saying he was happy with the decision and wanted to die. Nevertheless, he was reprieved and the sentence was commuted to life imprisonment; but whilst serving his sentence at Parkhurst Prison, he attacked a warder's daughter and, not before time, was sent to Broadmoor.

★ ★ ★

Reported crimes for 1923 had actually dropped to 15,383, but the annual cost of running the Metropolitan Police had risen, to a staggering £7,838,251.

But then, newspaper headlines from a bizarre and horrific murder reverberated around the world, and the case was dropped neatly into Wensley's lap on 1 May 1924. He was in his office when he received a visitor; it was an old comrade, the former Divisional Detective Inspector of 'L' Division, John Beard, who told Wensley that he had been approached by a friend, Mrs Jessie Mahon, who had handed him a Waterloo Station cloakroom ticket which had fallen from her husband's pocket. Suspecting (quite correctly) some kind of infidelity, she asked Beard if he could investigate further. He discovered that the ticket referred to a locked Gladstone bag; he had lifted the flaps at the side and saw that it contained items of women's clothing which appeared bloodstained. He had then returned the bag to the cloakroom, instructed Mrs Mahon to insert the ticket back in her husband's pocket and informed Wensley.

The case was given to Chief Detective Inspector Percy Savage; it was the first murder he would investigate. Savage – who made no mention of Wensley at all in his memoirs – said that he managed to get hold of a sample of the bloodied material and sent it to a Harley Street specialist, who stated that it was human blood. However, in *his* memoirs, Wensley stated that 'there had not yet been time to have them scientifically tested'. Of the two versions, Wensley's sounds the likelier. Meanwhile, two officers kept observation at the cloakroom, and the following day, when Patrick Herbert Mahon, aged twenty-five, retrieved the bag, he was arrested. 'Rubbish!' exclaimed Mahon, but was informed it was not rubbish and that he would do as he was told.

Wensley was dining when he was informed that Mahon was at the Yard, and he went there immediately. The bag was opened and in it was found a cook's knife and some bloodstained items of women's clothing, including a pair of bloomers, two pieces of white silk, a scarf and a brown canvas bag marked 'EBK', all of which had been sprinkled with Sanitas, a disinfectant.

Asked to account for his possession of these items, Mahon replied, 'I'm fond of dogs ... I suppose I carried home meat for dogs in it.' Unsurprisingly, he was told that this was not a believable explanation. After an hour, Mahon volunteered the first of several statements, saying that a woman had died following a quarrel during which he had been attacked and she had struck her head on a coal-scuttle.

The initials 'EBK' on the bag referred to its owner, Emily Beilby Kaye, aged thirty-four, a secretary, who over the years had accumulated considerable savings of £600. Mahon had been employed as a sales manager, and the two soon commenced an adulterous relationship. Good-looking Mahon had, in fact, been a serial adulterer from soon after his marriage in 1910 and, what was more, had been in trouble with the police, being bound over after forging cheques, followed by a twelve-month prison sentence for embezzlement. He had lost his job because of his succession of amorous affairs and in 1916 had broken into a bank and attacked a girl with a hammer. Sentencing him for this to five years' penal servitude at Guildford Assizes, Mr Justice Darling told him, 'I have come to the conclusion that you are not only a burglar, not only a coward but a thorough-paced hypocrite.'

In the two months before her death, Miss Kaye's bank balance had been whittled down, leaving a balance of £70; the rest had gone to Mahon. She had also discovered she was pregnant, and Mahon promised that they would go to South Africa together, where they would be married. In fact, he had no intention of doing this; he rented a bungalow at Pevensey Bay, using the name of Waller, and Miss Kaye moved in. And while Mahon was living at home in Kew, making plans for Kaye's murder, he met another woman, Miss Ethel Duncan, had dinner with her and induced her to agree to spend the Easter holiday with him at the rented bungalow.

But before that could happen, Emily Kaye had to die. Mahon hit her on the head with an axe, so hard that the shaft broke, and then dismembered her body. He placed her remains in a trunk – also marked 'EBK' – and then spent the night with Miss Duncan in the room next door. The following day, Mahon made an excuse for them to return to London, since the body was starting to decompose, and during the following week he worked hard to dispose of it, eventually depositing the Gladstone bag at Waterloo station on Sunday 28 April.

During the early hours of 3 May, Wensley and Savage travelled down to the bungalow, where they discovered a scene of such unimaginable horror that Spilsbury, himself inured to dreadful sights, stated it was the most gruesome he had ever seen.

There were bloodstains on the sitting room floor and on the doorframe, also a bloodstained saw and an axe with a broken handle. In the trunk were Miss Kaye's limbless remains. The heart and 37 pieces of flesh which had been cut or sawn were found in a hatbox and a biscuit tin, and other body parts had been boiled in a saucepan. In the dining room and sitting room fire grates, plus on an ash-dump outside, were almost 1,000 bone fragments. Spilsbury meticulously set to work and was able almost to reconstruct the skeleton and also to say that Miss Kaye had been between one and three months pregnant. Of the head there was no sign, and Mahon said he had burnt it. This may have been true; Spilsbury later put a sheep's head on a fire, and within four hours it had been reduced to unrecognizable ashes.

Charged with murder, Mahon calmly replied, 'I've already made a statement. It wasn't murder, as my statement clearly shows.'

At his five-day trial at Lewes Assizes, which commenced on 15 July 1924 before Mr Justice Avory, Mahon presented a picture of manly innocence, enhanced by an immaculate seven-guinea suit and a tanned complexion, aided, it was said, by staining his face with tobacco juice. He gave his evidence in a clear, compelling voice, but under some merciless cross-examination his defence started to crumble.

Mahon had said that following the 'accident' he had purchased a saw and a knife in London in order to dispose of the remains; but it was proved that those items had been purchased at least three days before Miss Kaye's death, thus showing premeditation. And when Spilsbury was asked about the likelihood of Miss Kaye dying as a result of striking her head on the coal-scuttle, he firmly replied that the metal used in the manufacture of the item was so soft that, 'No, in my opinion, she could not.'

Found guilty after deliberations of three quarters of an hour by the jury, Mahon was sentenced to death; and those who might have said, 'Hanging's too good for him' were right on this occasion, because he was hanged twice. As he stood on the trap at Wandsworth Prison on 9 September 1924, and the executioner, Pierrepoint, went for the lever, Mahon jerked his bound feet forward on to the stationary part of the platform. At that same moment the lever was pulled, the hinged platform dropped down and Mahon's body swung back, his spine hitting the sharp edge of the opened trap with terrific force, which killed him; half a second later, his spine was broken once more, higher up this time, as the rope around his neck tightened.

It was a bizarre end to what the Director of Public Prosecutions referred to as being 'one of the foulest crimes which has been committed in recent years'.

★ ★ ★

On 1 December 1924 Wensley was appointed chief constable of the CID, his role of superintendent being taken by John Ashley OBE. Wensley was the first officer to have risen through the ranks to be so appointed since Frederick Adolphus Williamson, who had briefly held the rank in 1889 and retired shortly afterwards.

No finer officer could have been posted to such a prestigious rank. From behind his desk, smoking either a cigarette or his large-bowled pipe, he ran CID operations effortlessly and smoothly. Once a week, the divisional detective inspectors from the twenty-two divisions would come to the Yard to be briefed and debriefed by the chief constable. Wensley's happiness was complete when, in 1927, his daughter, married to a CID officer, presented him with a grandson, Harold Frederick Wensley Cory.

A report from the Director of Public Prosecutions landed on Wensley's desk alleging that a former army officer referred to only as 'the Captain' had been the victim of a gang of blackmailers for over three years; they had obtained a total of £10,754 from him. The first time 'the Captain' paid up, he was lost; and over the next three years his panic increased as he swallowed every threat made to him. It was only when he approached a lawyer that he was strongly advised to report the matter to the authorities.

After weeks of work, the gang were arrested and all were convicted at the Old Bailey on 17 June 1927. In the dock stood six highly unprepossessing specimens.

The Lord Chief Justice, Lord Hewart, before passing sentence, stated that it was:

> The worst case of its kind which has come to my knowledge in an experience of more than twenty-five years at the bar and on the bench.
>
> You have pursued this wretched man relentlessly over a period of three years and a half, employing every varying device which ingenuity and relentlessness could suggest to you. It is difficult to understand why persons who are tortured

in the way the victim in this case has been tortured do not come forward and lay the facts frankly and fully before their solicitors and the police, or both. They could then, I am sure, rely upon the discretion of the Press. If they are prepared to take that course, they will have done something to stamp out one of the worst pests of contemporary civilisation.

George William Taylor, aged thirty-eight, was a professional blackmailer who was well-educated and spoke several languages. He had been sentenced to five years' penal servitude in Egypt for desertion and, in 1925, four months' imprisonment for pointing a revolver at a woman. He was sent to penal servitude for life.

Joseph Maples, aged thirty-nine, was also a professional blackmailer, whose real name was James Townsend. During the First World War he was said to have made £5,000 'by unknown means', and in one of his unsavoury schemes had used his attractive wife as a decoy – she had since left him. Maples had five previous convictions, including housebreaking, burglary and robbery with violence, and was sentenced to fifteen years' penal servitude.

Norman Stuart, twenty-six, was a musician who had done no work since 1923, and his wife was currently serving eighteen months' hard labour for blackmail. He was sentenced to twelve years' penal servitude.

Twenty-five-year-old Frank Leonard's real name was Abram Glown. A Russian alien, he was sentenced to ten years' penal servitude. Alfred Tannen, aged twenty-four, had also posed as 'Detective Lynch' of Scotland Yard. He was similarly sentenced to ten years' penal servitude.

The last prisoner was Arthur Brown, aged forty-three, known to his admiring associates as 'Newcastle Arthur' and to the unhappy victim as 'Detective Benshaw of Scotland Yard'. He had untruthfully told 'the Captain' that he could 'square the whole matter up for £1,400'. He was sentenced to eight years' penal servitude.

Women fainted in court as the sentences were announced, although Mrs Maples and Mrs Stuart were not amongst them, having business elsewhere.

\* \* \*

So that was a feather in Scotland Yard's cap; and so was the next case, which Wensley both supervised and participated in.

# Chapter 23

# The Body in the Trunk

On 10 May 1927, Wensley was informed that a trunk deposited at Charing Cross Railway Station was found to contain the dismembered remains of a woman, as well as a pair of shoes and a handbag. He went straight to Bow Street police station, whose jurisdiction covered the railway station; but because, of course, the murder could have been committed anywhere, it was quite clearly a case for the Yard. Wensley appointed Chief Detective Inspector George Cornish to investigate – and Cornish appears to have been in the mould of Percy Savage, because in his memoirs he, too, made no mention of Wensley in this or any other case.

Leonard Burt, then a detective sergeant (second class) – he would later be promoted to commander – was one of the junior officers deputed to assist in the investigation. He managed to resist the temptation to throw up when Sir Bernard Spilsbury carried out the post mortem. 'It was ghastly enough to be unforgettable,' he later said.

Three paper parcels contained the arms and legs, wrapped in towels and a pair of knickers with laundry marks 447 and 581 and bearing the name 'P. Holt'. A fourth parcel contained the head (wrapped in a filthy duster) and the remainder of the body. It appeared that the woman – aged between thirty-five and forty-five – had received a severe blow to her head, which caused unconsciousness, and had then been suffocated.

The trunk which held these ghastly remains was old and covered with identifying marks, none of which, however, had anything to do with the case. Naturally, the investigators were unaware of this, and there was a lot of work to do to identify the woman by following up all of the clues, which received great publicity in the evening papers.

A second-hand dealer from Brixton recognized the distinctive-looking trunk, which he had sold on or soon after 4 May for 12s 6d to a military-looking man, aged about thirty-six, with a small moustache. A bus conductor recalled taking a passenger from Brixton to Victoria on 6 May who brought a large, empty trunk on board, although the man got off at Rochester Row, before his destination. Next there was a taxi-driver, who had picked up two men from the Royal Automobile Club and had taken them to

Westminster police court on 6 May; he had then immediately been hailed by a man across the road, in Rochester Row, with a large trunk in the doorway to a block of offices. Helping the man get the trunk into his cab, the cabbie jocularly remarked on its weight and was told it contained books. He then conveyed both trunk and passenger to Charing Cross station. His first two passengers, who had gone to Westminster police court to answer motoring summonses, were traced, and the time that they arrived was fixed at 1.35 pm. As the cab left Charing Cross, the passenger threw a left-luggage receipt out of the window; this was picked up by a shoe-black, and it revealed that the trunk had been deposited at 1.50 pm.

Meanwhile, the bloodstained knickers were identified as belonging to a Mrs Holt, who lived in Chelsea and was very much alive. Obviously, the items must have been stolen by one of the ten servants she had employed over the past two years. All were accounted for save one, and Mrs Holt gamely identified her from the head in the trunk as being a Mrs Rolls. But that was not her correct name; a Mr Frederick Rolls was found, who stated that they had lived together for a time and she had taken his name for propriety's sake. She was in fact a prostitute named Minnie Alice Bonati, the estranged wife of an Italian waiter, Bianco Bonati. She had last been seen alive between 3.45 and 4.30 pm in Sydney Street, Chelsea on 4 May.

The police now turned their attention to the block of offices at 86 Rochester Row, where the man with the trunk had been waiting prior to hailing the cab. Just one of the occupants could not be found: an estate agent named John Robinson, who had left on 9 May. He had similarly left his lodgings in Kennington, but a search revealed a telegram addressed to 'Robinson, Greyhound Hotel, Hammersmith'. There they found a Mrs Robinson, who turned out to be John Robinson's wife and who agreed to assist the police when she discovered that their marriage had been a bigamous one. When Robinson asked her to meet him at the Elephant and Castle public house on 19 May, Cornish accompanied her, and Robinson (who had a small moustache and had previously served in the army) was arrested and taken to the Yard, where Cornish and Wensley interviewed him. He denied any knowledge of Mrs Bonati or that he had purchased the trunk; and when the second-hand dealer and the cabbie both failed to identify him, he was released.

The following day, all the evidence relating to the case was reviewed. The office at Rochester Row was searched again. The officers felt that if Robinson had murdered Mrs Bonati, it must have been there that he dismembered her body, but not a trace of blood could be found. Robinson was a heavy smoker and in a waste-paper basket were a great many cigarette stubs and spent matches. All of them were examined, and on just one match was found a bloodstain. After dismembering the body, had Robinson lit a cigarette and left a stain on the match from his bloodied hand? It was good, circumstantial evidence, and even better was the filthy, bloodstained duster which had been wrapped around Mrs Bonati's head. It was washed, revealing the name 'GREYHOUND' on it; it was identified as belonging to the pub which employed Mrs Robinson, and later, by a typist whom Robinson had employed, as being used in the office in Rochester Row.

It was the end of the road for Robinson. Re-arrested, he admitted meeting Mrs Bonati on 4 May; he had invited her back to his office and she had asked him for money. When he refused, there was a blazing row, she fell over and struck her head, and he left. When he returned the following day, he found her dead. It was a mirror image of the murder of Emily Kaye, backed up by the fact that Robinson purchased the knife for the dissection at the very same shop where Mahon had bought the knife and saw for his dirty work. Robinson showed the police where he had buried the knife, under a may tree on Clapham Common.

During a two-day trial before Mr Justice Swift at the Old Bailey, beginning on 11 July, the defence endeavoured unsuccessfully to discredit Spilsbury's evidence; but Robinson was found guilty and was executed at Pentonville Prison on 12 August 1927.

Then there was the case of Frederick Guy Browne and Patrick Michael (or perhaps William Henry) Kennedy, who on 27 September 1927 brutally murdered Police Constable George Gutteridge. It was a case that excited a great deal of public attention because of the horrifying circumstances of the killing; the officer had been shot twice in the face then, after Browne asked him, 'What are you looking at me like that for?', once in each eye. It was an enquiry which commenced in Essex, travelled to London, to Sheffield, to Liverpool and then back to London. In fact, it was Chief Detective Inspector James Berrett, the famous 'bearded detective', who ran the case, but with Wensley in overall charge of the operational work of the CID, the kudos rubbed off on him as well.

Murder investigations were reaping impressive results, although in 1927, when a number of 14 hp Lea Francis tourers with a top speed of 75 mph arrived at Scotland Yard for the Flying Squad, as well as a number of new vans, Major Thomas Vitty of the Engineers Department was treated to a furious broadside from the irascible commissioner. All of the vans and tourers were the same colour and all the registration numbers were consecutive. The panic-stricken major suggested that the tourers should be painted all sorts of fanciful colours, including crimson, and that the vans could be disguised by putting the names of businesses on the sides by means of transfers – difficult to substitute when moving from one district to another. Fortunately, the bellowing of a despotic commissioner and the wailing of an incompetent civil servant were soothed by Wensley dealing with the matter in a characteristically unflappable manner.

The tourers, he said, should be repainted in colours common to the manufacturer's specifications, and the registration numbers of both cars and vans must not, of course, be consecutive. In addition, slots should be cut into the sides of the vans to accommodate boards bearing the names of businesses commensurate with the areas in which the vans were patrolling – just as they had been with the prototype horse-drawn covered wagons of 1919. It was not rocket science, nor had there been any need to re-invent the wheel; and although the highly insecure Major Vitty later suggested to the readers of the *Daily Mail* that this had been his idea, Wensley added his signature to his report dated 8 November 1927, which ended with the words, 'Personally, I never knew it to fail'.

On 6 August 1927, it was a case of 'the biter, bit'; one night, whilst Wensley and his wife were sound asleep, a burglar used some steps to climb in through a fanlight – the only window that was not burglar-alarmed – and made off with Wensley's silver, antiques and medals. He commented, 'Whoever was responsible for the burglary, I am obliged for the sporting way they behaved.' Wensley was probably referring to the fact that his sons' medals had not been taken. These he kept on the wall, together with their photographs and records of service, just inside the door of the dining room – with the door open, it was highly probable the thief had not even noticed them. But he was not the only senior officer to have been burgled. Deputy Assistant Commissioner Sir Percy Robert Laurie KCVO, CBE, DSO had had a hamper stolen from his South Kensington home, and two of Wensley's contemporaries in 'the Big Four' – Superintendents Hawkins and Carlin – also suffered burglaries, the former losing property worth £100, the latter jewellery and clothing valued at £150 from his home in Clapham. The fourth member of 'the Big Four' – Superintendent Neil – carried out the investigation, but no arrests were made.

Wensley was now sixty-two years of age, and compulsory retirement was not far away. But he was content. The three major investigations referred to were the most headline-catching of 1927 (and just a fraction of the cases successfully solved by the Yard), the police were held in high esteem by the public and Wensley felt, with complete justification, that his chief constableship was giving great service to the Metropolitan Police, which he had now industriously served for almost forty years.

But with 1928 just around the corner, there were a number of scandals waiting to emerge, all of which would cause great harm to the reputation of the Metropolitan Police and would seriously threaten Wensley's position.

# CHAPTER 24

# Scandals

The Government was in a bad state in 1928, as was, in
particular, the Prime Minister, Stanley Baldwin. He was
in poor health and poorer spirits, badly advised by those
whose efforts should have been concentrated on getting the
economy back on track. Although there were half a million more
people in work than in the previous year, unemployment, at 1.3
million, was still too high.

The Metropolitan Police numbered 19,779 – 250 under strength,
but that was the least of their problems. At 9.45 pm on 23 April, two
officers in plain clothes, Police Constables Alexander McLean and
George Badger, carried out an arrest for outraging public decency
in Hyde Park. The persons arrested were Miss Irene Savidge, aged
twenty-two and employed by the Standard Telephone and Cable
Company, and her companion, Sir Leo George Chiozza Money,
aged fifty-seven, who was married and had previously been Lloyd
George's parliamentary private secretary.

The evidence given by the police on 1 May at Great Marlborough
Street police court was that Sir Leo had his hand up Miss Savidge's
skirt and Miss Savidge was holding Sir Leo's penis; and upon being
arrested, Sir Leo claimed, 'I'm not the usual riff-raff; I'm a man of
substance. For God's sake, let me go!'

Sir Leo was expensively legally represented in court, all of the
officers' evidence was hotly disputed, and the magistrate, Henry
Cancellor, not only refused to allow Miss Savidge to be cross-
examined ('in case she was upset') but dismissed the case against
the pair, awarded ten guineas costs against the police and harshly
criticized the two officers.

The resultant headlines castigated the police, and with Sir Leo
raising the matter in Parliament and demanding the two officers
should be charged with perjury, the Home Office quite properly
demanded an internal police enquiry. It was then that matters
started to go badly wrong.

Wensley selected Chief Detective Inspector Alfred Collins
to investigate the matter, with Detective Sergeant Clarke as his
aide. On the face of it, these were good choices. Collins had
been commended on ninety-three occasions, was a very good
investigator and was tipped for promotion. As a detective sergeant,

he had been involved in the Voisin murder case and was the officer who discovered Mme Gerard's head and hands. Collins had also figured prominently in the Engelstein fire-raising enquiry, plus the large blackmail investigation of 1927. Detective Sergeant Clarke had carried out the search of Robinson's office in the Bonati murder case, and it was he who had found the bloodstained matchstick.

The truth was as follows: the two constables had not committed perjury – Sir Leo Money had. Therefore, Collins wished to interview Miss Savidge – her evidence had not been tested – to see if she would corroborate the officers' statements. Wensley insisted that when Collins brought Miss Savidge into Scotland Yard, a woman officer should be present, an eminently sensible course of action. So Lilian Wyles was collected at Marylebone police court on 15 May by Collins and Clarke, and they drove to Miss Savidge's place of work at New Southgate.

But Collins and Miss Wyles did not like each other, and upon their arrival at the Yard, Miss Savidge was taken to the chief constable's waiting room, where Miss Wyles was brusquely dismissed and where, over the next five hours, the two men carried out their interview of Miss Savidge. It was an act of almost unimaginable stupidity which would give rise to a number of serious allegations.

Collins addressed her in ways which were both avuncular (calling her 'My dear') and suggestive, stroking her knee, asking her to stand up so that he could see the length of her skirt and questioning her regarding her sex life and the colour of her petticoat. He put his arm around her, to ask if that was the way Sir Leo had embraced her, and was by turns fatherly, hectoring and bullying. When she was given a cup of tea, Clarke offered her the only teaspoon, saying, 'Now, Irene will spoon with me.' This old-fashioned expression, meaning to lovingly embrace, was not even remotely funny; it was crass. (Clarke later claimed that what he had actually said was, 'Will you use this spoon with me?' – but few, if any, accepted this was true.)

Miss Savidge was so exhausted that she later said, 'In the end, I was so tired I did not care what the police put down'; and she left the Yard at 7.00 pm and returned home to her parents' house. Sir Leo called at midnight, and when he asked her why she had gone to the Yard, when she could not have been compelled to do so, she became hysterical and flung a cigarette box at him, before collapsing.

When Wensley discovered that Miss Wyles had been excluded from the interview he was furious, and vehemently castigated Collins for his jaw-dropping stupidity; Collins was unable to see the implications of his actions, but Wensley could, and he was right.

The following day, Collins telephoned Sir Leo's office to make an appointment, but was told that he was not there. Indeed, he was not; Sir Leo was at his solicitor's office, together with Miss Savidge, who was making a long, detailed statement regarding precisely what had happened at Scotland Yard. Later, the solicitor telephoned Collins, telling him that he had no intention of permitting his client to be interviewed regarding his 'past affairs'. Collins informed the Director of Public Prosecutions of this conversation, who promptly wrote to Sir Leo's solicitors insisting that their client make a statement to Collins, 'otherwise, other steps will be taken'.

But by now the storm clouds had started to gather, and the late editions of the evening papers of 16 May, then the morning papers the following day, roared their displeasure at the Metropolitan Police. On 17 May the matter of the Director's letter was raised in the House, and extracts of Miss Savidge's statement were read out; a debate would take place later the same day, in which the Liberal MP Sir John Simon pretty well summed up the feelings of the House when he rhetorically asked, 'If that had happened to my daughter, how should I feel?'

Miss Wyles was picked up at her hairdresser's by a Flying Squad car; the detective inspector in charge of the car had his unequivocal instructions from Wensley: Miss Wyles was to be taken directly to see the Home Secretary's private secretary and under no circumstances was she to be allowed to speak to any other person beforehand. She made a short statement and later, following an outcry from all of the political parties, the Home Secretary, Sir William Joynson-Hicks Bt, PC, DL – he was, inevitably, known as 'Jix' – announced the setting up of a tribunal of enquiry into Miss Savidge's interview.

On 18 May Miss Wyles reported to Wensley, then went to her own office, where she saw Collins, who made his second big mistake. He informed her that she would provide a fresh statement for the enquiry and that he would tell her what to say. This was the proverbial straw that broke the camel's back; Miss Wyles completely lost her temper and told Collins exactly what she thought of him. She then informed him that she would write a statement which would be the mirror-image of the one she had already written for Parliament, and that when she had completed it, it would be handed to Wensley and nobody else.

In her memoirs, Miss Wyles said that Wensley had entreated her to keep Collins calm, and that Collins himself had suddenly been transformed into a timid, cringing creature, one who obeyed her every word. Miss Wyles portrayed herself as a strict nanny, firm but unyielding, in charge of a recalcitrant, rather dim-witted child. It is unlikely that there was any reliability in this account.

The enquiry commenced on 6 June in one of the courts of the King's Bench Division at the Royal Courts of Justice, headed by Sir John Eldon Bankes GCB together with a solicitor, John James Withers CBE, MP, and the Labour MP, Mr Hastings Bertrand Lees-Smith. The latter was virulently anti-police and the enquiry's hatchet-man.

Miss Wyles corroborated the evidence of her two male colleagues and, possibly, the three of them lied their heads off. Nevertheless, Sir John and Mr Withers came to the conclusion that the police evidence had been truthful, while Lees-Smith, in a separate report, stated quite categorically that it was not. He also made fifteen recommendations, and nobody took the slightest notice of them. The matter was debated in the House, and the Home Secretary accepted the majority report.

The case led to a change in the practice of interviewing women, especially in cases where intimate matters had to be discussed; unless the interviewee expressly desired otherwise, a woman officer had to be present.

Some interesting points arose out of this case. Collins was never promoted to the rank of superintendent, although from his string of successes many thought he should have been. Clarke, however, was promoted: he later became divisional detective inspector of 'V' Division. Miss Wyles was also later promoted to Woman Detective Inspector (First Class) and upon her retirement was appointed BEM.

The day before the enquiry commenced, Wensley's MBE had been advanced to OBE, and he was not present at the tribunal. It was clear that Wensley – with considerable justification – was extremely concerned about the outcome of the case, not least for the reputation of the Metropolitan Police.

The matter was summed-up in the House of Lords by Lord Birkenhead, who said:

> If an elderly man takes a young girl thirty years younger than himself to lunch in a restaurant in Soho, a girl not belonging to the same class of life, not sharing, as one may surmise, his intellectual and economic interests, and sits in close proximity to her in Hyde Park; if there takes place between them, as accepting the evidence of the police as I do accept it, we must assume there took place, some caress of a kind which was distinguished by the young lady herself in her evidence as being a kiss, but not a kiss of passion, have they any great

ground for complaint if a policeman forty or fifty yards away misinterprets the precise nature of the caress? I must add this, that the charges of perjury against the policemen involved in this particular case I most absolutely repel.

In fact, reinforcement of Lord Birkenhead's views came five years later; by which time most people had forgotten this case. In September 1933 a flustered thirty-year-old spinster named Ivy Buxton got off a train at Esher and complained to a porter that a man had boarded the train at Dorking and then, in a tunnel, had tried to board her, passionately kissing her face and neck, against her will. The magistrates at Epsom court accepted her version and fined her attacker £3 plus five guineas costs. Justice – of a kind – had finally been meted out to Sir Leo Money.

★ ★ ★

If Wensley breathed a sigh of relief at the conclusions of the Savidge/Money enquiry, it was a tad premature. Just as the report was published, along came the next scandal.

Helene Adele, aged twenty-one, was arrested in July 1928 in Van Street, Holloway for insulting words and behaviour – her shouting 'something about five bob' at a man who ran away tended to show that she was a disgruntled prostitute. In fact, she later admitted that she was 'a girl of loose morals' and had 'often misconducted herself', including several liaisons with a garage manager (of whom more later), causing a judge at the Old Bailey to later remark that she was either a woman of the streets, or close to it. So there were similarities between this and the Savidge/Money arrest – immoral behaviour – but also one crucial difference. The officers who had carried out that arrest in Hyde Park had told the plain, unvarnished truth; Police Constables 541 'Y' John William Clayton and 383 'Y' Charles Victor Stevens, who arrested Miss Adele, had not.

Miss Adele had an arrangement with a taxicab washer that she could sleep in his taxi, which was garaged off the Caledonian Road. On this occasion when the officers visited the garage, PC Clayton got into the cab and suggested that Miss Adele have sexual intercourse with him. She volubly refused and threatened to report him, then rushed into the cab office, from where she was dragged out and arrested by the officers. There were independent witnesses to this outrageous act: the cab-washer stated that a man had got into the cab and accosted Miss Adele, but although Clayton was in full uniform, he was unwilling to say that the intruder was a police officer.

The case against Miss Adele at Clerkenwell police court was thrown out, the magistrate stating that this was a serious abuse of police powers. At the trial of the two constables, who were indicted for perjury and attempting to pervert the course of public justice, the manager of the cab office stated that the girl had shouted for assistance, he had seen the cab rocking but considered it wise not to interfere. Clayton had asked him to throw her out of the office because she was going to report him, but that he was 'going to knock her off, before she got the chance'. Other witnesses from the cab office came forward to corroborate the manager's story, saying that they had previously held back from telling the truth because they 'feared the constables' revenge'. A boy working in the garage found a piece of leather in the cab; it corresponded exactly to a piece missing from Clayton's belt.

Acting-Sergeant Smith very unwisely stated that at the time of the incident he had seen Clayton on his beat at 1.30 am, and that had he not, it would have been his duty to report him. He recalled the time because he had been en route to Caledonian Road police station for his supper. Unfortunately, two station sergeants stated that Smith had not consumed his supper at the station that night.

Both constables stuck to their original story – that neither had been inside the garage, that Clayton had arrested the girl in the street when she refused to desist from using immoderate language and that Stevens, who was working an adjoining beat, had heard the commotion and assisted in the arrest. In the face of the conflicting evidence, it did not sound very plausible.

The defence counsel stated that a guilty verdict would mean 'the condemnation of the entire Metropolitan Police', but in his summing-up Mr Justice Humphreys stated:

> It would be absurd to suppose that 20,000 police would not include some unworthy members. It would rather show that the same Force, especially those from Scotland Yard, had brought two unworthy members to justice.

The jury retired for only half an hour before returning a verdict of guilty on both constables for conspiring to bring a false charge against Miss Adele. In sentencing the prisoners on 14 September 1928, the judge stated that he agreed with the verdict. He voiced the opinion that no offence on the part of the constables could be more serious and he was glad to think that an investigation by the very Force to which they belonged had brought them to justice.

Both officers – Clayton with four-and-a-half years' service, Stevens with nine – had unblemished records (except for a small peccadillo by Clayton, who had been fined for smoking on duty), and both were now sentenced to eighteen months' imprisonment, in the second division,[17] said the judge, out of consideration for their previous character. In addition, Acting-Sergeant Smith was dismissed from the Force. Stevens sobbed and uttered a piercing cry when he was sentenced, falling and hitting his head on the dock rail, and had to be carried to the cells.

The *Daily Mail* could usually be relied upon to champion the Metropolitan Police's cause and they did so on this occasion; their leader read:

> It is a grave affair but its gravity should not be exaggerated. The general credit and character of the Force was not involved. The result proves that the authorities do not spare any pains to root out undesirables and they do not discriminate or favour their colleagues when justice needs doing. We still are entitled to regard the police as a highly honourable body, of which we have every reason to be proud.

A committee chaired by Hugh Macmillan MP was set up, following complaints from the newspapers concerning alleged malpractice by the police, but with one exception the police were exonerated from general wrongdoing. This was followed by the Lee Commission, headed by Lord Lee of Fareham, which considered the cases of Irene Savidge and Helene Adele and also debated whether 'the third degree' was ever used by police officers whilst interviewing suspects – the Commission came to the firm conclusion that it was not.

The Commission published its findings on 16 March 1929; but before that happened, there was a fresh allegation of police corruption, and of the three which occurred in 1928 this was by far and away the worst. And although Commissioner Horwood had already publicly stated that he intended to retire by his sixtieth birthday (and did, two days beforehand, on 7 November 1928), it appeared to the public that, what with the taint of the Savidge and Adele cases – and now, this new allegation, which burst like a bombshell – Horwood was making good his escape and leaving his successor to pick up the pieces.

★ ★ ★

---

17 Imprisonment in the second division meant that these prisoners would be segregated as much as possible from other inmates, would wear uniforms of a different colour and receive more frequent visits and letters.

The matter had come to light on 20 May 1928, when a number of letters (and especially one signed simply 'Richette') arrived at the Yard, alleging that a certain Station Sergeant George Goddard, aged forty-nine, had been accepting bribes from West End restaurateurs and club owners for turning a blind eye to activities which included permitting gaming, staging erotic cabarets and the flouting of the licensing laws.

However, although this was the first time letters had been received at Scotland Yard, other anonymous letters had been sent the previous year to Superintendent Barton, the head of 'C' Division, making exactly the same allegations. The superintendent had confronted Goddard with these accusations, and, not unnaturally, he had denied them. Barton accepted these denials because he wanted to believe them, and Goddard, now completely forewarned and with breathtaking arrogance, carried right on as before.

George Goddard had joined the Metropolitan Police in 1900 and, following a posting to 'S' Division in 1910, had been fined, severely reprimanded and cautioned for heavy drinking. But it appeared he had overcome this particular problem, and he had been promoted to sergeant in 1913 and posted to 'C' Division. From 1918 he had been given responsibility for administering the licensing laws in West End establishments and had collected ninety-one commendations for his work. True, there had been one further blip in his career: in 1921 Police Sergeant Horace Josling had accused him of accepting bribes from bookmakers. A subsequent Home Office enquiry, conducted in secret, referred its findings to the Metropolitan Police, Josling appeared on a police disciplinary board charged with making false accusations against another officer and was forced to resign. Goddard, completely exculpated from any wrong-doing, continued his perfidious activities in Soho.

One of the bribe-givers mentioned in 'Richette's' letter was Kate Meyrick, who operated a number of sparkling, expensive night clubs: the Folies Bergère, the Manhattan and the Silver Slipper and, most famous of all, the '43' in Gerrard Street.

Known as 'Ma' Meyrick and also 'the Night Club Queen', she had been born Kate Evelyn Nason in 1875 in a suburb of Dublin. Married to a doctor, she had three sons and three daughters, but the marriage foundered and she arrived in London in 1919. The 43 opened its door two years later, and the great and the good, including Augustus John, Jacob Epstein, J. B. Priestley and Joseph Conrad, flocked to it.

She was twice fined for breaches of the licensing laws, firstly in February 1922 and then in July 1924. On each occasion, Goddard had led the raids on the club. For the second offence Mrs Meyrick was fined £390, plus £10 costs, and disqualified from running a club for twelve months. She blithely disregarded the disqualification, and on 18 October 1924 her club was raided by the police once more; one month later, Mrs Meyrick was sentenced to six months' imprisonment.

With her Harrow-educated son and her Roedean- and Girton-educated daughters to maintain – they would soon be married into the aristocracy, many of whose members frequented her clubs – Mrs Meyrick wanted no more of this kind of disruption to her activities, and she proceeded to bribe Goddard on a breathtaking scale to ensure that adequate notice was provided of any impending police raids. It was successful; Goddard, who had been told to 'keep an eye on the club', submitted four consecutive reports saying that he had done so and that nothing was amiss.

Wensley ordered the Flying Squad to make very discreet enquiries into Goddard's finances and, in addition, raids – without the knowledge of Goddard – were carried out simultaneously at the 43 Club and the Manhattan on 22 May 1928 by the Flying Squad, resulting in Mrs Meyrick being sentenced to a further six months' imprisonment.

Detective Sergeant Fred 'Nutty' Sharpe of the Squad interviewed Mrs Meyrick in prison in an effort to get her to implicate her protector, Goddard, but this she refused to do. However, a further anonymous letter was sent to the commissioner on 23 September 1928, again urging action against Goddard and threatening that the writer's MP would be contacted if no action was taken. In fact, a great deal of information had already been gathered about him by the investigating officers. On his weekly wage of £6 15s 0d, Goddard had managed to purchase for cash a house valued at £1,850 in Valley Road, Streatham – to put this into context, someone earning that wage at that time would have been lucky to be able to purchase a three-bedroom terraced house costing far less than half that amount on a twenty-five year mortgage.

Goddard also bought a £400 Chrysler saloon car (for cash) and had financed two pawnbroker's shops, which were managed by his brother-in-law. He had bank accounts totalling £2,700 and a safe deposit box at Selfridges containing £471 10s 0d and some foreign currency. In fact, he had originally rented two safe deposit boxes at Selfridges, but a few days before their discovery he had closed one of them and transferred the contents to a newly acquired deposit box in Pall Mall. This box, rented in the name of Joseph Eagles, contained £12,000 in cash, many of the notes having consecutive numbers. This transfer did not go unnoticed by the Flying Squad.

Goddard was directed to attend Scotland Yard on 26 October 1928. There he met Wensley in company with Charles Cooper, the head of the Flying Squad. Telling Goddard that his safe deposit boxes were suspected of containing ill-gotten gains, Wensley said, 'I'm going to direct Chief Inspector Cooper to go with you and bring the contents of these safes to us for inspection.'

Goddard staggered and gasped, 'I'm done for!' Recovering his equilibrium, he then added, 'I'm quite willing to do as you request.' When the money was brought back to the Yard and counted, Goddard, referring to his impending disciplinary board, said, 'I shall give no trouble. I shall plead guilty to two charges before the board. I would rather have penal servitude rather than say anything, although I could. I don't want to disgrace the service.'

Three days later, on 29 October, Goddard appeared before a disciplinary board and pleaded guilty to neglect of duty by failing to give a satisfactory account of large sums of money received from unknown sources, and also to discreditable conduct by betting and associating with certain undesirable persons. He refused to say how this money had come into his possession and was dismissed from the Force in double-quick time, with forfeiture of all pension rights. Afterwards, Wensley saw a certain Police Constable 163 'C' John Wilkin and casually mentioned, 'Goddard said he was going to stand alone, rather than bring other people into it. I don't know who those other people are – do you?'

'No,' replied Wilkin, but he was being disingenuous. He had worked directly under Goddard and had accepted money and gifts, via Goddard, from licensed club owners to turn a blind eye to their activities; he was induced to tell all he knew at Goddard's forthcoming trial, in return for immunity from prosecution.

Mrs Meyrick enjoyed ten days of liberty following her release from Holloway prison, before she was arrested on 27 November, together with Goddard, Luigi Achille Ribuffi (Mrs Meyrick's business manager) and a Mrs Anna Gadda who 'kept a certain house, in Greek Street, Soho' – in more prosaic language, a brothel. Goddard was charged with receiving bribes of £260 from Ribuffi, £155 from Mrs Meyrick and £500 from Mrs Gadda; they, in turn, were all charged with bribing Goddard.

Mrs Gadda mysteriously disappeared, but the other defendants appeared at the Old Bailey before Mr Justice Avory on 21 January 1929 and pleaded not guilty, Mrs Meyrick tearfully denying bribing Goddard, as did Ribuffi, who said that he had never even met Goddard prior to this case.

Bank notes from Goddard's safety deposit boxes were traced back to Mrs Meyrick's and Ribuffi's possession. Goddard stated in his defence that he had made £2,000 by speculating in foreign exchange, that betting on the right kind of horses accounted for another £7,000, a music publishing business had paid him £5,000 and a stall at the 1924 Wembley Exhibition selling seaside-type rock had brought in £4,000. However, he was unable to substantiate any of these assertions. As for PC Wilkin's evidence, Goddard confessed that he was 'astonished'.

Summing up, Mr Justice Avory told the jury:

> It is clear that for years, Goddard has been systematically and deliberately amassing money by breach of the regulations under which he has held office, and for the purpose of his defence to this charge, he has had to admit that he has been in the habit of having monetary transactions with persons whom he knew had been convicted or at least suspected of keeping disorderly houses, and he has had to admit that some of the money has been made with street bookmakers whom it was his duty to arrest.

No one was particularly astonished when, after three hours' deliberation, the jury found the trio guilty. All were sentenced to hard labour: Mrs Meyrick and Ribuffi to fifteen months, and Goddard to eighteen months; he was also fined £2,000 and ordered to pay the costs of the prosecution.

But on 2 December 1929 Goddard was back in court, in the King's Bench Division of the High Court, flanked by two prison warders – this time as the plaintiff. The commissioner had confiscated all of Goddard's ill-gotten gains, on the grounds that they were the property of the Crown. However, Goddard had only been convicted of receiving £915 in bribes, and therefore, due to an anomaly in the law, the bulk of the money was returned to him. He retired to the country and lived the rest of his days on his investments.

PC Wilkin was 'required to resign'; this meant he kept his pension. Superintendent Barton was reprimanded for negligence, fined and transferred. Sergeant Josling, who had been so badly treated for telling the truth about Goddard and had returned to his former profession of schoolmaster, was offered his old job back. He declined, and was later awarded £1,500 compensation.

Mrs Meyrick received two more prison sentences before giving up the club scene. The Wall Street crash of 1929 decimated her investments, and when she wrote her memoirs, their publication was swiftly stamped upon. She died in 1933.

This was a case which caused the reputation of the Metropolitan Police immense harm; as a detective sergeant, Peter Beveridge recalled that East End tearaways would abusively bellow, 'Goddard!' when they thought they were a safe enough distance away to avoid retribution. They were wrong. They would later be seen and suitably spoken to, and the practice stopped.

None of these three scandals, not one word about them, found their way into Wensley's memoirs. Obviously, he was being very selective about what was published, but the fact remains that he was one of the few who emerged from these affairs with any credit; in every case he had acted decisively, and in the Goddard enquiry, within days of receiving the first anonymous letter, he had arranged for raids to be carried out on two of Mrs Meyrick's clubs and thereafter had scrupulously supervised the investigation.

But three earth-shattering scandals in one year after forty years of public service were a great deal for a man in his sixties to contend with, and soon it would be time to go.

# Time to Book off Duty

Although Parliament had officially cleared the Metropolitan Police of taint, the newspapers and the public had not. With Horwood's resignation, the Government offered the post of commissioner to eight candidates; all of them rejected the offer. So, initially, did the ninth, Field Marshal Julian Hedworth George Byng GCB, GCMG, MVO, 1st Viscount Byng of Vimy. Byng had had a highly successful army career and was enormously popular with his troops, but he was aged sixty-six, not in the best of health, suffering from a weak heart and emphysema, and was looking forward to retirement. It was only when King George V intervened that Byng accepted the post, with the aim of restoring the Force to being 'a happy family'.

The Labour party vociferously declared that the appointment of a former army officer was yet another attempt to 'militarize the police', and following a general election in May 1929 when Labour swept to power with 288 seats, Byng offered his resignation to the newly-appointed Home Secretary, John Robert Clynes PC, with the words, 'I really am the most readily sackable person in the world, so please don't hesitate.'

Clynes very wisely did not sack him; he could see the way the wind was blowing with this new, highly popular commissioner, who showed a real interest in the welfare of his men. Byng changed the beat system, incorporating bicycles and motorcycles so that excessive footslogging was reduced, started the chain of blue, 'Tardis'-style police boxes and improved and considerably strengthened the Flying Squad. He also made peace with the Newspaper Proprietors' Association, asking for fair play and requesting them not to sensationalize and blow out of all proportion every petty allegation of misconduct.

On 27 May 1929 Wensley donned a uniform for the first and last time since discarding his constable's uniform thirty-four years earlier. It was the uniform of a chief constable, worn to commemorate the centenary of the Metropolitan Police, and Wensley was one of 10,000 officers who paraded in Hyde Park. His uniform was adorned with his five medals: the OBE, his King's Police Medal, the Queen Victoria Golden Jubilee Police Medal of

1887 (with clasp, for the 1897 Diamond Jubilee) and the Police Coronation Medals of 1902 and 1911.

Then the uniform was taken off, the medals removed and put away, and it was almost time to go home. He said, 'I feel I want a rest and besides, my wife would like to see something of me, occasionally.' But not before Wensley had completed one last task, improving further his brainchild of ten years earlier.

★ ★ ★

The Flying Squad had gone from strength to strength. The old Crossley Tenders had more or less been discarded; instead, at Wensley's insistence, a whole new fleet of vehicles had been acquired, including a Bentley, a Lagonda, an MG Star and a 4¼ litre Invicta Tourer, capable of a top speed of 90 mph. One week before Wensley's retirement, the Invicta was put into service in stunning style, when the crew rammed a stolen Vauxhall and arrested a gang of violent shopbreakers. The officer in charge, Detective Inspector Edward Ockey, who was almost killed, was later awarded the King's Police Medal for gallantry.

The vehicles were fitted with Marconi wireless equipment, capable of receiving and transmitting; Squad arrests for 1929 were a record-breaking 515; and Wensley ensured that the Secretary of State's approval was forthcoming to increase the personnel to forty officers. Walter Hambrook, who had accompanied the Squad on their first outing, was taken from his position as divisional detective inspector at Albany Street police station, promoted to chief detective inspector and put in charge of the Flying Squad.

In 1929, Alfred Hitchcock's *Blackmail*, the first British 'talkie', featured a Flying Squad detective as its hero; J. Ord Hume had already composed *The Flying Squad Quick March* for both military and brass bands; and Edgar Wallace had added a play to his already famous book, *The Flying Squad*. The latter was turned into a film directed by Arthur Maude in 1929, and remade in 1932 by F. W. Kraemer.

The Flying Squad's star was in the ascendant, and in the ten short years of its existence it had become the one (small) unit of the Metropolitan Police whose name was on everybody's lips. Its success was due purely to the foresight of one man – Frederick Porter Wensley OBE, KPM.

★ ★ ★

In *Police Orders* dated Wednesday 31 July 1929 was the following announcement:

> The Commissioner has much pleasure in notifying the appointment of Mr John H. Ashley (Superintendent C.I. Department) to Chief Constable, *vice* Mr Frederick P. Wensley OBE, retiring on pension; to date from 1st August.
>
> Mr Wensley joined the Metropolitan Police on 16th January 1888 and was appointed to the Criminal Investigation Department on 3rd October 1895. He became Chief Constable in December, 1924.
>
> His ability and devotion to the work of his Department has been a notable feature in its history. The Secretary of State has expressed his appreciation of Mr Wensley's long and exceptionally distinguished service, and with this expression the Commissioner wishes to be heartily associated.

It was an extraordinary tribute; nothing has been seen like it before or since. And as a footnote, in the same *Police Orders*, fifteen Flying Squad officers were commended by the commissioner and thirteen monetary awards were granted, ranging from 7s 6d to 15s 0d.

It has been said that the commendations which Wensley received 'ran into the hundreds and are uncountable', and this is almost correct. Wensley kept a notebook which chronicled his commendations up until 31 July 1916, and at that time they totalled 242. However, he was commended by judges and the Director of Public Prosecutions many times thereafter, in the last thirteen years of his service, and it is not fanciful to suggest that the total number must have been approximately 300.

It was rumoured that a 'special extension' of five years' extra service was offered to Wensley, although this would have meant remaining at work until he was sixty-nine, which seems unlikely. So, leaving behind a completely reorganized CID with a strength of 780 men, Wensley was 'signed off' by his contemporary Percy Savage, and with an annual pension of £600 he returned to Lollie at their Palmers Green home. It must have seemed extremely strange to her that her husband – of whom she had seen so little during their married life – might be home for good. In fact, it seemed unlikely that he would be; even before he had officially retired, it had been mooted that Wensley should go to Chicago in an advisory capacity, to root out their indigenous gangs. Really, it appeared that he was the best choice; the celebrated lawman Wyatt Earp had died earlier that year. However, Wensley stipulated two conditions: firstly, that he receive a formal invitation from the responsible civic authority in Chicago and secondly, that he be left 'severely alone to do a job of work' and be exempt from any social or private engagements.

There were certainly problems in Chicago which needed to be addressed. On Valentine's Day that year, seven members of the North Side Gang were lined up at 2122 North Clark Street and gunned down by four bogus police officers, acting on the instructions of Alfonse 'Scarface' Capone, who at that precise moment was sunning himself in Florida. The intended target was the gang's leader, George 'Bugs' Moran; he escaped execution when he arrived late, saw the bogus police car and, believing it was a legitimate raid, made himself scarce. It was another attempt to take control of the bootlegging business in a city where many police officers took more in pay-offs than their city wage.

It was thought that Wensley could clean up 'the windy city' sufficiently in time to attract more visitors to the forthcoming 1933 World's Fair; but it would have been difficult for Wensley to receive an invitation from 'the responsible civic authority', as he had demanded. At that time, the city's governing Democratic Party was divided along ethnic lines – Irish, Poles and Italians – who controlled their respective neighbourhoods – and no such invitation was forthcoming. In desperation, the authorities implored former Chief Detective Inspector Charles Arrow, who had retired from the Yard twenty-three years previously, to come and 'clean up' Chicago; but as the seventy-year-old Mr Arrow informed them, he felt he was 'too old to undertake so formidable a task'.

Paris, too, was said to have asked Wensley to overhaul their police force. He was referred to there as *l'homme de fer* ('the man of iron'); but if they did invite him, this, too, came to nothing. Still the offers came in: in August 1931 Wensley was invited to go to New York as a consultant in District Attorney Thomas Dewey's battle against organized crime and corruption, but again he stipulated complete autonomy. 'I certainly do not think it is a superhuman task,' commented Wensley mildly, but the Mayor of New York was not willing to hand over the reins of such a task to an outsider. Again, this was fortunate; the Mayor, James John 'Jimmy' Walker, was obliged to stand down three years later following a corruption scandal.

In 1934 it was reported in the press that the services of Wensley, Chief Inspector Collins and Sir Basil Thomson had been retained by the *Paris-Soir* newspaper to conduct an independent enquiry into the mysterious death of Judge Albert Prince, found dead on the Paris–Dijon railway line. Prince had been enquiring into the activities of a fraudster named Alexandre Stavisky, who was found to have suffered two gunshot wounds to the head. The official verdict was 'suicide'; however, it was thought the police had killed him because of Government involvement in Stavisky's swindle.

It is difficult to say to what extent Wensley was involved in the investigation; he could not have been inspired by Collins after his performance in the Savidge/Money case. As for Sir Basil Thomson, his reputation was in tatters after he was arrested in 1925 in Hyde Park for committing an act of indecency with a certain Miss Thelma de Lava, for which she was fined £2 and he £5. Sir Basil had taken the case to appeal, but after Miss de Lava was called to say that nothing had happened and instead confirmed that it had, that was the end of Sir Basil's good name. In the French case, Judge Prince had been steadily selling off his investments, witnesses stated that he had often intimated that he intended to throw himself under a train, and his death was attributed to suicide. It was the last time that Wensley participated in an investigation.

These interludes aside, Wensley had got to work on his memoirs, and in October 1930 these were serialised in the *Sunday Express* over a period of weeks. Their publication caused a great deal of interest and excitement, not least with Sir Nicholas Grattan Grattan-Doyle, the MP for Newcastle upon Tyne North, and George Wilfred Holford Knight, the MP for Nottingham South. They both approached the Attorney General, William Allen Jowitt PC, KC, asking him to prosecute Wensley under the Official Secrets Act, saying that these revelations had betrayed vital confidences to the advantage of criminals and the detraction of criminal investigation.

Of course, they had done nothing of the kind, and the vast majority of Labour MPs disagreed with those two honourable members, as did the Attorney General and the commissioner, who thought that this type of publication was just the thing to rouse the flagging confidence of the public in the police.

In 1931 Wensley's memoirs, *Detective Days*, were published (in New York they appeared as *Forty Years of Scotland Yard*). The memoirs were syndicated all around the world and were a tremendous success, particularly appreciated by the author and creator of 'Tarzan', Edgar Rice Burroughs.

Wensley had not been forgotten; even in his retirement, when East Enders were arrested, it was quite common to hear them say, in an attempt to prove innocence or plausibility, 'But I know Mr Venzel!'

\* \* \*

So Wensley settled down to retirement; he operated an open-house policy to his many friends, who called to admire his large garden, in which he had installed a pond stocked with goldfish, a rockery, a summer house and trellis-work, and where he grew roses; there was also his collection of Goss china, old coins and stamps. He still dressed immaculately in a well-pressed grey suit, and carried gloves. Cigarettes had now been discarded in favour of a silver-mounted briar pipe. The years passed, and then, to Wensley's great distress, Lollie died at home aged seventy-four on 25 February 1943; her death was attributed to high blood pressure, inflammation of the kidneys and heart disease, and her married sister, Mrs Beale, was with her at the end. Lollie had not been well for some time; Wensley noted in his diary on 22 July 1937 that she had suffered 'a severe seizure', and she never regained her power of speech. He had already purchased a plot at Old Southgate Cemetery as a memorial to his two sons; it was there that Lollie was buried on 29 February.

Wensley, too, had suffered poor health; early in September 1939 he had experienced great discomfort in his leg, which led to him being bedridden for several weeks – this had made it impossible for him to care for Lollie and resulted in the employment of a housekeeper, Miss A.W. Hogan, who looked after them both.

In 1947 recipients of his letters noted that his copperplate handwriting had markedly deteriorated, as had his eyesight; the following year, a specialist was consulted. By March 1949 Wensley appeared haggard and his face had a vacant look. Senility had laid its heavy hand on him, and he became delusional; the sight of knives drove him to a frenzy, and at mealtimes a spoon had to be substituted.

On 4 December 1949 Wensley died, at the age of eighty-four. His daughter, Edie Cory, was present at his deathbed, in the beloved home of which he had seen so little. He had suffered from hardening of the arteries, and death came as a result of this, heart failure and senility. Wensley had previously given instructions that on his headstone should be inscribed, 'Faithful unto Death'. His estate was valued at £15,429 10s 0d.

# Epilogue

Frederick Wensley was still well enough remembered for his death to make newspaper headlines; the *News Chronicle* proclaimed, 'Wensley the great detective is dead', the news flashed around the world and the *New York Herald Tribune* gave enormous coverage to his career. Quite often, these reports were inaccurate, the most common error being that Wensley had been awarded the King's Police Medal for gallantry for his actions in saving Leeson during the siege of Sidney Street – whereas Wensley had actually been awarded the medal over a year earlier, for distinguished service.

Tributes from his contemporaries came flooding in. Detective Chief Superintendent Jack Capstick – known to the underworld as 'Charlie Artful' – recalled with pride how, as a new police constable having being commended by a Bow Street magistrate in 1925, he was taken to the Yard to be personally congratulated by Wensley. 'As a detective, he was one of the finest, if not the finest, in the Metropolitan Police,' said Capstick, who spent many years with the Flying Squad and headed the secretive post-war Ghost Squad.

'No one,' said Deputy Commander William Rawlings OBE, MC, 'knew as much about the East End as he did.' Detective Superintendent John Gosling, who, like Capstick, spent many years with the Flying Squad and Ghost Squad, and joined the Metropolitan Police just as Wensley was leaving it, put matters in their correct perspective. When Gosling praised Divisional Detective Inspector William Salisbury as being, 'The greatest of them all', he was careful to add, 'after Wensley'.

Having been appointed to the CID in 1923, Ted Greeno rushed off to be best man at the wedding of his brother, who asked him, 'Are you going to be another Nick Carter?'

Grinning from ear to ear, Greeno replied, 'No. Another Fred Wensley – if I can!'

And Woman Detective Inspector Lilian Wyles had this to say:

Because of his own wonderful successes in bringing so many criminals to justice, because he solved so many famous crimes a lesser man might overlook, Frederick Wensley will always remain Scotland Yard's greatest detective. His eyes, deep-set, clear and piercing, seemed to read every thought that passed through one's mind. No wonder criminals feared to face that dark, saturnine man with the soul-searching eyes! Famous criminal lawyers like Sir Edward Marshall Hall and Sir Richard Muir admired him and named him the greatest detective of all time.

So was Wensley 'the greatest detective of all time' – as he is often called? The short answer is, yes, of course he was. Wensley led and others followed. The great detectives – Fabian, Capstick and Greeno, to mention but a few – became household names and were associated with some of the Yard's greatest successes in the years prior to and following Wensley's retirement. It was due to Wensley's driving, inspirational personality; those officers wanted to be just like him.

'Don't be afraid to make honest mistakes,' Wensley would tell his subordinates. 'Decide upon a line of enquiry and don't let anything or anybody deflect you from it until you are satisfied that you have gone through with it to the end.' And on the subject of integrity, Wensley would add, 'You can't deceive yourself – others may not know, but you do.' It was a homily that could be attended to with advantage by today's detectives.

It took Wensley just over forty years to bring the Yard's Criminal Investigation Department to its zenith – for it to shine like a beacon to the rest of the civilised world, to show them that its methods and training produced detectives who could be counted upon to solve the most baffling of crimes. That is his epitaph; it is sad that no one at Scotland Yard can now remember his name.

# Bibliography

ADAMSON, Iain, *The Great Detective* (Frederick Muller Ltd, 1966)

BERRETT, James, *When I Was at Scotland Yard* (Sampson Low, Marston & Co Ltd, 1932)

BEVERIDGE, Peter, *Inside the CID* (Evans Bros. Ltd, 1957)

BROWN, D., *The Rise of Scotland Yard* (Greenwood Press, 1956)

BROWNE, Douglas G. and TULLETT, E. V., *Bernard Spilsbury – His Life & Cases* (George G. Harrap & Co, 1951)

BROWNE, Douglas G., *The Rise of Scotland Yard* (George G. Harrap & Co, 1956)

BUNKER, John, *From Rattle to Radio* (KAF Brewin Books, 1988)

BURNETT, R. J., *Wensley of Scotland Yard – The Life and Adventures of the 'Ace' Detective* (Unpublished typescript, Bishopsgate Institute, circa 1960)

BURT, Leonard, *Commander Burt of Scotland Yard* (Heinemann, 1959)

CAPSTICK, John (with Jack Thomas), *Given in Evidence* (John Long, 1960)

CHERRILL, Fred, *Cherrill of the Yard* (George G. Harrap & Co, 1954)

CONNELL, Nicholas and EVANS, Stewart P., *The Man Who Hunted Jack the Ripper* (Rupert Books, 2000)

CORNISH, G. W., *Cornish of the Yard* (John Lane, the Bodley Head, 1935)

DARBYSHIRE, Neil and HILLIARD, Brian, *The Flying Squad* (Headline Book Publishing, 1993)

DIVALL, Tom, *Scoundrels and Scallywags* (Ernest Benn Ltd, 1929)

EVANS, Stewart P. and RUMBELOW, Donald, *Jack the Ripper – Scotland Yard Investigates* (Sutton Publishing, 2006)

FABIAN, Robert, *Fabian of the Yard* (Naldrett Press, 1950)

FABIAN, Robert, *London after Dark* (Naldrett Press, 1954)

FIDO, Martin and SKINNER, Keith, *The Official Encyclopedia of Scotland Yard* (Virgin Books, 1999)

FIRMIN, Stanley, *Scotland Yard: The Inside Story* (Hutchinson & Co, 1948)

FRASIER, David K., *Murder Cases of the Twentieth Century* (McFarland & Co, 1996)

FROST, George, *Flying Squad* (Rockliff, 1948)

GOSLING, John, *The Ghost Squad* (WH Allen, 1959)

GRANT, Denis, *A Fragmented History of the Flying Squad, its Transport, Drivers and Detectives* (Boxing programme notes, 1976)

GREENO, Edward, *War on the Underworld* (John Long, 1960)

HAMBROOK, Walter, *Hambrook of the Yard* (Robert Hale & Co, 1937)

HART, E.T., *Britain's Godfather* (True Crime Library, 1993)

HATHERILL, George, *A Detective's Story* (Andre Deutsch Ltd, 1971)

HIGGINS, R.H., *In the Name of the Law* (John Long, 1958)

HILL, Billy, *Boss of Britain's Underworld* (Naldrett Press, 1955)

HONEYCOMBE, Gordon, *The Complete Murders of the Black Museum* (Leopard Books, 1995)

HOSKINS, Percy, *No Hiding Place!* (Daily Express Publications, undated)

HOWE, Sir Ronald, *The Story of Scotland Yard* (Arthur Barker Ltd, 1958)

HOWE, Sir Ronald, *The Pursuit of Crime* (Arthur Barker Ltd, 1961)

INWOOD, Stephen, *A History of London* (Macmillan, 1998)

JACKETT, Sam, *Heroes of Scotland Yard* (Robert Hale Ltd, 1965)

KENNISON, P. and SWINDEN, D., *Behind the Blue Lamp* (Coppermill Press, 2003)

KIRBY, Dick, *The Squad – A History of the Men and Vehicles of the Flying Squad at New Scotland Yard, 1919–1983* (Unpublished manuscript, Metropolitan Police History Museum, London 1993)

KIRBY, Dick, *The Guv'nors* (Wharncliffe Books, 2010)

KIRBY, Dick, *The Sweeney* (Wharncliffe Books, 2011)

KIRBY, Dick, *Scotland Yard's Ghost Squad* (Wharncliffe Books, 2011)

KIRBY, Dick, *The Brave Blue Line* (Wharncliffe Books, 2011)

KRAY, Reg, *Villains We Have Known* (Arrow Books, 1996)

LEE, Christopher, *This Sceptred Isle* (BBC Worldwide, 1999)

LINKLATER, Eric, *The Corpse on Clapham Common* (Macmillan, 1971)

LOCK, Joan, *Scotland Yard Casebook* (Robert Hale, 1993)

LUCAS, Norman and SCARLETT, Bernard, *The Flying Squad* (Arthur Barker Ltd, 1968)

LUCAS, Norman, *Britain's Gangland* (WH Allen, 1969)

McCALL, Karen (ed), *London Branch NARPO Millennium Magazine* (Orphans Press, Leominster, 1999)

McKNIGHT, Gerald, *The Murder Squad* (WH Allen, 1967)

MORRIS, R. M., *Wensley, Frederick Porter, 1865-1949, Police Officer* (Oxford Dictionary of National Biography, 2004-2012)

MORTON, James, *Gangland – London's Underworld* (Little, Brown, 1992)

MORTON, James, *Bent Coppers* (Little, Brown, 1993)

MORTON, James, *Supergrasses and Informers* (Little, Brown, 1995)

MORTON, James, *East End Gangland* (Little, Brown, 2000)

MORTON, James and PARKER, Gerry, *Gangland Bosses* (Time Warner Books, 2005)

MOYLEN, J. F., *Scotland Yard and the Metropolitan Police* (GP Putnam's Sons Ltd, 1929)

MURPHY, Robert, *Smash & Grab* (Faber & Faber, 1993)

NARBOROUGH, Fred, *Murder on my Mind* (Allan Wingate, 1959)

PEARSON, John, *The Profession of Violence* (Weidenfeld & Nicolson, 1972)

RAWLINGS, William, *A Case for the Yard* (John Long, 1961)

ROBINSON, Dr David J., *The Wensley Family at War, Work and Play* (Unpublished typescript, Bishopsgate Institute, 2007)

ROSE, Andrew, *Stinie – Murder on the Common* (The Bodley Head, 1985)

RUMBELOW, Donald, *The Houndsditch Murders and the Siege of Sidney Street* (WH Allen, 1988)

SAMUEL, Raphael, *East End Underworld* (Routledge & Kegan Paul, 1981)

SAVAGE, Percy, *Savage of the Yard* (Hutchinson & Co, 1934)

SELLWOOD, A.V., *Police Strike 1919* (WH Allen, 1978)

SHARPE, F.D., *Sharpe of the Flying Squad* (John Long, 1938)

SIMPSON, Keith, *Forty Years of Murder* (Harrap, 1978)

SPARKS, Herbert, *The Iron Man* (John Long, 1964)

SWINDEN D., KENNISON, P. and MOSS, A., *More Behind the Blue Lamp* (Coppermill Press, 2011)

TULLETT, Tom, *Strictly Murder* (Bodley Head, 1979)

WENSLEY, F.P., *Detective Days* (Cassell & Co, 1931)

WYLES, Lilian, *A Woman at Scotland Yard* (Faber & Faber, 1952)

YOUNG, Filson (ed), *The Trial of Bywaters and Thompson* (William Hodge & Co, 1923)

YOUNG, Hugh, *My Forty Years at the Yard* (WH Allen, 1955)

# Index

Abel, Elizabeth Jane, 66–7
Abel, William, 66–7
Abinger, Edward, 67, 76–8, 153–65
Abrahams, Barnet, 42–3
Abrahams, Soloman, 136
Abramovitch, Myer ('Myer the Insane'), 174–5
Adams, Thomas, 4–5
Adderley, Revd James, 8
Adele, Helene, 225–7
Alexander II, Tsar of Russia, 132
Allam, Det. Sgt. John, 56
Allen, Emily, 123–8
Alonsky, Samuel, 119
Ambrose, Dr Edward, 75
Andrews, William (associate of Harding), 169–72
Andrews, William – see Marsh, H.
Arbour Square police station, 75, 89, 105, 135, 137, 139
Armstrong, Major Herbert Rowse, TD, MA, 196–7
Armstrong, Katherine, 196–7
Arrow, Det. Supt. Charles, 177, 236
Ash, Henry, 94
Ashford, PC, 112
Ashley, Det. Supt. John, OBE, 184, 214, 235
Atkinson, PC 231 'H' Walter, 19, 43
Austin, Mary Ann, 46–7
Avenall, Edwin, 105
Avey, George, 65–6
Avory, Mr Justice, 170, 186, 213–15, 230–2

Bacchus, PC 359 'H' Ernest, 20–1
Badger, PC George, 221–5
Bailey, William, 34–5
Baker – see Briggs, J. (Sr)
Baker, Cecilia, 102
Baldwin, Stanley, Earl Baldwin of Bewdley KG, PC, FRS, 221
Bambery, Annie, 6
Bankes, Sir Eldon, GCB, KC, 112, 224
Banman – see Morrison, S.

Barker, Dr Aubrey, 176
Barnard, Herbert, 29–30
Barnes, Richard, 103
Bartley, Elizabeth, 6
Barton, Supt., 228–32
Baungart, Herman, 35
Baxter, Mr Wynne E. (Coroner), 47, 106
Beale, Mrs, 238
Beard, ex-DDI John, 211
Beaszon – see Blackcowsky, M.
Beattie, John, 34
Beck, Adolf, 16
Beckett, PC 414 'H' Zieba, 42–3
Beechenow, James, 117
Beilby, Albert, 87
Bellinger, Detective James, 149–50
Belper, Lord, 45–6
Bennett, Sir Henry Curtis, KC, 203–7
Benstead, Henry, 128–9
Bentley, PS Robert, 134
Bernstein, Dr, 135
Beron, Leon, 148–65
Beron, Soloman, 152, 158–9
Berrett, DCI James, 218
Bertillon, Alphonse, 16
Bessarabian Gang, 72–8
Beveridge, DCS Peter, MBE, 194, 232
Bietz, Jacob, 99
Bigham, Mr Justice, 76–8
Billington, James, 22, 105
'Billy the Greek', 182
Bingham, Lady Edith Ellen, née Drysdale, 208–9
Bingham, A/Commissioner Sir Trevor, 191, 208–9
Biron, Sir Charles (Magistrate), 169
Birkenhead, Lord, 224–5
Bishop, PC 455 'E', 7
Blackcowsky, Moses, 109
Blaschke, Conrad, 56–63
Bloom, Jacob, 115–16
Blue, Becky, 154
Bogard, Isaac, MM, 166–72

Bonati, Bianco, 217
Bonati, Minnie Alice, 216–18
Bone, Samuel Robert, 39
Bonn, John, 68–71
'Bouncing Albert' – see Hawkins, A.
Boustred, Insp. John, 46
Bowater, Rebecca, 20
Bowman, Samuel, 79
Bradford, Colonel Sir Edward,
    Bt., GCB, GCVO, KCSI
    (Commissioner), 7
Brannan, Superintendent, James, 3
Braum, Otto, 56–63
Braun, Frederick, 40
Briggs, John (Jnr) 86–7
Briggs, John, (Sr) 86–7
British Brothers' League, 132
Brodovitz, Henry, 73–8
Brodsky, Esther, 156
Brodsky, Jane, 156
Brogden, Det. Sgt. William, 14, 28,
    49–50, 150, 152, 162
Brook, Arthur – see Graham, R.
Brooks, Ellen – see Stevens, E.
Brooks, James, 68–71
Brootan, James, 105
Brown, Arthur, 214–15
Brown, Frederick, 35
Brown, William James, 53, 58
Browne, Frederick Guy, 218
Brozishewski, Barnett, 73–8
Brust, Julius, 209–10
Buller, John, 36
Burley, William George, 67–8
Burman, Jack, 167
Burt, Commander Leonard, CVO,
    CBE, 216
Burton, Charles, 84
Buxton, Ivy, 225
Byng, Field Marshal Julian
    Hedworth George, 1st Viscount
    Byng of Vimy, GCB, GCMG,
    MVO (Commissioner), 233
Bywaters, Frederick Edward Francis,
    200–7
Bywaters, Lilian (mother), 201

Calib, Lewis, 115–16
Callaghan, Charles, 111–12, 169–72
Callaghan, Michael, 24–5
Cancellor, Henry (Magistrate), 221
Cantwell, Thomas, 10–11
Capone, Alfonse 'Scarface', 236
Capstick, DCS John Richard, 239,
    240

'Captain', 214–15
Carlin, Det. Supt. Francis, 182, 191,
    197, 219
Carr, PC, 111–12
Carr, Mr J.W., 96
'Carroty Nell' – see Coles, F.
Castling, Alfred, 154–5
Caunter, Det. Sgt. Eli ('Tommy
    Roundhead'), 14
Cavalho, Aaron, 36
Cave, George, KC, MP, 164
Chandler, William, 179
Channell, Mr Justice, 17
Chapman, George – see Klosowski,
    S.
Chapman, William, 81
Chasleberg, Alex, 119
Chatfield, John, 33
Chesnovski, John, 175–6
Chilvers, George, 30
Choat, PC Walter, 134
'Chocolate Soldier' – see Horwood,
    W.T.F.
Churchill, Home Secretary Winston
    Spencer, OM, PC, MP, 141–2,
    161, 163
Cinnamon, Mrs, 150, 151
Clainowitz, Hyman, 78
Clarke, DDI, 221–5
Clarke, Dr Percy John, 129, 175
Clarke, PC 279 'H' William, 44–5
Clavell, Eva – see D'Angely, E.
Clayton, PC 541 'Y', John William,
    225–7
Cluer, Mr (Magistrate), 112, 114
Clay, PC 472 'H' George, 83
Clayton, Ethel, 164
Clynes, Home Secretary John
    Robert, PC, MP, 233
Cockfield, Harold, 155
Cohen, Harry, 120–1
Cohen, Louis, 115
Cohen, Michael, 119
Cohen, Samuel (interpreter), 75
Cohen, Samuel, (Jewish Assoc. for
    Protection of Girls & Women),
    120
Coleridge, Mr Justice, 130
Coles, Frances 'Carroty Nell', 42, 44
Collins, DCI Alfred, 221–5, 236–7
Colman, Hyman, 74–8
Colman, Israel, 74–8
Colman, John, 101
Connor, James, 48–52
Cooper, Det. Supt. Charles, 230

Cooper, Stephen, 167–72
Cornish, Det. Supt. George, 216–18
Cornwall, Edgar (Jnr), 25–7
Cornwall, Edgar, (Sr), 25–7
Cory, Edith, née Wensley, 214, 238
Cory, Harold Frederick Wensley, 214
Cox, Frederick, 47–52, 64, 182
Craggs, Edwin, 48
Crawley, Ellen, 34
Crichton, William – see Graham, R.
Croney, Charles, 118
Cronin, James, 25
Cronin, Michael, 44–5
Crook, Mr G.T., 194
Crouch, Henry, 94–5
Crundle, Robert, 30
Cunningham, William, 157
Curry, James Valentine, 100–1
Curtis, L. Perry, Jr, 9

Dacey, Martin, 117
Dalby, Alice, 80
D'Angely, Eva, 110–11
D'Angely, René, 110–11
Dangerfield, Athelstan, 55, 56, 57,
    58, 61–2
Dangerfield, Susannah, 62
'Darky' – see Pease, L.R.C.
'Darky the Coon' – see Bogard, I.
Darling, Mr Justice, 153–63, 179,
    186, 189, 197, 212
Dart, PC 45 'H' Stephen, 160
Davis, Bario, 109
Davis, Mark, 109
Day, Frank, 86
De Grey, Hon. John, (Magistrate),
    152
De Lava, Thelma, 237
Deitch, Nellie, 149, 154, 157
Delafuente, Abraham, 80–1
Delafuente, Henry, 80–1
Deller, PC, 112
Dellow, Florrie, 151, 157
Denman, Mr (Magistrate), 110
Deppe, Mr, 38
Dessent, Det. Sgt. Henry, 14, 87,
    150
'Detective Benshaw' – see Brown, A.
'Detective Lynch' – see Tannen, A.
Dew, DCI Walter, 177
Dewey, Thomas, 236
Dickinson, Mr (Magistrate), 65, 67,
    99

Divall, DCI Thomas, 15–16, 46–7,
    49–52, 56, 57, 64–5, 67, 81, 87,
    102–6, 110, 115–16, 119, 177
Dodd, Superintendent Charles, 12
Donovan, Conrad, 103–6
Douglas, William, 10
Downes, William, 25
Dreseer, Richard – see Muller, S.
Dries, William, 194
Driver, Alice, 51
'Drooper' – see Neil, A.
Drought, Dr Percy James, 200, 201
Dubof, Yourka, 134–45
Duggan, James, 24
Duncan, Ethel, 212
Durrell, Henry, 54, 56, 57, 58
Dutiel – see D'Angely, E.
Dyer, Amelia Elizabeth, 22
Dyer, Dr Sidney Reginald, 175

Eagles, Joseph – see Goddard, G.
Earp, Wyatt, 235
Edgar, David, 69
Edgar, Myer, 68–71
Edward, Henry – see Moffatt, H.
Edwards, James, 68–71
Elliott, Ass. Commissioner Frank,
    208
Elliott, PC 140 'H' William, 21–2,
    23
Elliott, Mr. (Barrister), 116
Ellis, John, 187, 198
Ellis, Thomas, 52
'Emms' – see Spencer, W.
Engelstein, Joseph, 209–10, 222
Esener, Arthur – see Hansen, E.
Evrart, Mr, 185

Fabian, Det. Supt. Robert Honey,
    KPM, 240
Farley, James, 98
Farmer, Emily, 101–6
Farmer, Victor Newton, 104–5
Federoff, Osip, 137–45
Filler, William, 116–17
Fitzpatrick, James, 105
Fitzwater, Francis, 82–4
Fleishman, Rebecca, 140
Flitcher, Joseph, 82
Flitterman, Eva, 152–3
Flying Squad, 9, 63, 182–3, 189–98,
    201, 209, 229, 233, 234, 235
Ford, William, 25–7
Foster, Detective Ernest, 201
Fowler, DCI, 182

Fowler, Henry, 22
Fox, DCI Fred, 177, 183
Franci, Gustavo, 40
Francis-Williams, Mr Recorder B.,
    KC, 95–7
Frank, Max, 153
Freeman, Insp. John, 124–5
Freyberger, Dr Frederick, 148
Friday, Berthold, 38
Friday, Hugo, 38
Fulton, Colonel Carrie, 54, 56

Gadda, Anna, 230–2
Gale, Sarah Ann, 19–23
Garalovitch, Philip, 73
Gardstein, George, 134–45
George V, HM King, 131, 142, 232
Gerard, Émilienne, 184–7, 222
Gershon, Betty, 139–40
Gibson, PC 23 'H' Harry, 169
Gilby, Charles, 81–2
Gill, Charles, KC, 43
Gill, Det. Sgt. John W., 14, 26, 33,
    36, 38, 45, 52, 56, 58, 64, 69–70,
    81, 119–20
Gillender, Mr, 113–14
Gillham, Charles, 102
Girdler, Detective, 66
Girtler, Lewis, 115–16
Gladstone, Herbert John, 1st.
    Viscount, GCB, GCMG, GBE,
    PC, JP, 110
Glown, Abram – see Leonard, F.
Goddard, SPS George, 228–32
Godley, Det. Insp. George Albert,
    110
Gold, Louis, 120–1
Goldberg, Morris, 76
Goldbloom, Jane, 120–1
Goldsmith, Morris, 77–8
Goldstein – see Svaars, F.
Goldstein, Joseph, 77–8
Gonzewski, Victoria, 175–6
Gonzewski, Vincent, 175–6
Gooding, Detective Frederick,
    107–8
Goodman, Dr Percy Tranter, 175
Gordon, Isaac, 137
Gosling, Det. Supt. John Neville,
    239
Gotthelf, Rosie, 176
Gough, DCI, 182
Gould, Det. Sgt. Alfred, 56, 81–2
Graham, Jennie, 94–7
Graham, Robert, 93–7

Grandahl, Anna, 41
Grant, Dr Charles, 74
Grantham, Mr Justice, 104–5, 143–5
Grattan-Doyle, Sir Nicholas
    Grattan, MP, 237
Gray, Thomas, 5
Graydon, Avis, 200–1
Great Scotland Yard, 2
Greaves, PC 86 'H' George, 160–4
Green, George, 77
Green, Pinkus, 45
Green, Thomas, 155
Greenbaum, Rose, 29–30
Greenberg, Matilda, 106–8
Greeno, DCS Ted, MBE, 195, 239,
    240
Gregory, Dr, 34
Griffiths, Thomas, 80
Grimes, PS Walter, 200
Grimshaw, George Stanley, 197–8
Gristis, Minna – see Vassilleva, N.
Grose, Esther, 157
Grose, Henry Charles, 75
Gurney, PC 51 'H' Harry, 169
Gutteridge, PC George, 218

Haimovitch, Joseph, 75–8
Hall, Sir Edward Marshall, 240
Hall, DDI Francis, 200, 205
Hall, Harold, 128–30
Hall, Lena, 154
Hall, Robert, 66
Hambrook, Det. Supt. Walter,
    192–4, 234
Hammerman, James, 10
Hancock, Detective John, 203
Hansen, Edwin, 41
Harben, Mr H.D. (Barrister), 130
Harding, Arthur, 111–14, 166–73
Harding, PC 51 'H' Harry, 43
Harnett, Mr (Solicitor), 106
Harold, Mary, 66
Harris, Henry Samuel, 133–4, 143
Hartley, Edward, 26, 28–9
Hartman, Emily, 54
Hatch, Ernest, 53
Hauten, Matthias, 56–63
Hawkins, Det. Supt. Albert
    'Bouncing Albert', 182, 191, 197,
    219
Hawkins, Harry Alfred, 194
Hawkins, PC 325 'H' James, 83
Hawkins, Mr Justice, 21–2
Hayes, Daniel, 38
Hayman, Edward, 154

Healy, John, 189
Hearn, William George 'Fatty', 36–7
Hefeld, Paul, 133
Henderson, Colonel Sir Edmund,
    KCB, RE (Commissioner), 15
Henry, Sir Edward, Bt., GCVO,
    KCB, CSI (Commissioner), 46,
    161, 165, 187
Hepburn, CSM Montague Cecil
    Keith, MM, RE, 190
Herbert, Revd George W., 3
Herbert, James, 117
Hermilin, Henry, 154
Hewart, LCJ, 214–15
Hill, Robert, 80–1
Hiller, William, 117
Hincks, Dr Tom, 196
Hodges, Dr William Cliff, 168
Hoffman, Karl, 143–4
Hogan, Miss A.W, 238
Hollander, Rebecca, 107–8
Holmes, Lizzie, 154
Holt, Mrs P, 217
Hooper, PC 111 'H' James, 102
Horwood, Beryl, 208
Horwood, Brigadier General Sir
    William Thomas Francis, GBE,
    KCB, DSO (Commissioner),
    208–9, 218–19, 227, 233
Hughes, Eileen, 68
Hughes, Percy, 68
Humphreys, Mr Justice, 226–7
Hunt, Det. Sgt., 110
Hutchings, Charles, 24–5
Hymens – see Weiner W.
Hymes, Ben, 95–6

Inskip, Sir Thomas, KC, 203–6

'Jack the Ripper', 5–6, 9, 12, 32, 42,
    47, 110, 191
Jackson, James, 33
Jacobs, Lewis, 115–16
Jacoby, Henry, 197
Jeffries, Detective Harry, 149–50
Jelf, Mr Justice, 51–2, 127
'Jew-boy' – see Stevens, J.
'Jix' – see Joynson-Hicks, Sir W.
Joab, Esther, 106–8
'Johnny Upright' – see Thick, W.
Jones, Sir David Brynmor, 113
Jones, Florence, 210–11
Jones, John, 117
Jones, PC 243 'H' Major, 69
Jones, PC 166 'H' Noah, KPM, 180

Jones, Dr Thomas, MRCS, 67, 124,
    126
'Joseph' – see Sokoloff, W.
Josling, PS Horace, 228–32
Joslovitch, Julius, 84–6
Jowitt, Attorney-General William
    Allen, PC, KC, 237
Joynson-Hicks, Home Secretary Sir
    William, Bt., PC, DL, ('Jix'), 223

Kane, DCI John, 177
Kaplin – see Soulman, D.
Karmaryzn, Sam, 33
Karowsky, Hyman, 99
Katz, Lizzie, 136
Kaye, Emily Beilby, 212–15, 218
Keating, Thomas, 38
Keith, Thomas, 65
Kennedy, Patrick Michael, 218
Kennedy, William Henry – see
    Kennedy, P.M.
Kennington Lane police station, 3
Kid McCoy – see Moses M.
Kigesky, Woolf, 76
King, Cornelius, 180
King, George, 167–2
King, PC 175 'S' Thomas, 57–60, 62
King, William – see Seaman, W.
Klosowski, Severin, 191
Knell, Insp. Frank, 118
Knight, George Wilfred Holford,
    MP, 237
Konopbaki – see Lewis, J.
Kovalsky, Morris, 180
Kron, Morris, 115
Krovesky, Simon, 74–8
Kuttner, Morris, 38

Lambeth, 2–6
'Landlord' – see Beron, L.
Lapsley, Det. Sgt. Harry, 28
Lasserson, Hermann, 174–5
Latinsky, Louis, 78
Latrine, Mr Justice, 29
Laurie, DAC Sir Percy Robert,
    KCVO, CBE, DSO, 219
Lawes, Mr E.T.H., 142
Lawrence, Mr Justice, 11, 92
Lawrence, John, 81
Lawrence, Henry, 81
Lawrence, William, 117
Lawrence, William Henry, 50–1
Lawton, Martha, 19, 23
Lazarus, David, 87–8, 89
Lechtenstein, Aaron, 181

Lee, DDI Sam, 86–7, 103–4, 107–8, 110, 115, 121
Lee Commission, 227
Lee, Lord, of Fareham, 227
Lees-Smith, Hastings Bertrand, MP, 224
Leeson, Det. Sgt. Ben, 52, 57, 72, 89–92, 108, 115, 136, 140–2, 145
Leigh, Robert, 84
Leman, Eli, 109
Leman Street police station, 9, 59, 76, 125, 136, 148, 160–1, 175
Lemmer, Mary, 55
Leonard, Frank, 214–15
Lepidus, Jacob, 133
Le Sage, Dr Charles, 20
Levi, Joe – see Smoller, M.
Levine, Arthur, 64–5
Levine, Sarah, 120–1
Levy, Abraham, 119
Levy, Isaac, 134, 143–4
Levy, John (robber), 37
Levy, John Goodman, 19–23
Lewis, Cooksey, 73–8
Lewis, Frederick, 48–52
Lewis, PC 332 'H' Henry, 83
Lewis, Jack, 118–19
Lewis, Jane, 84–6
Lipman, Marks, 76
Lipman, Michael, 38
Lipmann, Philip, 167–8
Lipshitz, Soloman, 115–16
Littmann, Jacob, 25
'Little Darky' – see Pease, L.R.C.
Lloyd George, David, 1st Earl Lloyd-George of Dwyfor, OM, PC, 188, 221
'Lollie' – see Wensley L.E.
'Long Fred' – see Lewis, F.
Long, John, 34–5
Long, John (killer), 100
Long, Samuel, 34–5
Lonsdale, Lord, 191
Loufer, Morris, 180
Loufer, Samuel, 180
Loughlin, Ch. Insp. George, 124–5
Loveland-Loveland, Richard, KC, DL, JP, 116
Lyall, Gladys, 98

MacIntosh, PC 323 'H' James, 123–4
Macmillan, Hugh, MP, 227
Macnaughten, Ass. Commissioner Sir Melville, CB, KPM, 31–2, 105, 141, 148, 161, 162, 165, 177, 181
Macready, General the Rt. Hon. Sir Cecil Frederick Nevil, Bt., GCMG, KCB (Commissioner), 191, 208
Maddocks, Sidney, 54, 57, 62
Mahon, Jessie, 211
Mahon, Patrick Herbert, 211–14
Mahoney, Annie, 178
Maples, Joseph, 214–15
'Marguerite', 185
Marks, David, 115
Marks, John, 89–92
Marriott, George – see Bonn J.
Marsh, Catherine, 37
Marsh, Henry, 37
Marshall, Thomas, 17–18
Martin, Oswald, 196–7
Matthews, Sir Charles, 165
Matthews, Henry, PC, QC, 11
McCarthy – see Bonn J.
McCarthy, Dennis, 99–100
McCarthy, Det. Supt. John, 182, 184
McCarthy, Rose, 99–100
McEacharn, Charles Malcolm, 123–8
McGuire, David, 81
McKay, Sub-Div. Insp., 110
McKenna, Det. Sgt. Henry, 51
McKenzie, Insp. Roderick, 150, 162
McLean, PC Alexander, 221–5
McNally, James, 84
Mead, Mr (Magistrate), 38, 76
Meiklejohn, Det. Sgt. John, 182
Mew, PS Walter, 200
Meyrick, Kate Evelyn, née Nason, ('Ma'), 228–32
Michaels, Reuben, 181
Mieland, Marks, 76
Miles, Charles, 25–7
Millar, Lucy, 53, 58
Miller, Lewis, 77
Milsom, Albert, 22
Milstein, Annie, 174–5
Milstein, Jack, 136
Milstein, Luba, 135–45
Milstein, Nathan, 136
Milstein, Solomon, 174–5
Mintz, Joe, 153–4, 155–6, 157
Mitchell, Thomas, 102, 106
Mitchell, Mrs (mother of Thomas), 106

Moffatt, Edward M. – *see* Moffatt, H.
Moffatt, Henry, 93–7
Moffatt, Maxwell – *see* Moffatt, H.
Money, Sir Leo George Chiozza, 221–5
'Monge' – *see* Oreman, S.
Monro, Commissioner James, CB, 13, 31
Montgomery, Insp., 28
Moran, George 'Bugs', 236
Morris, Mr (Barrister), 62
Morris, James, 38
Morrison, Stinie, 147–65, 181, 199
Morrissy, Daniel, 82–4
Moses, Max, 73–8
Muclock, PC 286 'H' John, 83
Muir, Sir Richard, KC, 101, 130, 153–65, 170–2, 240
Muller, Saul, 56–63
Mulvany, Superintendent John, 31
Mumford, PC 863 'W' Joseph, 148
Munro, Hector, 156
Murray, William, 65–6
Musheat, Nathan, 40
'Myer the Insane' – *see* Abramovitch, M.
Myers, Jacob, 32
Myers, Woolf, 55
Mygren, Francis Victor, 10
Mysore, Maharaja of, 180

Nash, Isidor, 35
Nealon, PC 727 'P', 193–4
Needham, William – *see* Marshall, T.
Neil, Det. Supt. Arthur 'Drooper', 191, 197, 199, 219
Neimann, Abraham, 76–8
Neville, Frances, 38–9
Nevy, Dolly, 154
'Newcastle Arthur' – *see* Brown, A.
Newell, DI, William, 138, 139
Newman, William, 167–72
Nicholls, Edwin, 48–52
'Night Club Queen' – *see* Meyrick, K.E.
Nixon, George, 44
Nursey, DS Richard, 155
Nutt, Albert, 125
Nutt, Mrs, 124

Ockey, DDI Edward Michael, KPM, 234
Odessian Gang, 72–8
Oreman, Samuel 'Monge', 73–8

O'Shea, Patsy, 178–9
Ottaway, Det. Supt. John, 134, 139, 146
Owen, William, 38

Page, Det. Insp. Frank, 201
Palmer, Edward, 64
Palmer, George, 64
Palmer, Henry – *see* Moffatt, H.
Palmer, Thomas, 95
Panton, James, 80
Parkes, Isaac, 178–9
Parnell, PC 256 'H' William, 99–100
Parsons, John, 53
Paul, Ada, 178
Paul, Ellen, 6
Payne, Detective, 12
Payne, Mr, 37
Pearman, Thomas, 45
Pease, Lilian Rose Caroline 'Darky', 178–9
Perkoff, Mr, 73
Perrin, William George, 79–81
'Peter the Painter' – *see* Piatkov, P.
Peters, Franz, 56–63
Peters, Jacob, 134–45
Petley, John, 66
Petropavloff, Alex – *see* Morrison, S.
Philbey, PC, 112
Phillimore, Mr Justice, 43
Phillips, George, 53, 58, 62
Phillips, Montague (Magistrate), 6
Piatkov, Peter, 135–45
Pickett, Insp. John, 75
Pierrepoint, Henry, 105, 213–14
Pilenas, Casimir, 138, 145
Piper, PC Walter, 133–4, 143
Pittard, Dora Finch, 200
Police Strike (1890), 7
Police Strike (1918), 187–8
Police Strike (1919), 190
Pollard, William – *see* Graham, R.
Pool, Hugo, 164
Poppie, Hulda, 101
Potter, Joseph – *see* Donovan, C.
Powell, Martha, 101
Premislow, Morris, 125
Pride, DDI George, 82
Prince, Judge Albert, 236–7
Proud, Elizabeth, 6
Pryor, PC 145 'H' Arthur, 73–4
Pye, Detective, Alfred, 109

Quinn, Charles Thomas, 10–11

Rae, Robert, 103, 104
Raggert, Herbert, 157
Rankin, Det. Insp., 94
Ratman – see Gold, L.
Rault, Nellie Florence Ruby, 189–90
Rawlings, D/Commander William, OBE, MC, 194, 239
Rayner, Frank, 114
Read, Det. Sgt., 185
Rebork, Max, 52–63
Reid, DDI Edmund John James, 12–13, 64
Reid, Sir Hugh Gilzean, 55, 58
Reidy, Dr Jerome Joseph, 131
Reiners, Henry, 81
Reubens, Marks, 123–8
Reubens, Morris, 123–8
Reuter, Ernest, 40
Ribuffi, Luigi Achille, 230–2
Richards, PS 14 'A' Sidney, 129
Richardson, PC 442 'H' Henry, 10, 19–20, 29, 37, 110
'Richette', 228–32
Richford, Thomas, 10
Ridgley, Elizabeth, 189
Ridley, Mr Justice, 175
Roberts, PC 474 'H' Bertrand, 80
Robins, PC 522 'H' William, 169
Robinson, John, 217–18, 222
Robinson, Mrs, 217–18
Roche, Berthe, 185–7
Rochford, Thomas, 41
Rockman, Abraham, 174–5
Rogers, Henry, 34
Rolls, Frederick, 217
Rolls, Minnie – see Bonati, M.A.
Ronan, Kate 'Kitty', 128–30
Rooney, Kate – see Ronan, K.
Rose, Ezekiel, 64–5
Rose, Det. Sgt. Thomas, 50, 57, 64–5
Rosen, John, 137–45
Rosen, Sam, 152–3
Rosenberg, Marks, 35
Rosenberg, Mr, 73
Rosenthal, Benjamin, 122
Rosenthal, Isaac, 122
Rotten – see Donovan, C.
Rowe, William, 54
Royal Commission (1903), 132
Royal Commission (1908), 110–14
Rumsby, George, 10
Rush, George, 79
Russell, Earl, 111–12
Rutter, Detective Henry, 126

Sacker, Daniel, 109
Salisbury, DCI William Abednego, 239
Salveskie, August, 56–63
Samuels, Harry, 168
Samuels, Kate, 168
Saunders, William – see Seaman, W.
Savage, Det. Supt. Percy, 17, 211–15, 216, 235
Savidge, Miss Irene, 221–5, 227
Scanlon, Dr John James, 135
'Schafshi Khan' – see Gardstein, G.
Schennick, William, 10
Schneider, Mme, – see Suck, S.
Seaman, William, 18–23
Sellars, DI Richard, 200, 201, 202
Selvitzky, Woolf, 76
Seymour, Henry – see Moffatt, H.
Shafer, William, 19
Shalinsky, Harris, 77
Shamos, Solomon, 74–8
Shannon, Kate, 38–9
Shapiloff, Lazarus, 40
Sharpe, DCI Frederick Dew, 9, 172, 195, 229
Sharpe, Montague, 53, 56
Sharper, Harry, 68–71
Shearman, Mr Justice, 203–6
Sheppard, Robert, 210–11
Shiel, Able Seaman, 95–6
Shonck, Philip, 167
Shor, Isadore, 77
Shrimpton, Gaius, 49–52
Shrimpton, James – see Connor, J.
Sidney Street, siege of, 139–42
Simmons, Harry, 119
Simmons, PC 75 'H' Henry, 123, 125
Simon, Sir John, MP, 223
Slade, Mr (Magistrate), 5
Smart, Detective, Thomas, 38, 50, 104
Smeller, Marks, 115–16
Smith, A/PS, 226–7
Smith, Catherine, 34
Smith, Detective Charley, 27, 30, 58–9, 80
Smith, George, 117
Smith, Dr Lewis, 19
Smith, Judge Lumley, 121
Smith, Mr. Commissioner, R.L, KC, 61–3
Smith, William, 48–52
Smoller, Max, 134–45
Snelwar, Alec, 153, 155

Snelwar, Becky, 153
Soane, Alfred Robert, 39
Sokoloff, William, 142, 144
'Soldier Billy', 182
Solomons, Henry, 27–9
Solomons, Isaac, 27–9
Solomons, Samuel, 27–9
Somerton, William, 45
Soubiger – see D'Angely, R.
Soulman, Rosen, 89–92, 97
Southey, William, 113
Spencer, Insp. Frank, 43
Spencer, Herbert Henry, 35–6
Spencer, William 'Emms', 167–72
Spilsbury, Sir Bernard, 17, 185–7, 189, 204–6, 213–15, 216
Sproul, William, 123–8
Stark, Det. Supt John, 134, 146
Stavisky, Alexandre, 236–7
Stein, Morris – see Morrison, S.
Steinaud, Morris – see Morrison, S.
Steinberg, Abraham, 78
Stephens, Alfred, 154
Stephenson, Catherine, 130–1
Stephenson, Jane, 130–1
Stephenson, Thomas, 130–1
Stevens, PC 383 'Y' Charles Victor, 225–7
Stevens, Ellen, 123–8
Stevens, Detective Frederick, 57
Stevens, Det. Sgt. Jack 'Jew-boy', 14, 113, 114
Stevens, William, 24–5
Stewart, PC 457 'H' Roderick, 174
Stolerman, James Bernard, 209–10
Stonham, Dr Henry Archibald, 36–7
Stop-at-nothing-gang – see Bessarabian Gang
Stores, Albert, 98
Stuart, Norman, 214–15
Sturdee, Arthur Frederick, 54–5, 57, 58
Suck, Sheena, 29–30
Sullivan, Mary Ann, 118
Summers, Harriett, 82
Svaars, Fritz, 134–45, 160
Swift, Sir Rigby, 211, 218
Swift, Thomas, 54, 61
Syme, former Insp. John, 160–1, 162
Symons, Mrs, 98

Tagger, Moses – see Morrison, S.
Tamplin, Thomas, 69–71
Tanenbaum, Simon, 74–8
Tannen, Alfred, 214–15

Tatum, Walter, 208–9
Taw, Jack, 154
Taylor, Frederick, 86
Taylor, George William, 214–15
Taylor, Thomas, 167–72
Thick, Det. Sgt. William 'Johnny Upright', 14
Thiel, PC Tommy, 187–8
Thomas, Det. Supt. Fred, 191, 197
Thomson, Ass. Commissioner Sir Basil Home, KCB, 32, 147, 181–3, 190, 236–7
Thompson, Arthur – see Burley W.G.
Thompson, Edith Jessie, née Graydon, 199–207
Thompson, DI Ernest, 135, 136
Thompson, Percy, 199–207
Thompson, Richard Halliday, 200
Thompson, Thomas, 37
Thompson, PC 240 'H' William Ernest, 42–4
Thornell, Det. Sgt. Roland, 56, 67
Timewell, James, 111
Tittle, PC 400 'H' David, 42–3
Tofler, Ann, 25
Tomacoff, Nicholas, 136–7, 159
'Tommy Roundhead' – see Caunter, E.
Townsend, James – see Maples, J.
Tramberg, Lionel, 126
Trassjonsky, Rosa, 135–45
Tresidern, Arthur – see Harding, A.
Tressadern, Arthur – see Harding, A.
True, Ronald, 197
Tucker, PS Charles, 134
Tucker, Emily, 67–8
Tucker, Matilda, 67–8
Turner, Henry, 45

Vasilev, Nina – see Vassilleva, N.
Vassilleva, Nina, 134–45
Vaughan, Revd Bernard, 142
Vaughan, Sir James (Magistrate), 35
Vekbloot, Marks, 174
'Vendettas', 172
Venn, William, 81
Venzel – see Wensley, F.P.
Vilben, Frederick, 25–7
Vincent, Sir Charles Edward Howard, KCMG, CB, 15
Vitty, Major, Thomas, 218–19
Voisin, Louis, 184–7

Wade – see Donovan, C.
Wade, Charles, 103–06

Wald, William, 56–63
Walker, James John 'Jimmy', 236
Wallace, Robert, 87–8, 89
Waller – *see* Mahon, P.H.
Warbrick, Mr, 22
Ward, DCI Alfred, 148–65, 181
Wardlaw-Milne, Mr, MP, 210
Warren, Sir Charles, GCMG, KCB
    (Commissioner), 2
Warshawsky, Gershon, 122, 127
Wax, James, 119
Wax, Joseph, 119
'Weasel' – *see* Wensley, F.P.
Webb, Katie, 178
Webb, Insp., 178
Weber, Charles, 17–18
Webber, PC, 194
Webber, John, 200
Weiner, Adolph, 53–63, 64, 182
Weiner, Bertha, 52–63, 64, 182
Weiner, Ludwig, 53–63, 64, 182
Weiner, Willie, 53–63, 64, 182
Weinstein, Mr, 72
Weinstein, Joseph, 73–8
Weinstone, David, 89–92
Weil, Max, 133, 143
Weir, Max, 77
Weissberg, Jacob, 154
Wensley, Edith Mercy 'Edie'
    (daughter), 30, 179, 238
Wensley, Second Lieutenant Frederick
    Martin, (son), 12, 179, 181
Wensley, CC (CID) Frederick
    Porter, OBE, KPM:
  Birth, 1
  Education, 1
  Employment, 1
  Joins Metropolitan Police, 1
  Appearance, 1-2, 194–5, 214, 238
  Sworn in as Constable, 2
  Posted to Lambeth as PC 153
    'L', 3
  Injured on duty, 3, 4, 5, 64–5
  Drafted into Whitechapel, 5–6
  Commendations & Rewards, 6,
    18, 30, 32, 52, 63, 98, 100, 116,
    117, 128, 146, 165, 176, 177,
    179, 180, 181, 195, 235
  Posted to Bow Street as PC 97
    'E', 7
  Posted to Whitechapel as PC 402
    'H', 7–9
  Married, 12
  Moves into 98 Dempsey Street,
    12

  Appointed to CID, 12
  Promoted to Det. Sgt. (Third
    Class), 32
  Cross-border operations, 47–63,
    106–8
  Threats against, 62, 170
  Promoted to Det. Sgt. (Second
    Class), 64
  Death of father, 55
  Undercover work, 89–92, 119–20
  Promoted to Det. Sgt. (First
    Class), 97
  Promoted to Det. Insp. (Second
    Class), 109
  Awarded King's Police Medal,
    131
  Promoted to DDI, 146
  Views on criminals, 130, 131, 166
  Promotion to DCI, 177
  Freemasonry, 177
  Moves to 'Lucholm', Palmers
    Green, 179
  World War One, 180–8
  Death of son, Frederick Martin,
    181
  Death of DDI Ward, 181
  Transfer to the Yard, 181
  Enquiries re formation of Flying
    Squad, 182–3
  Death of son, Harold William,
    188–9
  Promoted to Superintendent, 191
  Formation of Flying Squad,
    189–98
  Views on discipline, 195, 240
  Appointed MBE, 195
  Takes responsibility for CID
    Central, 197
  Promoted to CC (CID), 214
  Advice on Flying Squad vehicles,
    218–19
  Burglary at home address, 219
  Investigation of police scandals,
    221–32
  Advanced to OBE, 224
  Centenary of Metropolitan Police,
    233
  Medals, 233–4
  Commemoration in *Police Orders*,
    235
  Retirement, 235
  Invitations from abroad, 235–7
  Writes memoirs, 237
  Serialisation in *Sunday Express*,
    237

Death of wife, 238
Ill-health, 238
Death, 238
Tributes, 239–40
Wensley, George (father), 1, 55, 179
Wensley, George William (brother), 1
Wensley, Second Lieutenant Harold William (son), 39, 179, 188–9
Wensley, Jane née Porter (mother), 1, 179
Wensley, Laura Elizabeth 'Lollie' née Martin (wife), 12, 179, 190, 235, 238
Wensley, Matilda (sister), 1
West, Ellen, 26–7
Wheeler, Robert, 169
Whitbread, Det. Sgt. Henry, 29
White, Lady, 197
White, DDI Stephen, 13, 14, 27–8, 31–2, 33, 46, 64
Whitechapel, 5–6, 7
Whiteley, Cecil, KC, 203–6
Whitmore, Mr C.A., 112
Whittaker, William, 22–3
Wiggins, Harry, 102
Wilcox, John, 86
Wilkin, PC 163 'C' John, 230–2
Wilkins, Alfred, 128, 130
Williams – see Sullivan, M.A.
Williams, John Arthur, 100

Williamson, CC (CID) Frederick Adolphus, 15, 16, 214
Wilson, Charles, 82–4
Wilson, Henry 'Scotty', 64
Wilson, Rose, 26–7
Wilson, William, 41
Windebank, PC 402 'H' Henry, 9
Winterman, Morris, 115
Withers, John James, CBE, MP, 224
Wodehouse, Dep. Commissioner Major Frederick, 141
Woolbright, Robert, 86
Worsfold, Detective, Harry 103–4
Wright, Det. Insp. George, 190
Wright, Henry – see Thompson, T.
Wyles, W/Det. Insp. Lilian Mary Elizabeth, BEM, 202, 222–5, 239–40

Yates, Charles, 54–63
Yeldham, Elsie, 197–8
Yeldham, William James, 197–8
'Yoska' – see Sokoloff, W.
Young, Henry, 87
Young, Olive, 197

Zakeria, Mark – see Marks, J.
Zaltzman, Israel, 154
Zelkowitz, Joe, 76
Zimmerman, Annie, 149, 157
Zimmerman, Maurice, 157